THE INCREDIBLE RISE OF

MUMFORD & SONS

CHLOÉ GOVAN

OMNIBUS PRESS

London / New York / Paris / Sydney / Copenhagen / Berlin / Madrid / Tokyo

Exclusive Distributors
Music Sales Limited,
14/15 Berners Street,
London, W1T 3LJ.

Music Sales Corporation
180 Madison Avenue, 24th Floor,
New York,
NY 10010,
USA.

Macmillan Distribution Services,
56 Parkwest Drive
Derrimut, Vic 3030,
Australia.

Every effort has been made to trace the copyright holders of the photographs in this book but one or
two were unreachable. We would be grateful if the photographers concerned would contact us.

Typeset by Phoenix Photosetting, Chatham, Kent
Printed in the EU

A catalogue record for this book is available from the British Library.

Visit Omnibus Press on the web at www.omnibuspress.com

Contents

Introduction

"The Grammys? We're glad we didn't leave our hearts there"
– Marcus Mumford

No modern awards ceremony would be complete without a dose of excessive sex appeal and eccentric, almost farcical sartorialism – and the 2011 Grammys was no exception.

Lady Gaga, a fine example of the latter, was carried in by an entourage of scantily clad assistants, crouched inside a giant semi-opaque egg with its own oxygen tank. Meanwhile one helper assured bemused onlookers that the pop diva was in "an embryonic state", and wouldn't be coming alive until the performance began. And come alive she did, ripping herself from her oddly fashioned womb to break into song and start playing an organ decorated with disembodied heads.

In the outrageousness stakes, the performance was unparalleled. Yet some young singers – equally hungry for attention – were engaging in a very different game. Baby-faced Justin Bieber, for example – who at just 17 already boasted a fortune of almost £70 million – was playing the teenage heart-throb card. When he took to the stage that night, he was preceded by the deafening screams of his female followers – a sound so loud that it threatened to drown him out.

Like Justin and Gaga, the biggest players of the night were invariably either sexy or strange – and they were all celebrities. It took just one look at the set list to demonstrate that. Katy Perry was selling the "teenage dream", Usher was flaunting his chiselled chest and – as she got up, close and personal with rugged co-star Drake – Rihanna was salaciously inviting viewers to say her name. Yet in this playlist, packed as it was with household names, there were a few conspicuous surprises.

One such surprise was a conservative, unassuming, waistcoat wearing group by the name of Mumford & Sons. Their brand of bohemian casual raised a few eyebrows in typically image-conscious America. For them, a Grammys ceremony without glamour was the British equivalent of Wimbledon without strawberries, Ascot without fashionable hats or a royal Jubilee without pomp, pageantry or the slightest hint of elongated vowels.

While for some stars, their looks and egos preceded them, this musical foursome were incongruously down to earth. They were about to join the ranks of teenage groupie magnet Justin Bieber, for whom the ego-massaging screams of adulation of hysterical young women was merely something to be brushed off as a natural side-effect of a hard day's work.

Yet the past history of Mumford & Sons dictated that they'd be more at home in the dingy basement of a tiny 80-capacity nightclub, playing folk music with their closest friends. By all accounts, they'd now made it – but Marcus Mumford had different ideas and, unlike many of those in the audience, he didn't equate celebrity with success.

"LA is not us," he intoned. "Awards are not us. We are from England."

Explaining away what could have been perceived as an unpatriotic slight directed at his home country, he added, "We don't feel good at the awards dinner table. It's not where the music happens."

The music, according to the group, is what drives them – and exactly what distinguishes them from artists like Justin Bieber. Quietly contemptuous of his showbiz counterpart, Marcus delivered a powerful blow of annihilation to the teenage singer and his "Beliebers" without so much as a single slur. "For us," he admitted, "the acid test for any artist would be, 'Could we give this dude a mandolin and just jam?'"

In Justin's case, one might fear not – and it seems equally doubtful that Rihanna could successfully challenge Mumford & Sons to a game of Scrabble. Unusually well-read for musical stars, the group's songs are infused with references to Shakespeare and Steinbeck, while – sidestepping the generic skin-deep love songs – there's a sprinkling of spirituality too.

To their devotees, they're endearingly ill-prepared for the fast-paced and often fake world of showbiz and, staying true to traditional values, their biggest claim to modern living is owning iPhones. In other words, the group were far from the obvious candidates for a Los Angeles guest list.

All the more fitting, then, that one of the soundtracks which would introduce them to the public was Bob Dylan's 'Maggie's Farm'. The track fights in favour of individuality and rejects conventional societal values as staid and insipid, robbing people of all that makes them unique. It also denigrates those who succumb to corporate slavery and fights for the rights of the uncommon man.

The song was an appropriate way for Mumford & Sons to show the TV audience – 126-million strong in the USA alone – that they were taking on the world of celebrity on their own terms.

While the Beastie Boys fought for their right to party, Mumford & Sons were championing a more cerebral cause – the right to be themselves. Coming full circle, perhaps the group had more in common with Lady Gaga than they might originally have thought.

Yet while the Grammys might not have been complete without a jawdroppingly ridiculous outfit from Gaga, it wouldn't have been complete without a smattering of atypical musicianship either – and that was the place Mumford & Sons held in the modern music world.

Pop puritans might not have welcomed them at the prestigious award ceremony and they might not have endeared themselves to hardcore fashionistas with their pub attire, but – loath to embrace a world of glitz and glamour – they didn't care. "We're not rock stars," they confessed without a hint of shame, apology or regret.

And this casual comment would seem to sum up the very ethos of Mumford & Sons: it isn't about the money, the models or the trapping of fame – it's the music that commands their hearts.

While the average Grammys contender might have a glamorous, brightly burning, intensely public and yet ultimately short-lived moment in the spotlight, these softly spoken English gents were shying away a little from the media circus and, instead, quietly laying down the foundations of a long-lasting, altogether more hype-free career.

It was the classic case of the tortoise and the hare – Mumford & Sons might not have been the obvious favourites to win the race, but they too had earned their place alongside the pop giants at one of the music world's biggest events of the year.

They weren't interested in becoming the buzzword of the moment and attracting fickle followers of musical fashion, but instead in building up a dedicated fanbase for whom their songs' meanings were more than surface deep.

Plus, while the cookie-cutter pop stars might have been revelling in a glory moment like the Grammys, for Mumford & Sons it seemed to be merely a necessary evil, an uncomfortable distraction from more worthy causes. Causes like indulging in a bountiful brass section or succumbing to the seductive sounds of a mandolin.

Evidently the foursome lived and breathed music – but where did it all begin?

Chapter 1

Love Drunk And Sober

That was exactly the question an 18-year-old John Mumford was pondering when, in the early seventies, he made the move from London to Scotland and embarked on a degree in theology at St Andrews University.

The backdrop to his childhood had been the Swinging Sixties – the 'anything goes' era characterised by free love and loose morals. Rising up in defiance against the repressed era their parents had always known, this decade's repeat offenders lived up to every tabloid cliché. Capricious media headlines depicted them as dreadlocked and bedraggled 'wild child' figures who stayed out all night and slept all day. According to the stereotypes, it was a bohemian life filled with music festivals, bell-bottom jeans, hedonistic weekends in Marrakech and an insatiable appetite for cannabis. They worshipped at the altar of casual sex and hallucinogenic drugs – and all in the name of freedom.

Yet, unashamedly, John Mumford was seeking a different kind of liberation – and he was looking skyward. A deep, philosophical thinker, he revelled not in rock 'n' roll, but in finding Jesus.

The theology course satisfied his hunger, seeing him critically examine the arguments both for and against God's existence. Yet rather than challenging his views on religion, the debate made him even more of a believer than before. He was required to study the Bible, memorise its Gospels by heart and analyse the intentions of their authors. He would also translate God's works into contemporary contexts and discover how to apply the texts to the modern world.

This was the turning point for John – transforming the Bible from an unrelatable, outdated tome into what he felt was a guide for 21st century living. Beyond penning mere essays that only his tutors would read, he wanted to be the voice of his generation and bring God's teachings to his peers – and change the secular world. Perhaps, he reasoned, he should become a pastor.

The backdrop to this epiphany was St Andrews, a small university town about a two-hour drive from Edinburgh. The college's status almost matched Oxford and Cambridge academically and, despite its modest size, it had an upper-crust reputation, attracting the children of bankers, diplomats and businessmen. Not only that, it was also home to royalty – Prince William would later spend four years there.

The town was so diminutive that it had just three main streets and didn't even have a railway station to its name – but for the high-flyers that sent their sons and daughters there, its isolation only added to the sense of exclusivity and refinement. Yet while seclusion might be sophisticated, it could also be very lonely.

For a start, the town wasn't exactly renowned for its party atmosphere. In term time, when the tourist bus – which operates just two months of the year – had stopped pounding the streets, St Andrews was dead – and not just metaphorically.

It was home to a bitterly cold beach, which, due to Scotland's harsh and unforgiving climate, barely saw the sun, the ruins of a desolate 13th century cathedral – and very little else. Being the unlikely home to annual golf tournament the British Open, St Andrews had more golf courses than nightclubs – and at times, it seems as though John had more chance of bumping into sporting legend Seve Ballesteros than attracting an eligible female.

At first his degree had consumed his thoughts – with students required to learn Hebrew and Greek so that they could read the Bible in its original form, the course was a demanding, intellectually challenging one. For the first couple of years, mastering the intricacies of Greek grammar and syntax, not to mention discovering new Biblical passages that had been lost in translation, left him with little time for women.

Yet John had needs – and, according to his college friends, his strict committed Christian beliefs meant that simply masturbating over a copy of *Playboy* to ease the frustration was unthinkable.

Besides, in stark contrast to the average superficial teenage boy longing for a glimpse of leg, it was more than mere sexual relief he was seeking. As much as religion had filled John's life, he was now looking for a like-minded female companion with whom he could share his fervour.

By the time he entered his final college year, his isolation was beginning to irk. As fate would have it, the course was predominantly male and, aside from a couple of dingy bars, St Andrews boasted no nightlife at all. Just when it looked as though he would end his student years single, a friend came to the rescue, introducing him to wife-to-be Eleanor.

She was studying a postgraduate degree in History of Art at Edinburgh, having finished a History course at St Andrews the year before, and was back in town to catch up with old friends. A strong, feisty woman praised more for her strength of character than her good looks, she was perfect for him. Within weeks, she'd widened his social circle. Friends say Eleanor was the party animal of the pair and that, while she shared his religious convictions, she also encouraged him to step outside of his self-imposed boundaries and have some fun.

On the surface, they were polar opposites – John was intense and serious, while Eleanor was light-hearted and playful – but the two complemented one another, and the one thing they shared between them was an insatiable love of God.

They were, to coin a cliché, a match made in Heaven. Once the school year was over, the pair moved to Cambridge together – John to take a postgraduate degree that continued his studies in Theology and Eleanor to train as a teacher. She would go on to work in the teaching profession for five years, while her boyfriend – who was now working towards becoming an ordained minister – got by on a succession of low-key jobs.

By 1977, the moment he'd been waiting for arrived – and he was officially ordained during a visit to Salisbury Cathedral. Weeks later came an assistant position at the local evangelical parish church of Canford Magna, a sleepy village in Poole, Dorset. Despite the fact that she'd barely worked enough years to earn back the steep cost of her student living, Eleanor decided to abandon the teaching world and support her boyfriend's religious endeavours instead.

Indisputably, however, assisting the vicar at a tiny village church would hardly be lucrative. "They both came from well-heeled families," a friend revealed to the author, "and John was expected to follow the family tradition and do well in business. Going into the ministry and giving up all that – squandering the opportunities of a college degree, as they saw it – went against the grain."

Indeed, if they hadn't been so well-connected, the couple's destiny might have been a life of poorly paid curatorship. However, they'd formed a valuable friendship with a near royalty figure in the evangelical world, John Stott.

Named in *Time* magazine as one of the world's top 100 influential figures – alongside powerful magnates such as Bill Gates and revolutionary founder of Apple Steve Jobs – John was the author of 50 God-focused books and even had his own ministry group, which operated across North America. The son of a career-minded no-nonsense diplomat, he understood exactly the opposition John and Eleanor were facing from their families. Much to the consternation of his own father, he'd announced a calling in ordination – one too powerful to ignore. Soon afterwards, on this account, he sought exemption from war service – and cynical onlookers might have assumed a connection between the two. Was he really following a passion for God or was he just looking for an escape route out of the arduous life that faced him in the army?

He silenced some of his critics when, true to his word, he opened a central London institute for Bible study. Inspired by what he'd learnt in the Holy Book, he yearned to relate to the poor and dispossessed and once slept under the railway arches for a couple of days as a homeless person. It was beginning to sound like an early version of reality TV show *Secret Millionaire* – a concept where wealthy business-people briefly step into the shoes of those less fortunate – but, in post-war Britain, where times were still tough, emulating the homeless was decidedly not in fashion. In fact, to his wealthy, image-conscious and agnostic parents – who were not given to such sentiment – he was rapidly becoming a source of embarrassment.

Regardless, in the years to come, Stott would define himself as both financially and spiritually endowed – once even serving the Queen – and, by the time Eleanor and John met him, he was nearing the end of a worldwide missionary tour of universities that he'd begun 25 years earlier. Its purpose was to target young people and "share the good news" of God's presence on earth. He reported record numbers of students who'd converted after hearing one of his talks – and, when his mission reached Cambridge, the couple were only too glad to join him. This was a man held in such high regard that even bomb threats which put London on high alert didn't prevent droves from attending his sermons.

In spite of his popularity, he developed a particular fondness for Eleanor and, when she and John got married in 1978, he was the first guest ever to stay with them in the marital home. She would later describe Stott as "one of the most delightful and Godly men ever to grace my living room".

The newly married Mumfords' friendship with Stott widened their circle within the church world and, by 1982, they'd been introduced to John Wimber. Once the keyboardist in a group called the Paramours that included singers Bobby Hatfield and Bill Medley, he's been credited with having founded the Righteous Brothers, the name they later adopted. Hardly the most likely candidate to be a man of God, *Christianity Today* had retrospectively described him as "a beer-guzzling, drug-abusing pop musician".

Yet at the age of 29, Wimber decided his musical brothers weren't righteous enough – and "converted while chain-smoking his way through a Quaker-led Bible study". For someone born to atheist parents with an attitude to religion that bordered on disdainful indifference, it was quite a transformation.

By the time John Mumford had met him, he'd gone from a drug-addicted heathen to a pastor so well-known he practically commanded celebrity status. From pop star to pastor? John wasn't convinced. Yet after one gushing tribute by a fellow worshipper, he was persuaded to attend one of Wimber's spiritual kinship meetings in California. Having recently learnt to talk in tongues – something he'd previously thought impossible – he was now open to anything.

He watched, rapt, as prayer circles formed to bless the sick, while those being prayed for seemed to heal right in front of his eyes. Feeling like a news reporter for God's very own newspaper, John began to scribble furiously in a notebook, recording all that he'd seen.

He shared his experience with Eleanor and – when Wimber arrived for a meeting at a London church they were involved with,

Trinity Brompton – she went along to the event with him. What happened that day changed her life – and from then on, her faith was not a mere commitment, but an obsession.

"That meeting gave Elli the opportunity to try out faith healing for herself," a former friend explained to the author. "There was a medical problem with her ovaries and she would suffer with the most agonising period pain. But then she was chosen to receive healing."

To her astonishment, the pain in her body melted away. Within minutes, an ecstatic Eleanor had cornered Wimber, demanding he teach her all that he knew. By his account, healing was something any believer could do, simply by channelling the Holy Spirit. He obliged and she spent hours under Wimber's tuition, laying hands on church-goers and watching their prayers take immediate effect.

This was just the beginning of the Mumfords' transatlantic love affair – and over the next couple of years, they found themselves visiting California time and time again.

During one visit in 1985, Wimber invited them to a church he had just taken over – the Anaheim Vineyard. For him, it was merely one of many – he had recently become the leader across all Vineyard churches across the USA – but for the Mumfords, it was special. To Eleanor and John, God was urging them to be a part of the movement and to call Anaheim home. The pair looked at each other incredulously, before bursting into tears. In their eyes, God had spoken.

The couple hastily took leave from St Michael's Church in Belgravia, London, where they were then based, and signed up for an 18-month internship at Anaheim Vineyard. Like pop star Katy Perry's pastor parents – who lived a nomadic lifestyle, moving states regularly to spread the word of God across America – they were now travelling missionaries. Together with their firstborn baby son, James, they packed up and made the move in late 1985, convinced that they were following divine orders.

During their stay, the pair helped Wimber to set up the label Vineyard Records – then known as Mercy Records – which would enable his church movement to publish its own self-created worship music. They also busied themselves by learning all there was to know about church leadership.

Yet the internship wouldn't last forever. It was with regret that John prepared to bid Anaheim a fond farewell, but – as it turned out – it was a well-timed exit. By this point, he was desperately fighting off the embarrassment of mistaken identity, as another man by the same name – Bob Mumford – began to wreak havoc across America. The Mumford he shared his name with was far from righteous – in fact, he was one of five leaders of the Shepherding Movement, a notoriously sinister religious cult.

As John and Eleanor prepared to leave California, the scam had become so widespread that a ministry handbook had been penned by worried pastors, offering advice on how to free oneself from the group's clutches. The book described the movement as a "religious dictatorship" that committed others to "spiritual and mental bondage".

By most accounts – eventually, including those of the shamed leaders themselves – the cult had subverted religious teachings to brainwash naïve, trusting Christians, reeling them in with promises of a place in Heaven. However it didn't come free – to be eligible, followers had to submit themselves totally to the authority of their leaders. Usually a written Covenant Agreement was signed by each "sheep", pledging unconditional obedience to every whim of their "shepherd" – not to mention, of course, financial support. A signature was binding – and it became the green light for an unorthodox level of control.

The shepherds demanded as much worship and adulation as the God they claimed to act on behalf of – and sometimes more. According to one author, "They set themselves up as little Hitlers over the flock... even going so far as to demand submission to themselves rather than to the Lord."

He wasn't exaggerating. One recruit was quoted as saying, "If God Almighty spoke to me and I knew for a certainty that it was God speaking and my shepherd told me to do the opposite, I would obey my shepherd."

Like horses careering ahead, burdensome carts trailing behind them, to reach a strategically placed carrot that, cruelly, was always just a little too far out of reach, these God-fearing Christians fell for their shepherds' promises hook, line and sinker. To them, they were being offered an authentic chance of salvation. There'd been no voodoo, no hypnosis, but somehow these mere mortals had successfully duped thousands of gullible Americans – hundreds of pastors included – into believing they were a manifestation of God in human form.

With all the intensity of your average Sadhu, devotees vowed to live in submission to them, unquestioningly acquiescing to any and every request. At first, they were willingly placing their lives in the shepherds' hands. It seemed they sought an all-powerful, patriarchal figure to direct and guide them and to relieve them of all responsibility over their own lives.

This suited the shepherds, whose lust for power was so intense it had even seen them compared to Hitler, the Mafia and the Ku Klux Klan. By its own account, the group had been striving for a "Christian-controlled America", with themselves positioned at the helm. They'd engineered an image of pariah-like righteousness and Godliness, designed to impress and appeal to vulnerable church-goers who were keen to do right. Yet this carefully constructed PR image had subverted religion so much, it had become devoid of any worthy purpose.

No matter – five shepherds were all in search of inhuman levels of power and leadership, and forging a false association to God would doubtless help them to attain it. In fact, God's image had become a mere accessory or piece of furniture, a vehicle through which they could exercise their desire for dominion.

Guilt-ridden masochism intermingled with power-thirsty manipulation and sadism was quite a heady cocktail and not one you might expect to find in a law-abiding church. However, it wasn't to last. What had first posed as a consensual agreement, appealing to those who longed for a protective, nurturing authority figure to parent their inner child was now – undisguisably – an unwelcome and ill-intended campaign of control.

Countless Christians came forward to complain – and their testimonies were scandalous. They'd been coerced into giving vast sums of money to the movement, squandering entire inheritance funds to appease these five men. On occasion, their businesses had been lost, or they'd been made homeless.

The followers had been forbidden from making a single decision by themselves – even something as innocuous as whether or not to go on holiday. Buying a house, car or even an item of clothing required their shepherd's express consent – and if he agreed, he would then control how much they spent. It was little surprise that some of these aptly named "sheep" had become financially destitute. Ironically, they'd been told that they would face spiritual, physical and financial ruin if they *didn't* follow orders.

In the words of one victim, a group of inept scammers with "no more Biblical understanding than your average burger-flipper" had nonetheless launched a campaign of masterful deception that "heaped ruin on the heads of their flock".

A campaign of indignation circulated, witheringly likening the shepherds to Scientologists – and even Satanic ritualists. Furious pastors spread the word, distributing leaflets from door to door warning of their reputation – and fear and fury soon rose.

A petition soon followed to force the leaders out of their homes. Their houses were vandalised, death threats were scrawled across the bricks and crosses were burnt in their gardens. The message was clear – the shepherds were no longer welcome.

Later all but one of the leaders would plead guilty to wrongdoing, but when John and Eleanor were in the USA, the scandal was still in full swing. Even worse, Anaheim was no LA or Palm Springs – it was a small town with a sense of community, unaccustomed to controversy. It was a place where word spread fast.

The Mumford name was no longer a badge of pride, but a source of embarrassment – and for John and Eleanor, who had absolutely no affiliation to the Shepherding Movement at all, the link was one humiliation too many.

The sabbatical from British life was over – and it was time to return to the church they'd previously called home, miles away in London's Belgravia. However, according to the couple's account, God had other plans.

He had spoken to them, urging them to plant a Vineyard church in the UK – the first of its kind. Eleanor was the driving force behind the vision – she was desperate to put some of what she'd learnt in Anaheim to good use – but John Wimber, who was the leader of the Vineyard group, stood in opposition.

While Eleanor had declared, "It's not enough to read the books – I want to be in on the act!", her desire to become a church leader was controversial and, more importantly, directly in contradiction with Wimber's beliefs. He was her greatest spiritual influence – the guru she looked up to the most – and yet much of his work was based on the Bible's Timothy, who prohibited females from taking a leading role in the church. While the power imbalance might seem outrageous to modern sensibilities, the church was set in its ways.

In Timothy 2:11, the Bible states, "Let a woman learn in silence with all submission. And I do not permit a woman to teach or have authority over a man, but to be in silence."

That said, the Bible also stated that men and women were equal and should be held in equal regard. Not only that, but it was all in the interpretation. Translating the ancient text from Hebrew, alongside deciphering era-specific phraseology and colloquialisms – not to mention separating semantics from sarcasm – was a task akin to *The Only Way Is Essex's* Amy Childs trying to understand Shakespeare. Suffice to say, many feared that much of the Bible's true meaning had been lost in translation.

As for the passage that was standing in Eleanor's way, Timothy's words stated that a woman should not seek authority above that of a man and urged that she should be in submission to God – but that was a requirement of all religious devotees. The phrase seemed to simply imply that no-one – male or female – should assume authority over God.

In addition, some cynics believed that the Bible's message had been skewed by its authors to better represent their own interests, interpreted to suit their own agenda – and that, centuries on, it more closely resembled a game of Chinese whispers than God's actual words.

Nonetheless, Wimber's mind was made up. He publicly insisted, "I believe that God has established a gender-based eldership of the church. I endorse the traditional view of a unique leadership role for men in marriage, family *and* in the church." He later added, "I personally do not favour ordaining women as elders... I encourage our women to participate in any ministry, except church governance."

For Eleanor, the message was only too clear. Patently, he didn't approve of a female leader – least of all a heavily pregnant one like her, who in his eyes was a mere visitor from England. On one occasion, when the pair approached Wimber to share their convictions, insisting, "I think God has called upon us to plant a church in the UK," his answer left no room for misunderstandings – "I don't."

Not to be deterred, the Mumfords put together a 70-page proposal, together with an appendix detailing all the times God had spoken to them. It was a sound business plan, along with a spiritual message to tug at Wimber's conscience – and it did the trick.

Soon afterwards, Wimber revealed he felt God had spoken to him too – and that he approved of the project. It was now time for the three of them to present their findings at a board meeting, which everyone involved in Vineyard would attend.

Up until that point, there hadn't been a single Vineyard church outside of North America – and it had been Wimber's intention to keep it that way. However at the meeting, documenting the 33 times the Mumfords felt God had spoken, he began to pray.

"Lord God," he began, "we have done everything we know how to stop this. We have put every obstacle in their way and every time, Lord God, you have overturned it. Therefore, we take it that it is your will – and we are going to go with this thing."

Ultimately it was with Wimber's blessing that Eleanor and John flew home in June 1987, to embark on the journey. They were not alone – by this time, they were armed with their son James and a new arrival – six-month-old Marcus.

Music was already in Marcus' blood in more ways than one. He'd been exposed to a rich variety of Christian worship music while he was still in the womb and he'd been present – albeit subconsciously – at every meeting his mother had attended for Vineyard's record label.

Since his birth on January 31, 1987, he'd graduated to being around in person, watching his mother sing hymn after hymn in front of him.

Not only that, but a mere glance at Marcus' family tree confirms his musical leanings. He boasted musicianship on both sides of the family and one of his ancestors was a pianist, who tragically died in action during the First World War.

Plus, even at Marcus' tender age, when his parents opened the Vineyard SW London church, he had joined in the musical celebrations.

Eleanor had taken an "assistant pastor" role beside her fully-fledged pastor husband – perhaps so as not to publicly offend Wimber's regimented beliefs – but her enthusiasm for God meant that she maintained a direct leading role behind the scenes. A forceful presence in the evangelist world, she was a regular speaker at events too, and often headed prayer group sessions.

At first, however, the church project was amateur in the extreme. The Vineyard headquarters, low-budget and low-key, were based in an old, almost derelict school building with paint peeling off the walls and no signs to advertise its presence, aside from a blink-and-you'll-miss-it placard in the window.

However, what the church lacked in conspicuous magnificence, it made up for with music. Reflecting the Mumfords' musical ancestry, an entire band led worship, from a male vocalist playing both acoustic and electric guitar to a drummer, bass player and backing singer. No two Sundays were the same and for Eleanor, her fledgling church – based on her vision of a 'God's Britain' – quickly became all-consuming.

For some time, she and John quietly devoted themselves both to the church and to raising James and Marcus – but a chain of events was about to take place that would change the Vineyard movement for ever and that would culminate in the ultimate miracle.

The sense that Vineyard was building up to something special was characterised by several events. One of these was a visit to Fort Wayne, Indiana, statistically one of the USA's most feared locations. Renowned for brutal, territorial turf wars and casual drive-by shootings, it was a place where life counted for nothing and was valued merely at the price someone could be paid to direct a fatal gunshot. Sceptics felt local hearts were so hardened from a life of crime than their owners were a lost cause – but Vineyard thought differently.

A 10-year-old African American boy, who had recently lost a dear friend in gang warfare, was called to the altar to give a dramatic message – "turn or burn". At first, the young speaker's words were met with icy indifference. By the end he'd broken down in tears with frustration, begging God to "open their eyes or they'll die and go to Hell!"

This was the required turning point for some 15 convicted gang members, who reportedly rose and leapt towards the altar, crying "I want Jesus!"

These formerly impenetrable hearts now seemed to be seeking salvation, calling out to a long forsaken father figure to ease their pain and neutralise their anger. Within a month, dozens more "no hopers" were converted. It was an astonishing victory for Vineyard – and not the last.

John Wimber had contracted a life-threatening illness. Before long, cancer-ravaged vocal cords had left him unable to speak, while some 43 sessions of radiotherapy had rendered him so weak that he slept for 23 hours a day. Just when it looked as though he was on the verge of death, his wife resorted to intensive prayer, asking God to heal him and restore his voice. To his astonishment, the next day he was up and awake – and the day after that, he'd summoned the strength to go to church and deliver a life-affirming sermon. It was no short-lived fluke either – Wimber would go on to make a full recovery.

This type of miracle was the bedrock of the Vineyard faith. To them, it was testament that proved their commitment to God was not in vain. Yet the biggest miracle of all, which Eleanor would play an enormous part in unveiling to the UK, was yet to come.

In early 1994, Eleanor heard news of a revival movement of 'holy laughter' centred in Toronto, Canada, which saw worshippers literally 'struck down' by the power of the Holy Spirit. Instead of lacklustre seated prayer, visitors to Vineyard's tiny Toronto branch reported "breaking into uncontrollable laughter, shaking, crying, falling to the ground and roaring like lions".

Formerly sensible, tight-lipped pastors – those whose professionalism upheld the reputation of the church – were dissolving into spontaneous giggles and writhing, incapacitated on the floor. To cynics, it might have sounded like a trip to your average lunatic asylum – indeed, those who were not religiously inclined were raising their eyebrows in mockery and scorn – but for those who made it to the church, it was an event of unparalleled euphoria.

While Eleanor had heard about holy laughter before, she'd never experienced it – and she decided the news of the revival warranted some worship tourism. She consulted a pastor friend for advice, who promised to communicate with God on the matter – and he returned with the news that she was destined to travel to Toronto. She would be leaving the UK without her husband for the first time since her marriage – but seemingly with God's blessing.

The trip had come at the right time for Eleanor – and some might say it was synchronicity. Plagued by feelings of spiritual bankruptcy, she had sunk to a new low in her religious faith. She was close to clinical depression and, as she would later admit, was "burnt out and longing for a fresh understanding and vitality in my relationship with Jesus".

Perhaps this uncharacteristic phase was merely symptomatic of raising two young, boisterous boys. Regardless, the trip to Toronto was to be a well-timed escape route from the minutiae of her every-day life.

"I went because I had heard that there was a tremendous party going on," she later revealed during a sermon, "and all through my life, I've been one to get to a party."

"I knew if there was something happening, I wanted to be in the middle of it," she added. "I went in a state of personal bankruptcy.

I knew that I was bankrupt and I knew that I was needing the Lord badly and I had an incredible longing in my spirit for the things I had heard of. Some of the stories I was hearing were stirring me and just making me cry in the listening and I thought, 'I need to get there.'"

Terrified of disappointment and anxious not to set her expectations too high in case she was heading for a fall, Eleanor prayed silently through much of the flight. When she landed on the tarmac, she rushed to unburden herself of her bags at "a frightful little hotel in the middle of nowhere" and then returned immediately to the airport.

On arrival, she took a sharp intake of breath. This wasn't the promised land – nor was it even a bona fide church. For just a few yards from the airport runway lay a tiny, inconspicuous warehouse at the edge of a dingy, nondescript white office block. Behind its walls, it was buzzing with religious fervour, but from the outside it looked quite unremarkable. In fact, had visitors not noticed the diminutive paper Post-it note in the window inviting passengers to "come on in to the Airport Vineyard", it might have gone unnoticed altogether. The place looked more suited to a white-collar-worker than the devout wife of a pastor – and Eleanor's heart began to sink.

Swallowing a growing sense of foreboding, she walked through the doors of "the most comically improbable church you will ever see" and instantly the atmosphere changed.

"It was electric with expectancy and the pastors were just shining with the beauty of their Lord," she recalled. "[One] lovely pastor man said to me, 'What would you like? What are you here for?' and I said, 'I want everything you've got. I've only got two days and I've come from London!' Sort of defiantly. Behind this, I was saying, 'I've played it fair and I'm determined to get my money's worth. So what will you do?'"

She wasn't to be disappointed. That day, she was taken over by the same euphoria she had heard about, and sank to the floor, spontaneously laughing and cheering for God. By her final day in

Canada, she had resolved to take the experience back to Britain with her. She began to pray with an air of desperation, reciting, "God, who are we to say that this is Great Britain? We're not great. We're pathetic. We're pitiful. We're needy, needy people. We don't want GREAT Britain, we want GOD'S Britain!"

She scribbled furiously in a notebook during the return flight home when, to her surprise, just writing the phrase, "Come, Holy Spirit!" sent her into spasm again – and she collapsed right there on the aeroplane. "The Spirit of God fell on me!" she would recall proudly, "right in the middle of Air France!"

This infectious euphoria wasn't confined to Toronto any more. In fact, when she returned to London in late May 1994, she would be solely responsible for introducing the phenomenon to Britain – and this time the experience would be even more forceful than before.

Prior to her talk that day – a guest speech at Holy Trinity Brompton in Knightsbridge designed to spread the word to the nation – no-one in the UK had experienced holy laughter. Yet by the time worship hours were over, there wasn't a single person who hadn't.

Nicky Gumbel, a curate at the church, recalled, "Elli told us a little bit of what she had seen in Toronto, then she said, 'Now we'll invite the Holy Spirit to come' and the moment she said that, one of the people was thrown, literally, across the room. [He] was lying on the floor, just howling and laughing, making the most incredible noise."

Another eyewitness recalled, "That room sounded like it was a cross between a jungle and a farmyard. There were many lions roaring, there were bulls bellowing, there were donkeys, there was a cockerel near me, there were sort of bird songs… every animal you could conceivably imagine, you could hear."

Some of the congregation were jumping around, limbs flailing wildly, as if they were in a death metal group's mosh pit and – while they stopped short of crowd-surfing – it was indisputably unlike anything ever seen in a British church before.

Other worshippers lay spasming violently on the floor, tears of laughter streaming down their faces. People spoke of "electric shocks of liquid love", while some hallucinated, seeing the image of God in the room. Before too long, all the worshippers were forced to the ground. One minister was rendered paralysed and was unable to stand for over an hour.

While chaos reigned around the church, head vicar Sandy Millar sat oblivious in a nearby building, discussing funding for the worship services. The church's secretary managed to pick up the phone and call her, blurting out, "I know you told me not to disturb you at your meeting, but I thought you should know your entire staff are lying incapacitated on the floor."

No stranger to spiritual miracles, Sandy took the news in her stride. "Is it good?" she asked, unperturbed. "I think so," came the reply. "So what are you doing up?" she asked incredulously. "I crawled on my hands and knees."

It was as if a lightning storm had hit the building – electrifying everyone into violent movement before throwing them motionless to the floor. To uninvolved onlookers, it might have been hard to discern whether they were willing participants or victims.

It was drunkenness on a mass scale. One worshipper, a recovered addict who had dabbled in alcohol and Class A drugs before reverting to Christianity, recalled the experience as "just like being out of it on drugs".

For Eleanor that description might have been bittersweet – she had lived with severely alcoholic family members when she was growing up. "In my own family, I have seen drunkenness to a degree in my past which has so grieved and offended me that I'd never been able to watch drunkenness," she had confessed at that day's sermon. "I can't look at it in the street, I can't look at it on the television. It offends and it breaks my heart, because I've seen too much of the real thing. In the course of those three days in Toronto, God healed me of all that anguish… and I saw what it was to be drunk in the Spirit. It was a sweet and wonderful thing."

The biggest miracle for believers was that when they arrived at church, they were stone-cold sober. This was a unique kind of intoxication – one she felt "privileged to have witnessed".

It was Eleanor's testimony that had introduced a nation to holy laughter, which was then virtually unheard of on the British worship scene – but it was about to spread like wildfire. A few days later, her husband was giving a sermon at the Vineyard church in Putney and, again, miracles took place.

"After his sermon, Mr Mumford prayed for a tornado to visit the church," an eyewitness recalled. "Outside it was calm, but suddenly the curtains shielding an open door blew in and over my face and a huge wind rushed in, scattering service sheets and papers. Nearly everyone else fell over, stood rigid or were shaking, sobbing, clutching at their faces and waving their hands before them."

He continued, "I clambered over a couple of prostate bodies for tea and coffee and found myself giggling uncontrollably. I felt dizzy and grasped a chair in order not to collapse."

Everywhere that Eleanor and John worked, when they invited the Holy Spirit to join them, the hysterical laughter ensued. The spiritually inclined might argue that Eleanor had been called upon by God as a 'chosen one' to deliver the message of holy laughter nationwide. In fact, one journalist would later insist that her testimony of events in Toronto had been like "a lit match hitting the dry grass of the churches of England".

At that time the UK had been experiencing record apathy towards religion, with church attendance figures approaching an all time low. Perhaps it was understandable, too. It was an era when there existed a sizable generation of people who were old enough to remember the trauma of the Second World War – and many were overwhelmed by bitterness. They recalled poverty, queuing with their ration books for measly portions of rotting fruit. They recalled times when chocolate or a new pair of tights was seen as a decadent, obscenely over-indulgent luxury, barely seen in their society. They recalled their houses shaking violently under the strain of a bomb overhead – and some had lost friends and family in the army. It was a generation of have-nots, characterised by struggle and strife. If God existed, why had He brought so much pain and suffering upon them?

Plus with modern attitudes eclipsing Bible-based traditions, Britain was seemingly the most secular it had ever been. Yet Eleanor's impassioned words had touched notoriously cynical Brits and sparked a new evangelical trend.

A few days after Eleanor's talk, the Holy Trinity Brompton Knightsbridge published a front page feature in its parish newsletter entitled "Holy Spirit Fever Hits London". Soon after, all the major broadsheet newspapers had hit upon the story. *The Times* spoke of "a religious craze that involves mass fainting and hysterical laughter", reporting that one London vicar was "forced to cancel an evening service of Holy Communion, because so many in his congregation were lying on the floor".

The feature elaborated, "The service ended in chaos, as dozens of people burst into spontaneous laughter or tears, trembled and shook or fell to the floor."

Other media reports spoke of people so intoxicated that they had to be helped to their vehicles as they staggered 'love drunk' across the car park. Many were attributing the movement entirely to Eleanor, who revealed at one sermon that some of those affected were unable to drive at all.

She told of one woman who was pulled over by the police for dangerous driving after a "taste of the Holy Spirit". "She was reeling," Eleanor explained, "and unwisely, she decided to drive home. She drove up the freeway and she was all over the place and she was stopped by the police. She got out of the car and the policeman said, 'Madam, I have reason to believe that you're completely drunk.' She said, 'Yes, you're right.' So he said, 'Well, I need to breathalyse you,' so he got his little bag and as she started to blow into it, she just fell to the ground laughing. At which point, the policeman fell too and the power of God fell on him and he and she were sitting on the freeway laughing under the power of God. He said, 'Lady, I don't know what you've got, but I need it', and he came to the church the next week and he found Jesus… this is happening. People are going out and telling each other about Jesus with a recklessness that they've never known before."

Indeed, back in Toronto, events had reached fever pitch. Thanks to Eleanor's testimony, the UK media had caught on to the phenomenon and dubbed it the 'Toronto blessing', in honour of its origin. In the days that followed the publicity, worshippers from around the world descended on the church where it had begun. Direct flights from London to Toronto were often sold out for days on end and worshippers had to be turned away in their thousands as the tiny prayer zone found itself packed to full capacity. Some queued for three hours at a time, braving torrential rain, in their desperation to be the first through the doors of the diminutive little church, somewhere about as likely to have housed a global phenomenon as the average rabbit hutch.

Yet its size didn't detract from its popularity and some visitors, not to be deterred by the crowds, parked a mile away and made barbecue dinners camped outside the door. Realising they were totally unequipped to handle such large numbers, ministry staff hired a banquet hall to accommodate some of the extras.

Meanwhile in equally unlikely locations such as the sleepy town of Modesto, California, roads saw severe traffic jams totally incongruous with a quiet Sunday morning. On one occasion, a traffic helicopter pilot was interviewed on local radio to announce the mystery behind the pile-up. "We've found out what's going on!" he reassured. "All those cars jamming the road are trying to get to church!"

As the largely secular listeners choked back incredulous laughter – and not the holy kind – the voice on the radio continued, "There's a church down there holding a drama and we hear it's pretty good!"

However, outside of its home town, it was the UK where holy laughter seemed to have made the most impact. Like in Toronto, people were waiting for hours outside churches, in anticipation of a hit from the new legal high. They were worshipping with as much enthusiasm as a rebellious teenager getting their first puff of cannabis or a technology addict lining up outside the Apple store for the latest iPad model. It was like a mephedrone fix for the older generation too – and sure enough, it was just as addictive to its believers as any drug.

By now, Eleanor had gained notoriety as the first person to bring the pleasure to British shores. A popular phrase goes, "The best things in life are all immoral, illegal or fattening" – yet this was a morally sound rival to an illicit high. Eleanor also had a status as a faith healer because, allegedly, she had been able to encourage the entry of the Holy Spirit by laying her hands on members of the congregation. This physical intervention by a talented channeller of God was, according to many evangelists, what caused the phenomenon to manifest and then become infectious.

However, not everyone was enamoured by the 'miracles'. To some, it was just an embarrassing display of emotional incontinence, while to the unaffected outsider, it might have even seemed frightening. To those who considered themselves 'rationally minded' or didn't believe in God at all, seeing just one person writhing around as if they belonged in a straitjacket was intimidating enough, let alone accounting for an entire craze for the behaviour.

Were these worshippers having a collective seizure or stroke? Were they mentally ill? Hallucinating under the influence of drugs? Or simply love-drunk and taken over by the Holy Spirit?

One critic seemed to say it all, in atheists' eyes, when he simply stated, "If you saw this outside of a religious setting, you'd call a doctor."

Yet it wasn't just atheists who ridiculed and condemned holy laughter – it was other Christians too. The word 'evangelical' takes its origin from the ancient Greek, meaning "to have a message to proclaim". Yet to quote one believer, holy laughter was NOT that message.

"Nowadays evangelists don't have a message of *any* kind to proclaim," he asserted. "They only have an experience – and not even a Christian one at that!"

While her association with holy laughter had earned Eleanor and John admiration in some quarters, it was alienating them too. Believers and non-believers alike were fiercely disputing what was happening. Was this truly spiritual awakening – or just mass hysteria?

Firstly, there was widespread concern that holy laughter was not just meaningless folly, but was actively anti-Christian in its nature too. Some of those who had participated had reported being unable to free themselves at will from their hysterical stupor in the few days that followed church attendance. If it was a real phenomenon, did the reports of people 'trapped' by it not make it dangerous?

Fainting occurred en masse at the events and some believers even reported memory loss, forgetting who and where they were. The fate of others was to merely lie on the cold stone floor, unable to move for hours on end. Then there were the reports of dangerous driving, delirium tremors and slurred speech. Could any of these effects really be positive or indicative of God's will? If He had chosen to manifest himself to His people, would He truly have done so with such disastrous, chaotic consequences?

The Bible itself urges, "Let all things be done decently and in order" (1 Corinthians 14:40) and "God is not the author of confusion but peace." Yet, in contradiction, the evangelists who experienced holy laughter reported on the 'glorious chaos' God had brought to their church.

One follower, who in the height of trance barked like a dog and lifted up his leg to urinate like one too, did little to counter the reputation holy laughter was gaining for chaos and disorder. Eleanor was present at that session, but her faith in the practice was undeterred.

Yet a high so intense that its 'users' are under its control and cannot exercise free will against it had shadowy connotations of being enslaved by earthly, non-Biblical desires such as drug addiction. The Bible also appears to discredit anything that puts humans in 'bondage'.

Meanwhile one indisputably negative consequence of holy laughter was the case of one woman who fell backwards in religious fervour and smashed her head against a concrete pillar. She was rushed to hospital suffering heavy bleeding, concussion and suspected brain damage.

To add fuel to the fire of disapproval, there were sinister sexual connotations running through many of the activities. Another woman, whose commitment to modesty was usually so extreme that she would blush at wearing even a short-sleeved T-shirt in public found herself lying sprawled out across the floor of the church while her skirt rode up around her waist, her underpants on display for the entire room to see. Priests were believed to be taking advantage of the comatose state their congregation found themselves in – and that added to the rumours that they were preaching hypnotism for personal gain.

One recorded occasion that was perhaps more bizarre than torrid was a case of two women writhing on the floor making forceful pushing motions with their pelvises as if in labour. A male member of the clergy looked on, standing over them shouting, "Birth it! Birth it!"

What was more, some believed that followers felt obliged to go through the motions of holy laughter, even if they didn't feel anything, lest they were condemned as second-class Christians.

One junior pastor had admitted to ministry staff that she'd felt nothing while urging the Holy Spirit to come, but was told to fall on the ground anyway. Was she faking her experience to fall in line with what had now become not just a favourable response but an expected one? And were churches using holy laughter to get one up in the superiority stakes, competing with each other to be represented as 'holier than thou'?

Then there was the possibility of a placebo effect – that believers had artificially induced a trance-like state due to the strength of their beliefs. A plethora of scientific studies over the years have shown that, with some minor health conditions, genuinely believing that there is a cure or that a remedy has been administered can be sufficient to induce the healing process – even if they have consumed something as benign and ultimately inactive as a sugar pill, instead of a drug.

Perhaps experiencing multiple people laughing and losing their inhibitions had also set off a chain reaction as contagious as a yawn, behaviour which was then subconsciously imitated by the entire congregation.

Meanwhile some claimed these displays of emotional incontinence were inducing sin and Satanism and normalising hedonistic behaviour, the inevitable next step being seeking similar highs through mind-altering drugs. These critics thought they'd seen the phenomenon before – throughout history, it could have been likened to the occult, hypnotism and even voodoo. For example, 1800s preacher Maria Woodworth-Etter, who would conduct trance sessions during worship, was widely known as a 'voodoo priestess'.

A century earlier lived perhaps the most notorious hypnotic faith healer of all – Franz Mesmer, from whose surname the word 'mesmerise' is derived. The Austrian physician allegedly 'cured' his patients with the use of hypnosis. In Richard Cavendish's book *The Black Arts*, he describes the therapeutic process as follows: "Mesmer marched about majestically, passing his hands over the patients' bodies or touching them with a long iron wand... some felt as if insects were crawling over them, others were seized with hysterical laughter, convulsions or fits of hiccups. Some went into raving delirium, which was called 'The Crisis' and was considered extremely healthful." The key to his treatments was mind control.

Disturbingly for some, the modern day experiences in Vineyard churches seemed directly correlated with those of ill-repute – they seemed to have all the hallmarks of hypnotism and cult indoctrination. One journalist wrote indignantly of holy laughter, "We find that a Church of England Bishop is still having to race off to a church in Toronto where he can be found lying 'on the floor roaring like a lion'. This is not spiritual revival – that is demonic bondage!"

Eleanor herself was controversial in the debate when she suggested that church-goers should avoid analysing or questioning what they were experiencing for fear of "losing it" and that they should instead be "receptive and childlike [and] come as a child".

Complying unquestioningly without the use of independent thought might refer to the submission required of a committed Christian in worship to God – but it could also be interpreted as the signature style of mind control – a much more sinister prospect altogether.

Yet evangelical ministers committed to holy laughter argued that hypnotism was an impossibility when the person delivering the sermon was on the floor under the spell himself.

The debate raged on. Amid the chaos of writhing bodies and raucous screams, some ministers reacted with aloof detachment and a sense of inflated superiority, merely repeating the Biblical phrase, "God is not the author of confusion, but of peace."

One common symptom of the experience is for followers to talk in tongues – something the Bible might not condone.

Corinthians 1 claims, "Greater is he that prophesieth than he that speaketh in tongues... If I come unto you speaking in tongues, what shall I profit you, unless I speak to you either by way of revelation, or of knowledge, or of prophesying, or of teaching?... I had rather speak five words with my understanding, that I might instruct others also, than ten thousand words in a tongue."

Although the book seems to dismiss talking in tongues as irrelevant gibberish, another Bible reference seems to contradict his approach. In Acts 2, it is written, "There appeared unto them tongues parting asunder, like as of fire, it sat upon each of them and they were all filled with the Holy Spirit and began to speak with other tongues, as the Spirit gave them utterance."

This was the passage that Eleanor had in mind when she witnessed holy laughter for the first time in Toronto. During her testimony in London, she'd claimed, "I saw the power of God poured out just as it was in the book of Acts... I didn't see tongues of flame, but I suspect it was because I wasn't looking... we're in the days of the New Testament."

However critical observers sought science – and so far there was no evidence to prove that the phenomenon really was an encounter with the Holy Spirit – or indeed anything more than an hysterical fad.

Yet shockingly, a doctor who specialised in mood disorders – Grant Mullen – openly validated the movement, claiming, "I've seen powerful psychological changes take place spontaneously that could never happen with years of counselling."

Yet Mullen's testimony failed to address the burning question – was God healing these church-goers or was there a more rational explanation?

Primal therapy argues that neurosis is caused by the repressed pain of childhood trauma and that only by reliving the trauma and fully experiencing the pent-up emotions associated with it can sufferers release the pain and become healed.

In a reserved Western society, weeping and wailing is often feared or frowned upon and emotions might be swallowed to fall into line with social norms of a stiff upper lip, therefore grief sometimes goes unexpressed. Marcus himself would later concur, "I'm very English and we don't talk about emotions publicly." Psychotherapists who subscribe to primal therapy seek to relieve their patients of the burden of past traumas by encouraging them to "act out", sometimes seeing them scream for hours.

The therapy's founder, Arthur Janov, believed that – with the exception of genetic defects – there was only one cause of mental illness and that was imprinted pain. His theories attracted celebrity support before long, with John Lennon praising the therapy. "I no longer have any need for drugs, the Maharishi or the Beatles," he announced after taking part. "I am myself and I know why."

Such a public endorsement of psychotherapy by a famous figure was rare – and such fervour even more so. During one session, he agreed to be separated from his wife, Yoko, for three weeks so that they could both experience intensive therapy without distraction.

Perhaps church-goers were unwittingly advocates of the therapy too? Bound by the convention of a civilised society, many sufferers have little opportunity to unleash such intense feelings outside of the therapy room – until holy laughter time. Could the experiences have been a mass exorcism of emotional pain, made socially acceptable by its context as an experience of God?

Eleanor's own testimony unwittingly seemed to provide some support for that theory. She had harboured the trauma of alcoholism in her family – something so painful that she couldn't bring herself to even look at "party people" in the street without her heart lurching. In one of her talks, she had confessed to this weakness, only to reveal that during holy laughter, "God healed me of all that anguish and all that past as I saw what it was to be drunk in the Spirit."

It was the only way a parent could legitimately feel intoxicated around their children – although the occasional trip to a whisky distillery wasn't unusual for the Mumfords. On one family trip to

Perthshire, they visited Edradour — the smallest distillery in the country — which nestled on a hilltop glen above Pitlochry. Yet the young Marcus wasn't allowed so much as a sip. "I remember the smell was so vivid," he would later reminisce to *American Songwriter*. "We brought back little miniatures [but] I remember my parents let me just touch it to my lips — that was it!"

Back at home, it was business as usual. While Eleanor fended off criticism for her role as the UK's holy laughter ambassador, her son was still in single figures. At the time, he was attending Kings College, an exclusive private boarding school for boys in the leafy south west London village of Wimbledon. The location mingled the convenience of the city with the seclusion of the suburbs — and it just happened to be the same place that the parents of Marcus' future bandmate Ben Lovett had chosen to raise their son.

While Marcus' parents were borderline celebrities in the church-going community, Ben — by contrast — came from an ordinary, inconspicuous family. His father was a wealthy, self-made businessman, while his mother was a housewife, devoted to raising her children. At first glance, he and Marcus had little in common — especially because, as a child, Ben cared little for faith — but they bonded quickly over a shared love of music.

For Marcus' part, he had been raised on a heady combination of choir music — often directly off the printing press of the Vineyard record label — and classic rock and folk. The latter was provided courtesy of his mother's Bob Dylan records and, having learnt to use a record player at just a few years old, he would regularly play his favourites from her collection.

The most prominent of these would turn out to be Bob Dylan's acclaimed 1975 album *Blood On The Tracks*. He also fell in love with 'The House Of The Rising Sun', a traditional folk song whose origins are uncertain but which was turned into a worldwide rock hit in 1964 by Newcastle quintet the Animals.

All of Marcus' favourite artists were American and regular summer holidays in the USA throughout his childhood had helped to reinforce his fascination. "We came back every summer because we had lots of friends back in the US," he would recall. "So I'm well steeped in American music and culture. I would come home with bleached blond hair and ride a skateboard through this proper little British town."

Yet while he was influenced by looks and trends stateside, it was the music that would resonate with him the most. In an act of premature teenage rebellion, Marcus would add the soulful gospel sounds of Lauryn Hill to his list of favoured American music, purchasing the 1998 album *The Miseducation Of Lauryn Hill* at just 12 years old. "I was trying to be a badass," he would later joke to *Rolling Stone*. "I listened to that album religiously when I was like 12, 13. It was the first time I went to a store and bought my own CD."

Badass, Lauryn was not. With song titles such as 'Forgive Them Father', lyrical warnings to those who slept around, and continual references to Bible stories, she was a devout Jehovah's Witness. It was one of Marcus' earliest experiences of integrating God into music.

Ben on the other hand – an aspiring piano player – had a keen interest in blues and jazz. These two musical dimensions would be brought together by the pair's interactions at school.

Kings College was a leader academically – although arguably it had to be, to justify fees of £6,000 per term – and it achieved that status by accepting students not merely on their ability to pay their way but on the condition that they passed a strict entrance exam. The challenges didn't end once they'd earned a place, either. At GCSE level, Italian, Latin, Greek and Mandarin were just a few of the language options on offer – and those choosing Greek would find themselves memorising set texts such as *The Odyssey* in its original language and translating ancient mythology.

Yet while Kings College stood out for its academic rigour, it was also a leader in music – and it was the location where Ben and Marcus would first start playing together, in free jazz band Détente.

It all started with Ben's extracurricular music lessons. Nick Etwell, his piano teacher at the school, revealed, "I would teach Ben once a week. We had a really nice rapport and we thought it'd be nice to put a group together for him to play with other musicians. Being a piano player can sometimes get a bit boring, playing on your own all the time. So he got a little jazz group together with Marcus on drums and other friends Luke on sax and Ed on bass. I was their coach and I'd get them to play all the things I liked playing."

At the time, Nick had been working as a music teacher at the school purely to fund his real passion – playing trumpet in the funk, soul and organ jazz-style group the Filthy Six – and consequently he wasted little time in introducing the fledgling school group to some of the arrangements of his own band. He immediately saw potential in Ben ("my star pupil") and Marcus, whom he praised as "a great drummer".

Together with a young Matt Owens, who would later become a key part of folk group Noah and the Whale, Marcus and Ben devoted themselves to playing music and it seemed as though their blues, soul and jazz vibe was almost set in stone.

However, thanks to the influence of brother James, things were about to change. "He was a massive Bob Dylan fan and he and his friends would make me these mix CDs of obscure bluegrass and country," Marcus would later enthuse to *Music Snobbery*. Yet it was one soundtrack in particular that would change his life – that of the film *O Brother Where Art Thou?*

Set in the wheatfields of the Mississippi Delta countryside during the era of the Great Depression, the film followed a group of escaped convicts trying to form a blues group – and the music was just as Marcus might have expected from a movie about the Deep South.

Meanwhile the film's location mimicked that of the novels he'd read voraciously about his favourite era, thirties America. The plot, which was loosely based on Homer's *The Odyssey,* appealed to Marcus as he had just begun studying for an A-level in Greek. Exposure to this combination of influences – ancient Greek and vintage Americana – would prove a pivotal moment in inspiring his future songwriting.

Yet what mattered to him the most was the music. The film's soundtrack was packed with the folk sounds of its era, along with a sprinkling of bluegrass, country, swing and Delta blues. "It's a goldmine," Marcus would tell *The National.* "That was it. I just couldn't stop listening to it – and then I learnt to drive. I defy anyone to get in a car and drive with that soundtrack on. It creates a journey. And like John Steinbeck says, a journey is a person in itself. It has to have an element of the unknown and mystery. England doesn't have the wide open frontiers that America has, but with those bluegrass tunes on the car stereo, you're almost there."

There was one song in particular that would pull on his heartstrings – a version of the much covered 1913 bluegrass track 'Man Of Constant Sorrow'. It might have seemed odd to Marcus to see 10-times Grammy Award winning bluegrass singer Dan Tyminski's vocals lip-synced by Hollywood actor George Clooney, but nonetheless Marcus was hooked. He would play the song repeatedly on a loop while traversing open country lanes just outside of London and imagining himself not a few short miles from an urban metropolis, but in the heart of the Deep South.

Needless to say, mournful bluegrass songs reminiscent of thirties America weren't on every urban teenage boy's playlist. In fact, as Marcus would confess later, "No-one may age was listening to it." Yet unbeknown to him, another young music fan in West London was on exactly the same wavelength. That someone was Winston Marshall.

Winston was the son of Paul Marshall, a businessman known for co-owning one of the largest hedge-fund groups in the world. Paul's credentials were impressive; educated first at Oxford and then at the ISEAD Business School, where he was awarded an MBA, he'd started his career in politics, assisting the former leader of the Liberal Democrat Party, Charles Kennedy. By the time Winston was born, his father was in Fulham standing for Parliament.

Subsequently, following a stint as advisor to deputy prime minster to-be Nick Clegg, Paul made a name for himself as an investor, co-founding the £100 million company Marshall Wace LLP. Together with business partner Ian Wace, he managed funds that would go on to win multiple investment awards. As Paul's reputation soared, he would even be sought out later by media mogul Rupert Murdoch and his family, who requested advice on how to make a successful bid for BSkyB. Paul would respond by delivering a damning report on the quality of the family's PR.

Yet he wasn't the archetypal, ruthless businessman – he also had a passion for the welfare of children. After founding the ARK charity (Absolute Return for Kids), he became chairman of ARK Schools, an organisation which provides academies around the UK and fights to improve the standard of education in the inner city school system.

He'd noticed that for many, succeeding or failing was a postcode lottery and poorer children rarely had access to the education they needed to liberate them from poverty. He felt so strongly that he would co-author two books about the issue – *Aiming Higher: A Better Future For England's Schools* and *Tackling Educational Equality*.

Yet unusually for someone who campaigned for equality, he chose to send his own son to St Paul's School, one of the most exclusive options in the country. Admission to the school was predicated on a class-based system and, with fees of up to almost £30,000 a year, only the wealthy could apply.

Offering each student a place that cost more than the average Londoner's annual wage, wasn't this type of educational divide one Paul had been trying to stamp out? Tony Blair, former leader of the Labour Party, had been challenged on the grounds of hypocrisy when he defended the "excellent" quality of comprehensive schools but chose to send his own children to fee-paying ones – and now it looked as if Paul, who still had strong ties to the Liberal Democrats, might be facing the same accusations.

Yet there was equality in St Paul's history. The school was originally founded by a wealthy, eccentric and celibate priest, who spent all of his savings on building it next door to the cathedral of the same name. It had prided itself on its policy of offering education to children from any nation or background – and above all, it had done so for free. Children needed only to pay for their own wax candles to study by – it being the 1500s, there was no electricity.

Erasmus wrote textbooks for the school and it became the first place in England ever to teach Greek. It was the obvious choice for someone as passionate about education as Paul, as – even years on – the exam results spoke for themselves. The year that Winston graduated, it would make the headlines for being the highest-performing boy's school in the GCSE and A-level league tables for the second year running. Plus more students gained places at Oxford or Cambridge than from any other school in the country.

There was also a Biblical connection – and not just because of its proximity to London's most iconic cathedral. The school had originally provided 153 places, a deliberate reference to the miracle in St John's Gospel where Jesus turned his disciples' unsuccessful fishing trip into a plentiful one, yielding 153 fish from a river they'd thought empty. Some scholars claimed that, at that time, 153 species of fish were known to humankind, and the school used this as a metaphor to signify that any type of boy, no matter what his background, was welcome to apply – an inclusive policy that matched Paul's political proclivities. In memory of the Bible story, the school's official emblem became a fish.

Yet all of this was lost on Winston – according to his friends he had "absolutely no interest whatsoever" in religion and had preferred sleeping in late to attending the chapel.

This reluctance to embrace religion wasn't the only reason Winston stood out. For the son of an immaculately dressed, suited and booted businessman, someone who was no stranger to attending meetings at Parliament, his appearance made him the black sheep of his family.

Taking teenage rebellion to the max, he was sporting hip-hop style baggy jeans and long dreadlocks down to his waist. In the eyes of the conservative professionals who sent their sons to St Paul's, Winston was the poster boy for weed-smoking, gun-toting Rastafarian culture – and, possibly expecting a gangland turf war on their doorstep, some avoided him like the plague.

"He'd definitely get some odd looks," one friend confirmed. "There were people that didn't accept him because they automatically thought the hair and the general image meant that he was into drugs." Rising above any stereotypes directed at him, Winston was passionately defensive of his look – and once people got to know him, many cast aside their preconceptions.

In addition to the dreadlocks, Winston could rarely be seen without his trademark Reebok trainers – something that was decidedly at odds with the rest of his image. "You never quite knew what you'd get with Winston," his friend laughingly continued. "He was unpredictable. But he was a huge sport fan – and if God wasn't his religion, football probably was."

While his fellow students were studying Japanese and classical civilisation, Winston retreated into sport – and, of course, music. He too was passionate about soundtracks such as *O Brother Where*

Art Thou? – and in spite of having little in common with some of his more strait-laced classmates, he did find kindred spirits here and there to share in his love of music.

These included Charlie Fink – who would later become the frontman of Noah & the Whale – and Charles Costa, a slightly older boy at school who would later become the musician King Charles. The latter sported a "glam rock" hairstyle and had a penchant for light make-up, so Winston was not alone in having eccentricities. Yet he'd never found someone who loved the bluegrass genre quite as much as he did – until he met Marcus.

Ironically, considering Winston's disinterest in religion, the two 17 year olds' first encounter was at church. They'd later been reintroduced by mutual friends at the now defunct Push Bar – and they instantly bonded over *O Brother Where Art Thou?* "It was such a big influence," Winston would later rave. "It was huge… but [because no-one our age had it], when you found others that were listening to it, you felt more of a kinship."

For Marcus' part, he'd been given a first-class education in bluegrass by his brother, but he then discovered that Winston knew even more about the genre than he did. "My brother was at a college with a guy who made me a mix-tape with Alison Krauss and Gillian Welch and Old Crow Medicine Show on it… that was when I first discovered it," Marcus would later recall. "Winnie and I bonded over Old Crow really early on."

Winston would also introduce him to a bluegrass version of Gnarls Barkley's 'Crazy' – which was when their friendship was cemented. Soon the pair were calling each other constantly, in spite of attending different schools. Put simply, they understood each other when others didn't.

Bluegrass – along with rock, gospel, country and almost anything but the bubblegum pop that was trending among all of their schoolmates – was a major influence for Marcus, and listening to it was one of the defining moments that sparked his first flirtation with making his own music.

Combining his musical tastes with the ancient texts he was reading as part of his school curriculum, Marcus would also soon make his first foray into songwriting.

"I love classical history and I love medieval history," he would explain of his literary influences at that time. "Obviously you [also] study a lot of Shakespeare if you are an English schoolboy or girl, but growing up with *King Lear* was quite a big thing for me, as well as *Macbeth*."

Then he discovered a poet who would tap into his growing pains and teenage feelings of alienation, and in doing so, change his life. "I studied TS Eliot at school," he continued, "and he was the writer that made me want to start writing in the first place. I think he tackles the idea of being a nonentity quite well, maybe better than anyone else. So I started writing poetry that was so pretentious because I was also studying Latin and Greek, and obviously with all of Eliot's references, I was like [affects nerdy voice], 'Oh great, I can do this as well.' So I started making these awful poems."

Yet he was in for a crushing disappointment. When he plucked up the courage to show his work to a teacher, she butchered his efforts. "She just destroyed me," he recalled. "It was so pretentious and awful. And some of the first songs that I started to write were all kind of Eliot-esque. [When I listened back to them], they made me cringe."

Indeed, having his work critiqued so harshly was a sobering experience for Marcus, who had been bashful about it to begin with. As the end of sixth form approached, he'd started to tentatively hope that he might become a lyricist – but his teacher's criticism had cut like a knife. Humiliated and reluctant to ever make himself vulnerable on paper again, he wondered if he should take a more passive role in his love of literature and study a Classics degree instead.

Any seductive dreams of songwriting success were firmly dismissed as teenage fantasy. It was time to get real, he surmised, and – as painful as it was – he had to rise to that notion, enrolling at Edinburgh University instead.

Chapter 2

Fate Intervenes

Burying his instincts to pursue music, Marcus found himself enrolled on an intensive four-year course, studying the language, literature, history, art and archaeology of the ancient world. His first year was focused on Greece and the Roman Empire, whilst he'd also elected to study Latin.

The course had its perks – there would be organised study tours to countries such as Egypt and Iran all under the guise of work. Plus he would build an understanding of age-old civilisations by studying a series of epics, plays, poems and letters – something which appealed to Marcus' existing interest in writing literature-inspired lyrics. However, in some ways this aspect of the course only reminded him of what he'd turned his back on – and there was a nagging suspicion that he'd made the wrong choice.

Not that he could back out now, of course. His parents had spent more than £175,000 on his secondary school education alone – for the average worker, an equivalent of seven years' pay – and there was an unspoken, yet heavily weighted, expectation that he would produce a return on their investment.

Seeing the course through seemed inevitable and yet Marcus didn't have a career path planned. As much as he was trying to follow God, he knew that his future did not lie with the ministry and, due to his creative side, a high-flying business career would have slowly suffocated him.

What was more, to add to his confusion, his peers openly mocked and even scorned those who opted out of university life. "Everyone seemed to know what they were going to do afterwards though," one friend explained to the author. "Lots of people had jobs waiting for them in their parents' businesses as soon as they graduated. They knew where their lives were headed and what they wanted to get out of college – and they would laugh at people who didn't. Marcus tried to go with the flow and he was good at the work, but I think everyone could see his heart wasn't in it."

In spite of his uncertainty, he knew the only alternative was to become a dropout – and to endure all the social stigma that came with it. Yet there was one crucial turning point that gave him the courage to break away.

Since Marcus had left, Ben – who was still living in London – had started his own band, Hot Rocket, and was gigging on a regular basis. Seeing his friend's success and happiness showed Marcus how much he wanted to be involved in music too – and it was the push that finally prompted him to swallow his fears about leaving education.

"Ben and Marcus were like brothers ever since they met," his friend revealed to the author, "and seeing him get his own band together gave him a twinge of sibling rivalry. They'd always been involved in music together and yet now his best friend was moving on without him."

Up until that moment, Marcus had been faithfully attending every lecture – albeit with growing reluctance – but at every chance he got he was furiously scribbling lyrics on the back of envelopes in his college dorm room instead.

He would later admit that talking about his feelings went against his British temperament and was "so not cool", and thus his lyrics captured an alienation that he dared not admit to anyone around him. He'd told his closest friends that the college experience had left him "more lost than he'd ever been" but most of his candour was saved for the privacy of his poetry.

One of the very few peers to have seen a little of his work revealed to the author, "He would write about feeling inadequate, not being able to measure up to other people around him. I think he feared that everyone else having a sense of direction made them superior. There was a guilt trip that he wasn't living his life the way he wanted *or* the way his family wanted; he was failing on both counts. I think at that point he felt like a fraud. He would get lonely and start to feel that he was in the wrong place at the wrong time and that life was passing him by. Some of the lyrics were the Cure meets Nick Drake meets Leonard Cohen. Utterly depressing!"

To elucidate his belief even further that life was passing him by, he'd encounter his old friend Winston whilst in Edinburgh – and he was in the city to play a concert with his new band. "[It was] called Captain Kick & the Cowboy Ramblers, which was a bluegrass sleaze rap band," Marcus later recalled fondly, "who were, let's say, iconic in their status!"

Winston, who was still sporting waist-length dreadlocks, had reinvented himself as "Country Winston" and was playing a mixture of guitar, banjo, harmonica, dobro and mandolin, as and when the mood took him.

His bandmates included "Hillbilly" Harry Cargill, who alternated with him on all the same instruments, and the dubiously named Tom "The Kid" Fiddler who also moonlighted as a fiddle player for Noah & the Whale. On guitar duties were Davie Crocket, Zadok "The Hick" and Jersey "Big Tongue" Ben, who also doubled as the group's "Bad Ass MC" in representation of the rap corner.

Then there was Leeroy Ouseley on mandolin, Sheriff Dawson on bass, Tom Miller on the "rock organ", "Rambling Uncle AIDS" on the piano, "Deputy Sheriff Max Jazzriel" on the double bass and the saxophone and Uke Smith on the ukulele. Also in the group were "Blue Louis Green" on percussion and guitar, "MC Lil Haystack" as a DJ and MC and Max McGraw "The Honky Tonk Whore", who took up piano and organ. Finally "Hangman The Whale" was content to join in on "anything with strings". Vocals were performed by almost the entire group.

Heavily inspired by country and bluegrass, their influences included hit-makers such as Shania Twain, Dexy's Midnight Runners, Neil Young, Willie Nelson, Johnny Cash and – incongruously – the Grateful Dead, as well as less well-known acts such as the Soggy Bottom Boys, Union Station, Rednex, Hayseed Dixie, Jerry Douglas, Doc Watson, Blue Highway, Duelling Banjos, the Bluegrass Boys, the Humblebums, Bill Monroe, Ben Harper, Nitty Gritty Dirt Band and the Mississippi Sheikhs.

With such a broad spectrum of influences, it was little wonder Marcus, as he watched silently from the sidelines, was impressed. However, what captured his attention the most was that this 16-piece band, complete with an additional driver and tour manager, had all met at the same place – a blink-and-you'll-miss-it bar by the name of Bosun's Locker.

A tiny basement bar below a pasty shop, it was so small that it barely attracted a glance from the busy Londoners in the streets above – but for those in the know, it was rapidly becoming notorious.

"It was an amazing time," musician friend Kevin Jones reminisced of the era. "A tiny 40-capacity venue. It was like the beginning of the folk scene… all these solo singer-songwriters trying things out. It was a really good vibe."

Perhaps one of the reasons for its success was that the crowd came together as fans of a musical genre, experimenting and exchanging ideas. They were playing to honour music rather than to be competitive and self-celebratory, and that was the key.

"People would just jump up and play," Kevin explained. "It wasn't really big enough for bands, so you'd just have solo artists, but instead of working in isolation, they'd all swap ideas. No-one was really snooty about what anyone else was trying to do. It's amazing to think of how many people emerged from that tiny room."

What was more, Winston – who also ran a regular club night at the venue – was believed to have been the one who'd given birth to the "scene". "Winston started it," Kevin asserted. "He was really into banjos from the beginning. I don't think you could pin the craze on anyone else!"

It was also the location where Ben had started gigging with his indie band Hot Rocket, comprising fellow Bosun's Locker devotees Kevin Jones on guitar and Luxembourger Chris Maas, who'd previously gigged with hip-hop MC Example, on drums.

Unsurprisingly, Marcus was keen to be in on the act. After a heart to heart with Ben at Edinburgh nightspot Sneaky Pete's – run by an acquaintance of Ben's from Devon – he decided to leave Scotland behind and allow himself to be introduced to the music scene back home.

"I do remember asking where he was!" his tutor Andrew Erskine later told the author of the first time his student failed to turn up to class, "and being told that he had gone to be a rock star, which I assumed was a joke – until my brother bought the album!"

By early 2006, Marcus was back in West London, a world of promise now stretching out before him. Yet at first, as a newcomer to the scene, he struggled to slot in with what the others were doing. "I had one guy come up to me," he later admitted, "[when] I was playing a song on my own, and he said it was the most horrible thing he'd ever heard!"

Humiliatingly, in a venue of that size, the snub wasn't something the Bosun's crowd would quickly forget. Consequently, Marcus' early memories of the venue were a little less favourable than those of his peers.

"You'd struggle to find a scene less like an actual scene anywhere," he would later tell *The National*. "Scenes are supposed to have a look and an ideal and a certain exclusivity. We didn't. We welcomed anyone and we played whatever came to hand. But yeah, if 80 people in a hole in the ground underage drinking is a folk scene, that's what it was."

"A lot of us were underage and it was the only place where we could drink," Winston would add mischievously. "The only other qualifier to be there was you had to be willing to engage in some way."

While he, Marcus and Ben were able to legally drink – and, in fact, openly admitted to doing so soon after they reached double figures – they had personally encountered and worked with several young teenagers at the venue.

One of these was Alessi Laurent-Marke, whose first name was an allusion to her parents' favourite Italian design company. Inspired by Meg from the White Stripes, she'd been a keen percussionist from the age of 11, while love affairs with vocals and guitar soon followed. She'd soon find fame in Alessi's Ark, signing to Virgin in 2007 and going on to release her own material, but her days at Bosun's Locker, where she jammed with Winston and Ben, represented a short-lived era of pre-fame innocence.

That was exactly what the tiny bar represented to most of those who encountered it – a place for aspiring musicians to gather their confidence, meet like-minded music lovers and find their feet. Once Marcus shook off his initial performance anxiety and inferiority complex and started to see it that way too, he found himself very much enjoying it – apart from the overcrowding. "We were all just chilling out and it was a really fun time," he recalled, "but [the club] was always really rammed. You could only fit about 80 people and usually there were about 120 people there. Those were our first experiences with shit sound and a lot of people talking over you!"

Another of the underage performers at the bar was Laura Marling, a 15-year-old singer-songwriter who also played guitar. Introduced by mutual friend Winston, Marcus and Laura hit it off straight away and began to shirk the Bosun's tradition – dictated by lack of space – of showcasing solo artists only by both cramming on to the tiny stage at once to make music together. She would serenade him with song, while he took up the role of percussionist alongside her.

A large crowd of university-aged men befriending 15-year-old girls might have raised a few alarmed eyebrows – particularly as one of Winston's bandmates called himself Tom "The Kid" Fiddler and had jokily claimed that he played both "fiddles and little children", but – in spite of the somewhat tasteless paedophile jokes – the relationship between the boys and the younger performers was entirely innocent. In fact, it was only years later that romance would blossom between Marcus and Laura.

Marcus soon made another valuable connection at the bar too, when he met singer and songwriter Alan Pownall. In the years to come, Alan would support artists such as Florence + the Machine and would even receive a personal invite from multi-platinum star Adele to join her on tour. However back then, fresh out of art school in Italy, Alan was just starting out and was looking for a bassist and drummer for his backing band. Marcus won the position of percussionist, while another young hopeful, Ted, agreed to be the bassist. It was an ill-fated line-up and, within just 24 hours, after playing one show, both of them were fired. "Luckily I think we all got fired at one point or another," Ben would later reassure his bandmates, "and just became a reject band!"

At the time, Marcus struggled to find it quite so funny. On the plus side, the one-off concert did introduce him to a future Mumford & Sons bandmate.

Ted – full name Edward James Milton Dwane, but affectionately known as T–Bear to his friends – was another public school boy who'd attended the top-ranking Milfield School in Somerset. His father, also called Edward, had set up a construction company the year before he was born and by the time Ted arrived into the world on August 15, 1984, the family had become affluent.

Yet Ted had no interest in following in his father's footsteps as a self-made businessman – and, as soon as he left school, he enrolled in a course at the Academy of Contemporary Music College in Guildford instead. Already a part-time guitar and banjo player, his aspiration had been to learn the art of playing bass.

In a world saturated by bass players, Ted had originally taken up the banjo in a bid to be different. "He thought it would make him stand out," one schoolmate told the author. "After all, how many banjo players are there out there? In the end though, he knew his heart lay with the rhythm and sound of the bass."

Graduating in 2004 with a diploma in Bass Performance, Ted then reunited with his secondary schoolmates Hannah Miller and Ruth Skipper – all three had attended the co-ed Milfield School – and joined their experimental progressive folk group, the Moulettes.

Originally none of the members had taken the project seriously – for example, Hannah had just started a seven-year degree in Medicine and was using the band as a fun distraction to while away her time before qualifying as a GP. Gigs were sandwiched between her college commitments, while the group's members seemed to be on constant rotation. At the time when Ted joined, two members were leaving, while another – drummer Oliver Austin – had just been recruited. Operating now as a four-piece – although it wasn't the last time this precarious line-up would change – the group played a series of free gigs in London, Manchester and beyond.

Ted threw himself into each one with near feverish excitement. Although he was yet to earn any money from his musical endeavours, for him the pleasure of having a platform on which to play music was reward enough.

Playing in the Moulettes also satisfied his thirst for "real" music, free from the overzealous production values of, for example, an *X-Factor* winner's CD. "Electronic music or a DJ playing CDs doesn't excite me," he would later tell *The National*. "Acoustic instruments are really raw and have a much bigger energy, that is something I can understand."

Thus his group – featuring Hannah on guitar and cello and Ruth on bassoon and harp – seemed to have answered his prayers.

That said, earning recognition as a newcomer to the music scene wasn't easy – especially when concerts were necessarily organised around his bandmates' college commitments and tended to be infrequent – but, as his friend and fellow musician Nick Trepka recalled, his optimism was relentless.

Nick and Ted had originally met via a mutual friend, Joe Lewis, who'd been in Ted's year at Milfield School. "Joe and I met in Edinburgh and I first briefly met Ted when he came to visit Joe there," Nick told the author. "His infectiously sunny disposition made a strong impression on me and it's never really abated the whole time I've known him."

Before long, the friendship between Nick and Ted had deepened, and – together with Joe and his girlfriend Rose – they moved in with each other at a flat in London. Nick, a freelance producer, engineer, songwriter and musician, spent his time in the capital "gigging, working on Denmark Street and looking for recording work", although he was rarely too busy not to maintain the tradition of jamming with his housemates.

"Joe and I played music together [too] and there was a lot of music happening in the house," he reflected, "starting with the three of us working on a barber shop style version of Irving Berlin's 'The Song Has Ended But The Melody Lingers On' – just for fun. Ted and I spent a lot of time jamming too, mostly blues. He was a very agile and imaginative guitar player and it was always a pleasure to play with him."

The pair were prolific songwriters too, sharing their efforts on a regular basis and becoming a "sensitive, encouraging sounding board for each other". To add to the vibrant musical culture that ran through the household, the Moulettes would often stay over, cramming themselves into the overcrowded flat on gig nights or staging impromptu soundchecks and rehearsals in the living room. The logical next step was for Nick to produce them, which is exactly what happened.

"I recorded an early demo EP for them at another friend's house," Nick continued, "a very lo-fi affair to tide them over until they could afford a more polished recording."

Yet Ted was keeping his options open – although he was an official member of the Moulettes, he was also a stand-in bassist for Laura Marling. His jams with her could often be seen at Bosun's Locker, occasionally also featuring Marcus on drums.

The rapport between Marcus and Ted at these shows was evident. Like his friend, Ted had emerged from education not fully satisfied and with a fierce sense of ambition and a belief that Bosun's Locker, as tiny and innocuous as it might have seemed, was a gateway to living out his dreams.

The venue had become not just a place to perform, but a way of life, with almost all of the pair's closest friends now involved with the scene. At the time of the ill-fated concert with Alan Pownall, Winston and Marcus had been sharing one flat, while fellow Bosun's Locker friends Alan and Jay Jay Pistolet (future frontman of the Vaccines, real name Justin Hayward-Young) lived in the one above.

On the nights that they weren't performing at the venue, Marcus would gig with Laura Marling, socialising little with Alan on this account, but for Ted – in spite of being unceremoniously fired – his friendship with Alan endured.

Out of this camaraderie had come the proto-punk group Sex Face. "Unfortunately it never made it out of the rehearsal room," Alan chuckled. "I always describe it as we had to break up as it was too brilliant. I think the real reason we had to break up was because it wasn't good enough. I was trying to learn how to play the bass and Ted was playing the guitar and we had a friend on drums. We were going to be this magical three piece, but in reality there was no direction."

The concept of the group had originally reared its head during the trio's schooldays when all three had some "teenage angst" to offload, accounting for their raw, distinctly non-folk sound. By the time it had taken shape, it was entirely incongruous with Ted's goals. He was already a qualified bassist, yet the line-up required him to play guitar – and the idea of playing in a punk band was probably starting to wear thin. "The idea was to shave our heads and be punks," Alan joked, "but we couldn't find any clippers."

Despite the demise of Sex Face – which none of the boys had taken particularly seriously – Alan and Ted maintained a strong friendship. "Marcus was playing drums with Laura so we didn't see much of him," Alan recalled, "but me, Ted and Winston became very close. Winston is probably my favourite person in the world. We ate together, drank together, slept under the same roof and played music together – what more could you want?"

Yet before they knew it, the scene that had brought all of them together was about to split in two, with the closure of Bosun's Locker. Nevertheless, when one door closes, another opens, and that was exactly the case for the group of musicians who'd found themselves displaced. In the end, it had been Ben who'd taken "the logical next step" by launching Bosun's successor – the club night Communion.

The club's closure had left a gap and providing another place to play would simply fill it, but there was much more to the Communion ethos than that. Ben and fellow Hot Rocket member Kevin Jones had become increasingly outraged about what they believed to be the exploitation of new bands trying to make it in the music industry.

"We were fed up of playing shows were you ultimately had to pay to play," Ben told *Time Out*, drawing on his own early gig experiences. "You'd turn up and the promoter would be like, "Why haven't you brought 30 people?" You'd be hassling friends and family to get people to the gig. There's no platform for an unsigned music scene in the main cities – it's all hyped acts or showcases behind closed doors. I read about artists that are doing it "the old-fashioned way" and touring, as if that's a unique thing to do – well, that should just be the way it is."

Yet, as he'd found out himself, touring came with its own problems at the hands of ruthless promoters. Everywhere they played, Hot Rocket had been obligated to bring along a pre-agreed number of people to the show – and if they failed to make the quota, they wouldn't get paid. For those just starting out who lacked a disposable income or a large pre-existing fanbase, following their dreams could quickly become financially unsustainable.

Convinced that talented musicians were being bypassed left, right and centre due to low visibility and a hostile climate, Ben started to research the London gig scene – and was horrified at what he found. "I learnt that there are approximately 10,000 active bands playing each year in London alone," he exclaimed. "Some people would struggle to name one of those from 2011, most could name five or ten and a few could name maybe 20 or 30. Those aren't good odds for new bands."

He continued, "Communion was born out of shared frustration. We felt that although Myspace and YouTube opened up the playing field for songwriters online, people's discovery of these new artists was only skin deep. Those artists lucky enough to be hyped up would find themselves playing to barely anyone in a London venue one second, then playing in front of the flock of A&R scouts who determine who receives a record deal, then competing for space in the dwindling number of magazines and newspapers and reduced radio playlists."

To make matters worse, Ben felt that the average club night was focused purely on profiteering, doing little to benefit the consumers and at times downright discriminating against the performers.

"The curation is a huge problem," he would explain to *Pop Matters*. "No care or attention has gone into thinking how the artists will stand up next to each other in terms of the genre or the style. You might see a three-piece metal outfit, followed by a folk electronica outfit. To someone who has paid a ticket to go to the event, you're not encouraging people to stay and appreciate the other bands. When you're booking the act, you're putting pressure on the metal act from out of town to bring as many people as they can. They are stressed before the show, and the people they hassled to come to the show aren't going to stay and see the other acts."

In Ben's eyes, the system made it near impossible for a fledgling band to spread their visibility outside of their home town. After all, at home, bringing along friends and family to satisfy profit-fuelled promoters' agendas was child's play, but attracting a large crowd in an unknown city, on the other hand, could be near impossible. The culture of the music business was creating a Catch 22-style vicious circle, whereby those bands who were not lucky enough to be spotted by a record label straight away couldn't get noticed outside of their neighbourhood at all.

Yet Ben felt a rush of paternal pride every time he caught sight of an exciting new act he felt deserved the spotlight – and his instinct was to take over where Bosun's Locker had left off by "nurturing" this emerging musical talent.

He found a like-minded ally in bandmate Kevin Jones, as well as a producer he'd met earlier in April 2006 by the name of Ian Grimble. The group had been approached by Ian after he'd caught a Hot Rocket live show and had been keen to produce their debut album. Coming from someone who'd previously worked on Travis and Manic Street Preachers albums, it was "flattering" and, all in all, an enormous coup.

They'd stayed in touch and now, together, the three of them would embark on a mission to create ethical club nights, free from exploitation. Under their wing, no longer would groups desperate to make a mark be intimidated into bringing everyone they knew to the show, only to receive a measly couple of pounds per band member for their efforts.

The idea was to build up a community based on a shared love of music and to introduce audiences to those groups that they felt deserved more recognition. They knew exactly what they wanted to do – and now all they needed was a name.

One drunken night, Marcus did the honours. "We were in the Rose and Crown in Wimbledon," Ben recalled to *Chords And Candles*, "and we were all hanging out. Marcus was like, 'Why don't you just call it Communion?' and that sounded like a good idea. Community, communion – it kinda made sense."

Following on from where the Bosun's Locker club nights had left off, the name was a very fitting way to describe their ethos. "There was a lot of competition on the indie scene, but the Bosun's group were always helping each other out, playing on each other's records and writing songs for one another," Kevin Jones recalled. "[It's] always been the idea to make Communion a big family – not in a hippy way, but in a way where everyone helps each other out. I think that makes you stronger than the sum of your parts. The idea of the club night was to continue that community."

Thanks to Ian's connections, the trio's vision became a reality and they were offered a monthly residency at the Notting Hill Arts Club in west London. With a capacity of 200 people, it was more than double the size of Bosun's Locker but – crucially – it retained its intimate community feel.

The most rewarding part of the launch, of course, was scouting for talent. Ben recalled, "We would go out and find our favourite artists – some that we knew, some that had been recommended to us by friends, others that we just saw from going out and about in London. We would see them playing for four people – often their aunts and uncles and best friends – and we'd go and approach them and ask if they wanted to be part of a line-up that would be part of a multi-band line-up on a Sunday night."

The most exciting element of what Communion did was the chance to pluck unknown yet promising acts from total obscurity and give them the opportunity to make themselves known on a larger scale. In doing so, Ben had the sense that he was discovering – and then imparting – top secret but valuable knowledge.

He was a cheerleader for ethical promotions, too – and from the outset, he felt Communion's attitude to the bands was the antithesis of everyone else's at that time. "There is so much saturation in London, so many acts and promoters," Ben would later lament to *Pop Matters*, "yet we very rarely went to an event that was any good. Venues appeared to be at best half-full, bands wouldn't be getting paid, and promoters were either completely nonchalant or angry that the bands hadn't brought more people in. There was this big misunderstanding of everyone's roles."

Ben, Kevin and Ian made a mutual agreement that all performers would be paid regardless of how many punters they'd brought through the doors. "Every band was paid upfront before the doors opened," Ben clarified, "based just on the fact that we loved what they do, not on their crowd pull."

To prove yet further that their motivation was not merely lining their pockets, the trio faced fans – and themselves – with a challenge. Shows would be held on Sundays, the quietest night of the week. "We wanted to test the gig-goer, as much as we wanted to test everything else," Ben revealed, "to see who would commit to going to a show on a Sunday night, instead of a Friday or Saturday where people are often just out to socialise anyway."

Yet he was left with no doubt that true music lovers would pass this test of their commitment. In fact, fittingly named for a club that opened its doors on a Sunday, Communion's very foundations were built on faith. His conviction was that there would "always be an appetite for top-notch songwriting" and, inspired by the talent he was seeing as he scouted around London's lesser-known clubs and bars, he knew that he could provide it.

That first night, an unseasonably warm late spring evening in 2006, it was just like Bosun's Locker Mark 2. Marcus had been invited to sing solo, while Andrew Davie from Cherbourg played ukulele and Laura Marling chimed in on backing vocals. There were no boundaries – everyone mucked in together.

"There's a strong friendship network that underpins the whole thing," Kevin would remark admiringly. "All the musicians who came down to Communion really responded to that. It's a reaction against that kind of corporate promoting and all those indie bands who slag each other off – you're not going to get as far that way as if you help each other out."

The feel-good factor was common to the audiences too and, thanks to a manageable entrance fee of just £5, the club was packed – a sell-out on its debut night. "We noticed all of a sudden that there was a genuine bond building among fans who paid a very small fee to see the artists," Ben explained. "Almost like a thanks between the people who paid their five pounds at the door, and then got to get in and see a whole bunch of fantastic new artists. And the fans would keep going back and following these artists, as the artists went on to even better things."

However not everyone was quite so delighted. "Of course we're getting people who've got their back up a bit – I've got a guy standing outside my house with a baseball bat right now," Ben joked. "Some promoters are angry because we're calling all of this into question, and making them think about doing some real work – real booking, curation and promotion again. But it's all good. We're happy to do that. Really we're just bringing good vibes, we're not here to start a fight, but of course they'll be a little annoyed that we're trying to write the rules."

In spite of some promoters' resistance, however, the phone soon started ringing off the hook with calls of gratitude from record labels. To their eyes, A&R scouting had become a dying art and they'd been relying on *NME* – as well as the occasional showcase – to point them in the right direction, and often belatedly, of new talent. Communion, on the other hand, which relied on the mutual admiration between its artists to get recommendations, was always in the know. As the club night's notoriety spread, just playing a show on a Sunday came with the promise of being spotted – and even signed.

Communion soon became notorious for producing breakout artists. Throughout 2007, Noah and the Whale were commanding serious attention, and by the following year, they'd scored a Top 10 hit with the folk-pop anthem 'Five Years On'.

Then there was Laura Marling, flanked by Marcus, who was "depping for her other drummer who was doing his GCSEs"! Her debut album, *Alas, I Cannot Swim*, was released in October 2007, to much fanfare and a hotly tipped launch party at the Soho Revue Bar.

Unfortunately, Laura herself failed to attend – she'd been intercepted by security and banned from her own concert on account of being underage. "We played in an alleyway instead, outside these sex shops!" Marcus would later recall incredulously. Meanwhile, not to be deterred, Laura would reschedule her Revue Bar concert, returning on the day of her 18th birthday.

Yet that first night, sitting cross-legged on the pavement with a topless peepshow bar on one side of her and a sleazy cinema, with blow-up dolls in the window, on the other, might not have been the most glamorous way to formally launch a career – nor the most family friendly – but nonetheless it worked. Her fame accelerated rapidly and before long, the album would earn a nomination for the Mercury Music Prize.

Then there was the success of the founders themselves – Hot Rocket had performed artist slots on MSN Live Sessions and XFM that year and had even made an appearance at the Exit Kernow Festival, the all-day, all-night party set on an ancient round field in the heart of Cornwall's farmland, with stone barns surrounding the vicinity of the stage.

In October 2007, the band's debut single, 'Do Do Do', aired on indie radio, to feverish approval. The group, once described as "Charlie Chaplin meets the Strokes", also took the London music scene by storm with an EP featuring the tracks 'Love And Sympathy', 'School Song', 'Tammy' and 'Hail Of Gunfire' as well as the single 'Do Do Do'.

One critic mused that the boys were purveyors of "sparkling indie pop with an undeniable dark edge", while another vowed, "This band stands head and shoulders over all the arty, pretentious prats that tend to top the reviews. Great, bouncy, catchy, danceable, clever but unpretentious poppy rock!"

Clearly, the performers who played Communion were almost universally making waves. Yet the most famous group ever to emerge from the club night would, of course, be Mumford & Sons. Their first incarnation consisted of Marcus, Ted and Winston under the moniker of Marcus Mumford and His Merry Men.

"There was something special about the chemistry between the three of them," a friend and regular punter at Communion recalled to the author. "When they were all together in a room, it just went off. Ben was passionate about their sound – not only were they all his close friends, but he loved what they were doing. However at that point, he was committed to Hot Rocket and touring the country with them."

This in itself might have been a barrier to joining the others. Yet increasingly, the Mumford three piece was competing for Ben's attentions. He might have loved watching them, but when he took to the stage with them, it became clear that he was the missing puzzle piece that completed the musical picture. After joining them for a low-key concert at London's Monkey Chews – with a singer named Holly, who would later become Marcus' brother James's wife, in tow – Ben decided he knew where his heart lay.

That same month – October 2007 – Ben broke away and found himself holed up in Putney's RMS Studios with his three bandmates to be. Turning his focus away from Hot Rocket at a time when their popularity was at its height – not to mention when they were in the middle of a sell-out UK tour – might have seemed unthinkable, but Ben's every instinct was telling him that this line-up was right.

He wouldn't be disappointed. Together the quartet produced three songs – 'White Blank Page', 'Awake My Soul' and another track that sadly would never make it into the public domain, 'The Liar'.

"We sang in harmony in that studio and it clicked," Ben would later enthuse. "Four felt like a family. And then we just kept this ethic of jamming, writing, performing from scraps of paper stuck to the kick drum and then honing it afterwards. I'm going to sound like a complete wanker now but I don't care: the idea is we serve the song, and the songs were served by us being a four."

Now that they'd found the right line-up, it was time to give their project a name. Although they'd founded at Ben's club night, Marcus was the unspoken leader, the one who organised studio sessions and networked to find them gigs. He was a pivotal father figure to the foursome – and consequently, tapping into a trend that dated back to the Bosun's Locker days, he decided to adopt the group members as his musical sons. The move mimicked Sons of Noel and Adrian, another fledgling band out on the music scene, and a number of others – there'd even been a group with "and Daughter" in its name.

"We called ourselves Mumford & Sons because we liked the idea of an old-fashioned family-owned store," Winston elaborated to *The National*. "If it really was a store, it would sell cheese and whisky, cigarettes and tools. A general store selling stuff you really cannot live without. And we tried to make music that felt sort of natural and necessary."

The idea that cigarettes and whisky were essential household items might come as a surprise to some – but the Mumfords were adopting the philosophy of cheerfully debauched rock veterans Oasis, who famously penned the track '(All I Need Are) Cigarettes And Alcohol'. Perhaps the group was simply getting into folk 'n' roll character.

Despite sarcastic murmurs among early listeners that the Mumford sound was reminiscent of "sorrowful old men", Marcus was indisputably too young to have three 20-something sons. However, as ludicrous as it might seem, and as much as the name conjured up images of a vintage furniture shop, an old-school timber yard business or a family-run construction company, this was the way Mumford & Sons wanted to be known to the world.

It was under this persona that they wowed Ted's friend Nick Trepka. "I think I first met them around the start of 2008 when I was seeing off an old girlfriend at the door, and they were standing outside about to knock," he recalled to the author. "After I closed the door I remember Winston saying, 'Who's the broad?' I liked them straight away."

While first impressions were positive, that was nothing compared to his reaction when he heard the music. When he saw the four play together in a room, he instantly shared his friend's conviction that the chemistry in this band was right. "Seeing them play live for this first time was unforgettable," Nick continued. "It was the only time I could remember leaving a gig with tears in my eyes. It was profoundly emotional; I found 'Liar' particularly devastating. It just resonated with me."

The earliest version of the track compared love to a fortress, the strength of which the song's character had never before had to test. Yet honesty – or the lack thereof – can crumble the best-laid defences, as he soon discovers when his relationship ends in tears.

No-one in the group other than Marcus knew exactly what had inspired the song. "I'm very English," he would later joke to *Rolling Stone,* "and we don't talk about emotions." However, everyone understood the sentiment – and before long, the four-piece was sharing it.

They hit the road with people such as Laura Marling, Johnny Flynn, Jay Jay Pistolet, King Charles and Peggy Sue to name but a few, resolving to play wherever and whenever possible and do all it took to increase their exposure.

Some of the concerts were back-to-basics, but arguably no-one was more equipped than the Mumfords to eat humble pie. After all, their earliest performances had been to as few as three people. "You shouldn't feel precious about either where you're playing or who you're playing to," Marcus later told *Performing Musician.* "You've just got to carpet-bomb at first… say yes to every gig and just play."

He added, "Don't be snooty about where you play or who you play to, because there's always someone who's a potential candidate to be converted to your type of music. Even if you're playing to a crowd of 50 people and 49 of them are chatting away to their mates and are more obsessed with getting drunk than listening to the music, there'll still be one person there who will like your music and even become a fan!"

This approach was exactly how they attracted the attention of manager Adam Tudhope, who organised a headline show for them at a nightclub that was definitely not a dive – London's Luminaire.

Although they were yet to release any formal material, the gig – held on July 7 – was a sell-out from word of mouth alone. This momentous occasion marked a turning point for Marcus and his musical sons – they were no longer merely four friends jamming together for fun, without a sense of purpose or direction beyond the next show – that night had unified them as a band. "There was something about that night," Ben recalled to *The Guardian* nostalgically. "It felt like, 'OK, we're a band now, this is a proper gig.'"

The atmosphere was not lost on reviewers, one of whom labelled them "folk-infused enjoyment embodied". However the most special thing of all about the show was that it tied in with the release of their first EP, *Lend Me Your Eyes*.

Aiming to give listeners a snapshot of their sound, it included the three demos they'd recorded previously, along with another recently penned song, 'Roll Away Your Stone'.

The group had been approached by the newly founded boutique record label Chess Club, which specialised in releases on limited edition vinyl – just the type of small-scale investment the Mumfords needed to get their career started. As it was a small, passion-led label, it was much more about delivering the music than masterminding an image or arranging a heavy-handed, cringe-inducing PR campaign. As Ben's partner in Communion crime Kevin Jones would later note, "Major labels get it wrong a lot of the time because they try to project their own vision onto the artist. It's like if you're going out with someone and you think, 'If only they had a different haircut, were a foot taller and were wearing better shoes, then they'd be perfect.' That's not the right way to approach it [by] trying to change the artist… as soon as we start styling bands and generally being idiots, then we've lost our way."

To make sure there was no chance of the group losing its individuality, Ben produced the EP himself. Despite having little production experience, he knew what he wanted – an EP that showcased their raw energy as a live act and didn't dilute the bare bones of their sound.

"I've never really studied it or anything," Ben told *For Folk's Sake*, "but I've got a real chip on my shoulder about producers not understanding the music. When I don production, I get really protective of it – I think it's really important that the producer doesn't stamp their own sound on it. [With my involvement], it'll be more representative."

Ted concurred, "When you start adding more and more people into the mix, it dilutes it. No-one knows what we want to sound like as well as we do."

Thus it was a group effort, with Winston even trying his hand at the EP's artwork. Yet there was room for one outsider whom the group knew understood their sound – Nick Trepka. "Ted asked me if I'd like to go along and help out," he told the author, "and I went along for two days of the session. I helped with setting up mics to record Winston's dobro and banjo, and was an extra voice in the group vocal harmonies for several songs. It was a very buoyant atmosphere."

What was more, despite priding themselves on being a traditional grassroots band, the Mumfords didn't miss a beat when it came to cultivating social media. "Between recordings they were tending to their Myspace page," Nick continued, "which must've exceeded 10,000 plays not long beforehand. Interest in the band seemed to be rising exponentially, the messages from their fans full of adoration and superlatives."

Surrounded by only their closest friends and allies as they read the messages of support, everything about the project felt right. They'd chosen to work with Chess Club because of its previous work with trusted friend Jay Jay Pistolet on his 2007 EP *We Are Free*. The label had also released the much-admired *Unfinished Business* EP by White Lies.

Later, the label would add to its collection even further with three Cherbourg EPs (*Last Chapter, Into The Deep* and *No More Flowers*), Peggy Sue's *Yo Mama* and the Middle East's *Blood*, to name but a few.

Thanks to their involvement with other acquaintances on the music scene, the Mumfords and Chess Club were not merely business partners but friends. Even the studio had been just right – the House of Strange was a cosy basement below a Victorian dog biscuit factory, offering a labyrinth of vintage pedals, amps and "more percussion than you'll ever need" to serve its cramped stage.

All in all, the recording had been a great success, and – while its official release would be on July 14 – some copies were made available in advance to tempt punters at the Luminaire show. Watching in amazement as their new-found cult following's enthusiasm unfolded, and seeing the EP fly off the shelves that night at the show, the quartet knew they had to peel away from their respective side projects and make a commitment to each other.

Hot Rocket had already dissolved, with its members now focusing on developing the Communion nights, but Ted had to make the decision to part with old friends the Moulettes. "As Ted's commitments to the Mumfords grew and as tantalising hints of their growing recognition started to filter through, Ted could devote less and less time to the Moulettes," Nick explained to the author, "and eventually he had to part ways with them, which I'm sure was a decision he was reluctant to have to make."

Winston had been a perpetual session artist, with side projects everywhere but nothing too serious, so it was easy for him to break away. However Marcus was contractually obligated to Laura Marling for just a little longer – the following month would see him join her on drums on tour in America.

While Laura's success would ultimately peak at a lower level than the Mumfords, at that time her star was rising faster – and she was the headline act. Yet her position on centre stage during her solo sets, with Marcus assisting in the background, highlighted her social awkwardness.

This forced him to step out of the shadows to compensate – and before long, filling in for her taught him the art of engaging with an audience. "I got a lot of confidence being on stage with Laura," he would later confess to the *Herald Sun*. "She wouldn't say a word at gigs. We were doing shows where it was just the two of us. She wasn't talking to the audience so she asked me to."

Yet to Marcus' surprise, it wasn't just nerve-racking, but "fun" – and he soon grew to relish the idea of onstage banter. "I enjoyed the fact you can engage with hundreds of people," he added, "and you can talk to each other and communicate."

Marcus also learnt to multi-task, playing what one magazine would later describe as "an unholy amount of instruments". "You can't really count the ones that I don't know what I'm doing on," he would later chuckle to *Entertainment Weekly*. "Laura would show me the two buttons that I press on the accordion, then I make a noise and it's in the right key. Sometimes I would even put stickers on the buttons so I knew what to press. But really, I can only play the drums. I can fake-play the guitar and the mandolin and ukulele and the banjo, but I don't really know what I'm doing a lot of the time."

From an outsider's perspective, this was far from a professional outfit – one band member was haphazardly bluffing his way through instrumentals, while another was too fearful even to say hello to the audience. Yet what shone through was the passion and the raw talent – and not only were the concerts sell-out successes even on the other side of the world, but the shows gave Marcus knowledge about how to master the onstage experience, something which he would later pass on to his "sons".

When he returned to the UK, all four returned to the studio to create their second EP, *Love Your Ground*. While the first EP had been hastily compiled to keep up with the sudden and rapidly rising demand of fans who'd seen them on the road – an urgent bid to hold their attention before they moved on – this second effort, also commissioned by Chess Club, had a far more leisurely vibe.

The four retreated to a mansion belonging to Ben's parents, a hideaway deep in the Devonshire countryside, and began to explore the nature of their shared sound. "Having grown up listening to classic rock and even choir music, you are aware of the idea of harmony, but then finding the dudes that it actually sounds right with is quite a difficult thing," Marcus told *American Songwriter*. "It doesn't always work with groups of people. [Yet] when we sat down, the four of us, and we all open our mouths and sing, to our ears, it just started working quite quickly, because we have quite different voices. Ted's got a really gravelly, bluesy type voice in a certain register, then Ben's above that. Ben has a more technical approach to harmony. Me, Winston and Ted will kind of vibe it out about whatever sounds best, whereas Ben will figure out who is gonna sing the sixth or whatever."

When they'd first started performing together, they hadn't expected to be harmonising – in fact, while Ben and Marcus had shown off their voices every week in the school band, Ted had never even thought about singing before – but the harmonies had evolved naturally over time. Now this second EP provided the chance to hone them.

They'd also be capturing many new songs, which until then had only ever been performed in a live context – and committing them to tape. A couple were tracks which would later become well-known classics, such as 'Little Lion Man' and the B-side 'Hold On To What You Believe', although others wouldn't make the grade on future albums, making the limited edition EP the only formal recording of them in the band's career.

These included 'Feel The Tide', a message of hope in a place of darkness – Marcus' first ever song, which he had written naked on his bedroom floor – and 'Banjolin Song', so-called due to its marriage of banjo and mandolin elements. The track referenced a love so strong that it ripped someone apart, limb from limb and – thankfully for the band's fans – encouraged the character to sing.

Finally, there was the title track, 'Love Your Ground', which urged someone to accept and stay true to what they had and not to betray their roots, lest they rot away. "It's about loving your ground and just being happy with what you've got," Marcus would evaluate to *For Folk's Sake*. "It's easy to be happy, I guess, when you're affluent, middle class English people – but it's the idea of not being always dissatisfied."

Meanwhile Ben concurred, "I have to say that when we sing 'Love Your Ground', it really means something. Something about those three words seems to tie everything together quite a lot."

Plus the group had now bonded more than ever before. When the recordings came to an end, the Mumfords, masquerading as West Country farmers with their old-fashioned speech, posted a triumphant message to the growing number of internet followers to reveal exactly what had taken place. "This here EP marks the second occasion on which we were lucky enough to write, record and release a few songs to the wider world as Mumford & Sons," the note read. "When we decided to start our family trade, we four brothers wanted to do it as well as we could and with as much love as we could. The recordings of these here songs was done down at a lovely little house in Devon with a view of the sea and a nice patio, and we were extremely kindly hosted by Mr. & Mrs. Lovett."

Just as he had done for *Lend Your Eyes*, Ben commandeered production duties – although he had a little competition from his adoptive family, who jokily challenged him on that front. "Ben was producer-in-charge of the whole thing," the note read teasingly, "but we would all like to take unjust and disproportionate credit, so let's just say we all produced it. Ted takes sole credit for being in charge of whisky-bottle-shaking, and now we all know his five favourite vegetables. Marcus takes credit for keeping Mrs. Lovett awake whilst singing in the pantry at three in the morning. Country [Winston] for busting the Reebok Classics even in a sail-boat. Meanwhile we picked up a serious sense of loving the ground we were on, whether in the city in which we lived with all its faults, or in the countryside in which we recognise our heritage."

The EP was released on November 3. Like its predecessor, it flew off the shelves, and – as an increasing number of promoters booked the Mumfords to play gigs – they realised it was time to get a team together.

Central to this process was a search for a guitar technician and the obvious choice was old friend Adam Stockdale. He'd first met Marcus when he was onstage with Laura Marling; Winston had been there that night too, adding his signature-style banjo playing to the mix.

Adam had been working for the Kooks, whom fellow Virgin artist Laura was supporting. Once the Kooks tour was over, he received a phone call from a close friend, George Sewell, with whom he'd worked on a former Maccabees tour. For George's part, he'd met the Mumfords when they'd supported the Maccabees earlier that year – and he also knew them from previous work with Laura.

The web of networking was a tangled and long-winded one, but this chain of events culminated in Adam receiving a call from George, asking him to be their technician. He gladly accepted. "I went to rehearsals, built some pedal boards and my first show with them was the Hoxton Bar and Grill [on December 9, 2008]," Adam recalled to the author.

He had an instant rapport with the band, sharing a passion for photography with Ted and an interest in sport with all four. "There is a lot of tour footy which all the lads play," he added. "It can get rather competitive! There are also a lot of in jokes. We almost have our own language because of the colloquialism. Thumbs up is a big thing! Also, salutes to anything British. And we go, 'Wonder and disgrace' a lot!"

The group's tour crew had become the extended family – and, with everyone counting themselves as close friends, there was little chance of monotony or serious loneliness on the road. In fact, with the speed at which their fame was accelerating, there was barely any time to reflect. Talking of their "mad journey", Adam recalled, "I think we all, band included, feel like we are chasing our tails. Every time we prepare for the next thing, by the time you get there, it's already surpassed the point you thought it would be!"

The touring had intensified, with the band pausing only to release a third EP, *The Cave And The Open Sea*. The two-track introduction to the Mumford sound, which was released on April 6, 2009, contained title track 'The Cave' and 'My Heart Told My Head (No, Not Up For It)', which was an early version of 'Winter Winds'.

As the Mumfords' fame spread, the Camden nightclub KOKO approached them, hoping to poach Ben to host the Communion evenings there instead. However, he wasn't convinced by their flattery. "The question was," he would later recall, "do we go up or do we go across?" Deciding on the former, he declined KOKO's offer and resolved to expand Communion solo and on his own terms. Ideas began to formulate in his mind involving "spreading the melody" in other cities.

"We kept getting offers to do other places in London, but we didn't want to overexpose ourselves or take on anything too big," co-founder Kevin Jones recalled. "We really liked it the way it was, but we were kind of ambitious as well, so we figured, 'Why not go to other cities and try it there instead?'"

Following a few frantic phone calls between Ben, who was on the road, and Kevin and Ian Grimble – who were back home holding the fort and taking care of the minutiae of the business from day to day – the decision was made to launch a trial night in Brighton too. Following its success, Communion spread to Leeds, Dublin, Bristol and various other locations around the UK – and it would subsequently arrive as far afield as New York and Sydney, too.

2009 would also see the launch of Communion Records – as Ben had hoped, the brand was definitely going up. The decision to start their own record label came from a feeling of frustration that they couldn't see the bands that they wanted to nurture through the entire process. "There's a joy in putting on bands that you think are great," Kevin had explained, "but at Notting Hill Arts Club you can only reach so many people, whereas in theory if you put a great record out, you can reach a lot more."

One of the artists to be scouted was Matthew Hegarty – a landscape gardener turned musical star, whose group Matthew and the Atlas would become just one of dozens of artists given a voice by the Communion label. In fact, Ben and his business partners were already planning a compilation CD to give the musicians they believed in a chance to showcase what they could do to the wider world outside of a small nightclub.

With all of this happening around him, Ben was starting to become quite an adept multitasker and 2009 would also see him collect more production credits. Every time he went home to Devon, he had made the most of the countryside solitude to go back to work, recording Peggy Sue's *Lover's Gone* at the Barn Studios there. He had also used his parents' house as a makeshift studio to produce and engineer Cherbourg's *Last Chapter Of Dreaming* EP.

"The band actually wrote most of that song from scratch while they and Ben were in the studio," one anonymous insider told the author. "They all listened to an audio of a Bob Dylan poem called 'Last Thoughts On Woody Guthrie' for inspiration, which is where they got the line "Last Chapter Of Dreaming" from."

Ben also recorded Alessi's Ark's *Notes From The Treehouse*, including a cover of Lynyrd Skynyrd's 'Simple Man', which featured contributions from both Ben and Winston. His efforts didn't stop there either – shaking off the stereotypical tag as a folk keyboardist, Ben would subsequently join Alessi on the track 'Time Travel', playing the ukulele.

When he wasn't producing, engineering, recording or playing in the studio, he was gigging – and both the rigours and the rewards of his touring schedule never ceased. As arguably the busiest member of Mumford & Sons, he couldn't be blamed for taking a little downtime and eventually – much to the concern of his bandmates, he did exactly that.

One night, while the tour crew were frantically looking for him and sending out search parties, believing he'd been involved in a nearby stabbing – he was safely tucked up in the tour bus, sound asleep.

"One night we had a very late bus call to leave London and everyone had been out beforehand," Adam Stockdale revealed to the author. "Anyways, Ben was pretty hammered and had fallen asleep in the back lounge. The driver woke him before we left and Ben asked to stop at Marks & Spencer on Shepherd's Bush Green to get food. So anyways he did and he waited there for a while, assuming Ben had jumped off and would get back on. Time went on and on and there was a stabbing at the garage next door. The police and ambulances showed up. The driver doesn't know what is happening or if Ben's involved. More time passes, still no Ben, so the driver checks the bus and he had just woken up and got into bed, having never got off the bus. Haha!"

As the band's hysterical laughter subsided, they realised the episode, as funny as it was, might have been trying to tell them something. Had they been working too hard and travelling just a little too much?

Even if all four answered in the negative, an opportunity to get off the rollercoaster, but without leaving behind the music, was coming up – and sooner than any of them had thought.

A primal live moment for Marcus as he takes to the drums at a 2008 live show. The pendant around his neck bearing the sign of the cross symbolises his ambivalent relationship with religion. JAMES QUINTON/NME/IPCMEDIA

The boys tread the red carpet at London's Grosvenor House on September 7, 2008, to support Marcus' then girlfriend Laura Marling, whose debut album, *Alas, I Cannot Swim*, was shortlisted for the Mercury Music Prize. BRIAN RASIC/REX FEATURES

Humble beginnings: Marcus accompanies Laura onstage for the 2008 South by South West (SBSW) festival in Austin, Texas, at self-modelled "dive bar" the Meaneyed Cat. EBET ROBERTS/REDFERNS

The following year, it's Mumford and Sons themselves who are invited to shine at the SBSW Festival, this time at the Friends bar on March 18, 2009. ANDY SHEPPARD/REDFERNS

Continuing the party in Austin, the Mumfords pose for an outdoor shoot as part of the 2009 SBSW Festival, gripping the odd obligatory bottle of beer. WENDY REDFERN/REDFERNS

London Calling: Ben plays the accordion at London's Hard Rock Calling Festival in Hyde Park on June 27, 2009.
MARC BROUSSELY/REDFERNS

"Country Winston" is in his element in the state that gave birth to country music, performing at the 2010 Bonnaroo Music and Arts Festival in Manchester, Tennessee. TIM MOSENFELDER/CORBIS

East meets West: The Mumfords and Laura Marling team up with a group of Delhi-based musicians, seeing Muslims, Christians and Hindus unite without conflict for a musical fusion project. Their performances together at London's Roundhouse in Camden on July 9, 2010 promoted the release of the EP, *The Dharohar Project*. BRIAN RASIC/REX FEATURES.

Ted strums the double bass onstage at Washington Sasquatch Music Festival on May 29, 2010. ANIL SHARMA/RETNA LTD./CORBIS

Marcus cracks a broad grin onstage at Chicago's Lollapalooza Festival on August 8, 2010. TIM MOSENFELDER/GETTY IMAGES

A moment of group elation as the Mumfords pose for pictures to celebrate the nomination of debut album *Sigh No More* for the Mercury Music Prize on September 7, 2010. CHRIS JACKSON/GETTY IMAGES

The Mumfords prepare to take a bow as they close Glastonbury Festival June 2010. RICHARD JOHNSON/NME/IPC MEDIA

Chapter 3

A Question Of Faith

The touring had been relentless, barely leaving the band time to catch their breath – but none of them wanted it to stop. After all, the inevitable next step was recording an album – a daunting responsibility – and with it came doubts and fears. It would be the opportunity of a lifetime, but they were dragging their feet with reluctance, because – according to Marcus – "We just enjoyed playing live too much."

The group might have sounded like newly graduated, work-shy university students, about to make the transition from a life of perpetual partying to the real world of work and trying desperately to delay the onset of the daily grind, but their caution turned out to be good business acumen. Simply, they didn't want to be in the firing line for criticism – and, heeding both industry advice and their own intuition, had been taking it slow.

For example, vocalist Rita Ora would attract derision for taking on a guest judging role on ITV talent show *The X-Factor* at a time when her experience of the music industry was virtually zero. She'd had just one single under her belt – a collaboration – and, at just 21, had been totally unheard of a few months previously. The burning question by her detractors was: what qualified her to critique others when she'd only recently gained a record deal herself? What did she know about becoming a superstar when – despite potential – she wasn't yet one herself?

Mumford & Sons had the same dilemma – in their case, they were about to make the transition from merely listening to albums to contemplating actually recording one. How could they have confidence in songs that hadn't been road-tested? They were a grassroots band without a tried and tested style of manufactured beats to rely on to boost their popularity – in fact, they could think of nothing worse than the perceived insipidity of being catchy and on trend – so the only way to test whether audiences truly connected with them had been to take their music out on the road.

Doing so had given them the chance to build up a fanbase and name for themselves – a premade audience for any material they might release – but, even more importantly, it was a way to learn on the job. They could be shown the ropes and make the inevitable foolish mistakes of the early days whilst still shielded from the glare of the media spotlight – and all this took time.

The embarrassment of accidentally breaking instruments on stage, becoming tongue-tied at the intimidating sight of an expectant crowd and playing the wrong chord as they struggled to adapt to the demands of a 6,000 strong audience – all of these hiccups were played out while the group still had the luxury of anonymity. They were honing their live act to perfection – and there was no-one on hand with a clipboard to document every mistake in tomorrow's newspaper. For now, at least, they'd be granted a reprieve from public scrutiny.

Meanwhile, touring one small town after another – without seeking fame and glory or taking inflatable egos with them – quickly paid off. Island A&R Louis Bloom confirmed, "They were literally picking up fans every time [and] the buzz got bigger and bigger."

As their fanbase grew, so did their skills and confidence – not to mention that their work was growing and developing each time they took to the stage. Liberated from the artificial atmosphere of forced creativity they might have encountered in the studio, the songs were coming alive organically. "They knew they'd get writer's block if they had to work under pressure and in the studio, time is money," a friend of the band revealed to the author. "They'd feel pressurised to create something perfect on demand, while keeping their eyes on the clock. Yet creativity is not an exact science and it doesn't conform to a timetable. Being on tour inspired them, because they were relaxed and enjoying themselves, which is when most of their best work was written. They were at their best musically when they weren't even trying."

Louis Bloom concurred that they needed time to experiment and develop. "I was always questioning if they had the songs," he recalled, referring to their potential in the early days. "They needed to get the body of work together before they were ready to go into a recording process."

This is what musical puritans might have called 'real' showbiz. There was no-one on hand to mollycoddle them to visual perfection and they weren't simply waiting for an unsung hero to produce a number one hit – unlike manufactured superstars, their chances of success lay firmly in their own hands.

Yet over time, no-one could deny the transition. Songs that had been mere skeletons when they'd started out were now fully-fledged crowd-pleasers – and some followers knew every word.

By now, it was time for Mumford & Sons to shake off the comfort blanket from their shoulders and knuckle down to the one thing they feared most – recording the album.

"Up to that point, it was like two amazingly talented, international level footballers playing in a casual after-school club," a friend told the author. "The magnitude of it all hadn't sunk in yet."

As if to punctuate that point, Marcus would later use school metaphors in interviews, typecasting himself as an over-awed pupil in the company of more established names. According to him, the opportunity to work with his idols was "like the headmaster knocking on the door".

However, while the group might not have noticed yet, there were some music moguls around who were equally impressed with them. It was one such connection that would lead to the financing of their studio time. The band's manager Adam Tudhope stepped in and persuaded Louis Bloom – who had been watching their increasingly polished live shows like a hawk – to take a leap of faith and invest in the recording. However, as yet, they weren't signed to any label.

"I said I would finance the record outside of the deal," Louis recalled, "as I knew the negotiations would go on for a while and I didn't want to miss the opportunity."

What sealed the deal for Louis was that Adam had secured the help of super-producer Markus Dravs. A legend in the recording world, he'd been responsible for albums by Coldplay and Björk and had also masterminded *Neon Bible*, the 2007 album by Arcade Fire.

Louis set out his terms – if the recordings were successful, the band would sign a deal with Island to represent them in the UK. This painfully conditional offer stepped up the pressure for the foursome. The record deal was dependent on delivering the right material but – having thrived off the raw energy of playing live for the past 18 months – they didn't see themselves as a studio band.

In spite of that, here they were about to undertake the longest audition of their lives – the studio was booked for a month – and, in front of a producer they idolised, were quite literally ready to sing for their supper. What was more, there was almost £20,000 at stake if they failed. Even their families were dubious about whether they could really pull it off.

"We were really worried, we all were," Marcus would confess later to *The Guardian*. "Moreover, our fans were, our families were, everyone was. We all discussed it. We're this rootsy band… how are you going to do that on record?"

It was with reluctance that he added, "We didn't really know, especially not in the time that we did – we didn't have endless time, or endless cash."

No longer safely cocooned in the womb-like environment of the stage, it had seemed that the band's worst fears had all come true. Yet if they were going to prove themselves as credible musicians, expressing themselves smoothly on CD as they did on stage was a necessary rite of passage.

Fortunately the producer, Markus Dravs, was an expert at soothing their insecurities. He reassured them that he too wanted their music to retain its "rootsy" feel, but that he knew how to translate that into a studio sound. He also wanted their genre to stand strong against the Jay-Zs and Kanye Wests of the world and measure just as tall – they were going proudly into battle against commercialised beats.

Marcus recalled, "He said, 'Here's the deal: I feel like in your music, there's this unrelenting drive sometimes, these big-sounding instruments, and I don't want it to sound like a hip-hop record, but I want it to be able to stand up next to a hip-hop record."

They were speaking the same language – but it wasn't all plain sailing. Unfortunately, to say that the group was hopelessly unprepared for the world of showbiz was an understatement. In fact, when they first set foot in the studio, Ted didn't even have a musical instrument to his name. When he came face to face with the brisk, no-nonsense Markus, he was in for a reality check.

"Ted's double bass had broken at a gig and he hadn't had the money to pay for a new one," a friend told the author, "so he showed up to the studio empty-handed. He'd been improvising by borrowing his friends' basses for the odd gig here and there, but not to have one for the first day of recording just looked a bit unprofessional."

It didn't create a very good first impression on Markus, who just wanted to get down to business. "He asked him what instrument he played and he said, 'The double bass,'" Ted's friend continued. "He asked, 'Well, where is it?!', only for him to admit sheepishly that he didn't have one. Markus told him to stop messing around, get his act together and come back when he'd grown up and was ready to record an album!"

"Of course everyone saw the funny side later, but at the time it was a bit of a blow to the ego for both of them – Ted because he was treated like a naughty schoolboy and Markus because it looked like the group hadn't really bothered to prepare – even though they were working with someone like him, a veteran."

The initial awkwardness was easily laughed off and brushed aside, but perhaps it was the reality check they needed to get serious. Tellingly, Ted would later recall of the band's philosophy prior to recording, "We never had any conversation about taking it seriously and we never planned for anything. I just concentrated on where our next gig was going to be." Presumably his efforts were also focused on where he might go to borrow a double bass for the evening.

However the now notoriously lackadaisical Ted had one sentiment that everyone agreed with. "You can't plan on getting signed," he asserted. "The only ambition should be to make a good album."

That was exactly what the group were hoping to do when they began their sessions at London's legendary Eastcote Studios. The venue had been a temporary home to Laura Marling before them, as well as more well-known artists such as Brian Eno and the Arctic Monkeys – and it had a reputation for its association with vintage instruments, something which Mumford & Sons would be using aplenty.

"We used a 100-year-old harmonium that I love," Marcus recalled fondly, "although it [was] at my parents' house, because I can't fit it in my flat!"

The penchant for borrowing instruments clearly wasn't a one-off either. "We borrowed a bunch of vintage guitars off people we know," he continued, "[because] we don't own that many old instruments. We tour with relatively new guitars that are about 10 years old."

Hearing the haunting echo of centuries-old instruments bouncing off the walls and relishing it, the band set about performing the songs they'd crafted on the road and come to love. Most of the tracks were already "fully formed" by the time they'd booked the studio, so it was a mere matter of fine-tuning.

Marcus had played a leading role in creating the lyrics, based on his varying emotional states at the time, as well as the knowledge he'd accumulated, during his short stint at university, of classical literature. Music-wise, however, there had been no boundaries. Banjos, guitars and ukuleles – everyone alternated between whichever instruments took their fancy. What resulted was a group where Marcus had emerged as a firm leader, but all band members had taken an equal role in the musicianship.

By now, the 'one big happy family' that clichés are made of were ready to commit their work to record – but the atmosphere wasn't as light as the group's strong friendship might imply. During the writing process, one of the key themes had been the confusion and conflict Marcus was experiencing in his relationship with God. His parents' beliefs had had a profound effect on him and yet, like many Christians, he was going through a period of questioning, fluctuating between accepting and celebrating God and then denying Him and turning away.

The same conflict had played itself out publicly with several other musicians too. For instance, Brian Molko – the singer of alt-rock group Placebo – was born to uncompromisingly religious parents who could not accept his 'ungodly' penchant for cross-dressing and his desire to listen to rock, something they dismissed as "the devil's music". Brian, then a lonely, angry young soul struggling to embrace the fate of living in sleepy Luxembourg, didn't believe that God had shown him much mercy in life. Consequently his early songs were fuelled with angst-fuelled rebellion, and lyrics spoke of a need to "shed the sceptre of Jesus" and to eliminate every trace of God's influence in his life. Later he became a born-again Christian but spent much of his life flitting between three standpoints – devout religion, uncommitted spirituality and downright rejection of God.

Then, of course, there was Bob Dylan, a man who had visited the very Vineyard church run by Marcus' parents. He was born a Jew and had flirted with Christianity before eventually declaring in the nineties that he'd given up religion altogether, finding faith only in music.

A more recent example was pop star Katy Perry. Her pastor parents had been deeply religious, evangelical Christians, much like Marcus' own family, but they took their beliefs to a whole new level. Katy was forbidden from watching TV or listening to any music that lacked a God-focused theme. Watching *Sister Act* was acceptable, while listening to Madonna was definitely not. "My mom just sees her as that woman on billboards with her legs spread," Katy would later reveal.

Unlike Marcus' more liberal upbringing, hers had been one of censorship – and yet in spite of her sheltered early years, she'd quickly begun to question all the things that her parents had urged her to accept in the name of God. Were gay people really wrong, she wondered, as she began to bond with homosexual friends? Were Jewish people truly evil, as she'd been led to believe? Her every instinct told her otherwise, but acknowledging that meant abandoning her roots and turning away from everything she'd ever known that reminded her of home – a formidable prospect.

Likewise, did Marcus dare to contemplate that all he'd grown up believing might be based on a lie? Katy had, after some soul-searching, chosen the secular spotlight, a world of topless photo-shoots and archetypally sleazy showbiz – but she kept a tattoo of Jesus on her wrist to remind her of her roots and she seemed convinced that she'd return to God one day. Would the same fate befall Marcus?

It seemed that over the period that he'd written the songs for the album, he had experienced all of the above standpoints on religion and more besides. There were several reasons for his scepticism. Firstly, he'd seen religious extremism at its worst and had witnessed war, terrorism, political unrest and global suffering. A few short years earlier, he'd been shocked by the London bus and tube bombings by Muslim terrorists in 2005 and the bomb attacks on New York's Twin Towers earlier the same decade.

Both events were considered crimes against Christianity, fuelled by religious hatred and a desire for world domination by one religion. Marcus was questioning, when most believers had been born into their belief system and had seemingly accepted it blindly, what gave followers the right to claim that their religion was superior to all others?

How could any living human being know which was right – and didn't this uncertainty, not to mention the ensuing chaos it caused, undermine a person's faith in God altogether? A devout believer in Morocco might be a Muslim, but if the same person had been born in a sleepy village in middle England, he was highly unlikely to hold the same beliefs. For all but a small number of converts then, religion was a mere postcode lottery, determined more by geographical boundaries than sound theological reasoning.

In addition, as Marcus knew from his early studies in theology, there were numerous similarities between the religious books of Christianity, Judaism and Islam. Therefore it seemed a reasonable theory that, although there were cultural differences in the way religion was practised and variations in the telling of the stories themselves, all were ultimately worshipping the same God. Why them, had a private matter of who the people of the world prayed to become such a contentious issue?

In Ireland in the past, conversion to another religion could have meant the difference between life and death. As the Protestant-Catholic debate raged on between northern and southern Ireland, followers of the 'wrong' religion or those who strayed into the wrong territory could face not just prejudice, but violence, abuse or even murder. They had become embroiled in a 'holy war'.

Marcus wondered whether the perpetrators of such crimes truly had God at heart. Was this really a crusade in the name of God, or merely a covert operation to gain dominance, control and leadership over others? Not only that, but Marcus recalled the extremism of the religious leader in the USA who'd shared his father's name – someone who'd manipulated followers to surrender control of their lives over to him under the guise of being a 'shepherd'. He'd gained total dominion over hundreds of people and thieved from them under the false pretence of religious virtue.

It seemed God could be subverted in some cases for personal gain. For example, the suicide bombers who'd paralysed London and New York had publicly declared a war on Westerners and their alleged lack of morals, but cynics might say they'd acted in their own interests. Frustrated and demoralised by life, they believed their actions would lead them to a limitless supply of beautiful virgins in Heaven. Yet indisputably, they had breached the code of conduct that was universal across all faiths – to practise peace and non-violence.

Seeing people use religion to justify what seemed to be some of the most appalling crimes against humanity left a bitter taste in Marcus' mouth. Some Christians argued that a secular society spelt an immoral one, but – seeing the havoc caused by religious wars – Marcus might well have wondered whether atheism or agnosticism was such a bad idea after all. Maybe the souls of non-believers were empty and hollow, but they had one thing the devout seemed to lack – freedom. In comparison, their lives looked liberal, tolerant and conflict-free.

The logical conclusion that followed was a bitter pill to swallow. If Christians couldn't practise what they preached – peace, love, tolerance and forgiveness – then was there any point in being one?

Marcus' parents were devoted evangelicals, but the history of this sect had undeniable flaws. In the 1600s, for example, scientist and mathematician Galileo Galilei announced the results of one of his experiments – the now well-known fact that the Earth revolves around the Sun. Much of the religious world – evangelists and Catholics included – reacted in indignation. Who did this man think he was to contradict the words of the Bible? After all, there were numerous assertions there to the contrary. Psalm 104:5 reads, "[God] set the earth on its foundation and it can never be moved", while Ecclesiastes 1:5 readers, "The sun rises and the sun sets and hurries back to where it rises."

To pastors, this new claim was nothing short of blasphemous. In fact, at one sermon in Italy, it was announced that "geometry is of the Devil" and that all mathematicians should be "banished as the authors of all heresies".

Galileo's claims incited a misplaced drive for justice – he was tried before the Roman Inquisition in 1633 and was ordered to "abjure, curse and detest" his work, before being held under house arrest for the rest of his life. All of his published experiments were banned and he died a captive. It took over 300 years before the world heard a half-hearted apology – delivered by Pope John Paul II, the words merely gave a begrudging acknowledgement that "the Creator, stirring in the depths of his spirit, stimulated [Galileo], anticipating and assisting his intuitions". He said little of God's seeming failure to protect him from the public's fury. What was more, the apology had arrived almost four centuries too late.

It wasn't the only time that science had come into direct conflict with the Bible. For example, the carbon dating of fossils has repeatedly indicated that the world is billions of years old. Yet evangelists dispute that, insisting that – as it depicts in the Bible – the world is just 10,000 years old.

Numerous books published for and by evangelists have denied the claims of scientists, preferring to believe the direct translations of the holy book. The conflict only gave atheists greater ammunition with which to mock Christians. They saw them as naïve idealists. As one blogger claimed, "Let's be honest, being a Christian is hard. It's difficult to live in a world that treats your faith as a sign of weak intellect." This was exactly the dilemma that Marcus, a man who was undoubtedly well-educated, was beginning to face up to.

The story of Galileo was another illustration of how religion could unwittingly be used to stifle, persecute and oppress. Plus sadly, it was far from the only case of its nature. Why would a good God allow suffering in the name of religion – and why, if He was all-powerful, did He not step in to intervene?

Holy war aside, there were countless examples of murder, terminal illness, guilt and poverty worldwide. Even if it was argued that God had granted His people free will in good faith and shouldn't be held responsible for their actions, the world was full of natural disasters as well – earthquakes and famine to name just two. Perhaps the world had a natural polarity of good and evil and one couldn't exist without the other – but that theory wasn't enough to ease Marcus' nagging doubts.

According to a fellow Christian friend of the singer, all the theology in the world didn't answer certain questions for him. "He knew that suffering was a way to evolve as human beings, so that we could learn from our mistakes and be brought a step closer to spiritual perfection," he told the author. "He'd been taught all about Jesus' sacrifices and martyrdom and how he died for us on the cross, so he was familiar with the theory that suffering was all part of God's master plan. A lot of people take comfort in that and don't question any further, but I don't think Marcus could swallow it. He felt like, why had God created a world that was imperfect in the first place? If we'd been created perfect, we wouldn't need to evolve and therefore wouldn't need to suffer. If God was all-powerful and all-loving, why did he allow suffering to continue? Wouldn't he have stamped it out if he'd had the power to?"

Indeed, to say otherwise might imply that human beings were mere pawns in an elaborate, cruel game. It evoked imagery of a deity figure masterminding a survival of the fittest computer game, watching voyeuristically from behind a screen as the people he'd created struggled to win and reach atonement, while others less fortunate dropped like flies along the way. It could even imply that God revelled in the blood and gore.

It all pointed to one thing – that religion was innately unfair. Marcus had seen inequality and injustice both divinely and within the church himself. Not only was pain and grief an all too inevitable part of being alive, but some of the seemingly unethical power imbalance was being driven by those who considered themselves closest to God.

The church had largely banished women from roles of leadership, claiming it was God's will. Marcus had seen his mother, who'd taken the snub in her stride and hadn't lost an iota of her faith, take a back seat in the place of worship she loved so dearly, stifling her instincts to lead – and all in the name of religious tradition.

All of this, paired with the exploitation he'd seen, turned Marcus against the church. "He still had faith," his friend revealed, "but he was very uneasy about organised religion. For him, faith was a private thing – and he wasn't sure he wanted to go to church any more."

These were disquieting thoughts for someone whose entire family was devout. His parents were pastors and his brother James was now following in the same footsteps, gaining employment at the Holy Trinity Brompton Church in Knightsbridge. Prior to that, he'd studied theology in both the UK and USA and had completed a master's degree in Philosophy: Right And Wrong.

Marcus, on the other hand, stood out as the black sheep of the family. In the sum of all the evidence, he was still a man of faith but he had a whole host of desires and ambitions that contradicted God. Regardless of his beliefs that his maker existed, he was a wilful man with his own agenda in life and he struggled with the notion of giving up too much of himself to God.

Following the Bible correctly involved total submission and commitment. The teachings claimed that doing so meant giving over a part of oneself and surrendering autonomy – Marcus' soul would not be his own.

Increasingly for Marcus, there was a feeling that his free will was being stifled – buried under the weight of other's expectations – and yet when he rebelled against this perceived spiritual bondage, the guilt of failing as an orthodox Christian was overwhelming.

Was the roadblock in his life the everyday temptations that sent him further away from God or the religious devotion that restricted his freedom? According to the Bible, earthly pleasures and possessions would enslave him, take away his freedom and distract him from the righteous path: the attainment of true joy and alignment with God in Heaven.

Yet while sex, drugs and rock 'n' roll might have enslaved him, closing his eyes to the ultimate goal, so might following God. His faith required devotion, a giving over of oneself that would not be partial. With a background as devout as Marcus', there was no middle ground – either you were a good Christian or you weren't one at all.

What was more, a good Christian had little autonomy. His desires and needs would automatically be secondary to serving God and the community. Consequently the restrictions that living a conventionally Christian lifestyle placed on Marcus also stood in the way of his freedom. Which would truly free him – religion or individualism? Would he place his destiny in the hands of God, keeping the umbilical cord uncut between himself and the patriarchal figure he had never seen but had to trust existed – or would he veer from that path and be responsible for choosing his own?

Should he, like Bob Dylan – whose songs were a regular fixture on his parents' playlist – turn away from God a little and find sanctuary in music instead?

Dylan had been a cheerleader of the Vineyard movement for years, but by 1997 had made a public statement to disassociate himself from it. He'd claimed, "This is the flat-out truth. I find the religiosity and philosophy in the music – that's my religion. I don't adhere to rabbis, preachers, evangelists and all of that. I've learned more from the songs than I've learned from any of this kind of entity. The songs are my lexicon – I believe the songs."

What had caused his change of heart? Certainly Dylan's short-lived identity as a born-again Christian had been publicly mocked by fellow vocalists. When he'd written an impassioned song in explanation of his beliefs – the 1979 hit 'Gotta Serve Somebody' – John Lennon had replied with another song, the caustic 'Serve Yourself'. In it, he criticised those who thought they'd found their maker in Jesus, Buddha, Mohammad or Hare Krishna, jibing that they'd forgotten the role of their mother in their birth. He also blamed religion for starting fights, declaring that he wasn't going to study war any more.

Perhaps it was a convincing argument for Dylan, as years later he'd taken the same stance. Dylan was someone Marcus admired hugely as an artist, so it was natural for him to want to know why his idol had been such a keen advocate of his parents' church, only to retract his position later. He needed some answers – and yet no satisfying ones were forthcoming.

Looking on the bright side, this period of constant questioning certainly didn't make for dull songwriting. Marcus was gravitating between desperately searching for God and fulfilling a deep-seated need to serve Him, furiously turning away from the constraints He provided and then offering a guilt-ridden apology to the man he saw as his maker for leaving his faith behind.

His struggle between accepting God and denying Him plays itself out throughout the album, but nowhere more intensely than on tracks such as 'Sigh No More', 'The Cave' and 'Roll Away Your Stone'.

Of course, the latter had already made its way onto the band's eponymously titled debut EP, but the final recording for the album was more emotional than ever before. The track sees a conflicted Marcus deep in conversation with God. At first the title, a reference to the resurrection of Jesus, might seem to be a celebration of the virtue of religion, but – as ever in life – the reality was infinitely more complicated.

The Bible tells of Jesus dying on the cross and being buried, after which a stone was rolled across the entrance to the tomb and sealed by a priest. Breaking the seal would be impossible, but such was the faith of three women travelling to the tomb to pay Jesus a visit that they were already asking along the way, "Who will roll away the stone?"

However, on arrival, they discovered the stone had already been moved and the tomb was empty – Jesus had subverted the impossible and risen from the dead. The Bible says that he was killed to pay a debt for the sins of humankind, but rose again in order to acquit them. Yet according to the book of Samuel, the rolling away of the stone was not just symbolic of faith in God's existence, but also of the contraction of guilt for sin. Likewise in the song, Marcus was defiantly losing his guilt.

He claims in the lyrics that God has warned him of the dark nature of greed, materialism and earthly temptations. Yet he has filled his world with various shades of lust – for women, money and much more besides – but found it ultimately unsatisfying. He has filled the foretold void in his soul with things that are flawed – for example, sugar might be sweet-tasting but will ultimately prove sickly, something of which man will rapidly tire. It might delight the senses, but it is a poison in disguise, bereft of any real nutritional value. More wholesome goods might not be as tempting, but it is these that will fortify the soul.

In spite of God's plea to him to embrace the road that leads back home, he announces with resignation that his bridges have been burnt for good. Accusing God of taunting him with protests that this is how grace works, he then asks himself whether he is content to live the life of a metaphorical eunuch forever, someone who is castrated of his free will.

Did Marcus now see the orthodox practice of religion as something that targeted needy people and robbed them of their souls? As his close friend testified earlier, he was a man of faith but was in opposition to organised religion.

The psychologist Alfred Adler famously defined religion in terms of it satisfying people's "child-like dependency". To the casual observer, unlikely celebrity believers such as Russell Brand might support this theory.

It seemed as though the comedian's neediness – his broken soul – had repeatedly driven him from one addiction straight into the arms of another; sex, heroin, compulsive womanising and finally God, the one that he hoped would solve all his problems and succeed where the other dependencies had failed. Russell was seeking love, but all the while seemed too self-absorbed with his own unmet needs to offer anything of substance in return. He was a seeker and religion was yet another means by which he could fill an empty, unresolved soul. Was it really about serving God or merely about a man plagued by insecurity who needed a patriarchal figure to feed his neediness and pin all his hopes for the future onto? Could following God be just as much a trap that binds as any other all-consuming addiction?

In the song, Marcus seems to be claiming he won't succumb to neediness any more, that he will no longer fall into the trap of relinquishing his desires to please another.

The line "Stars hide your fires, for these are my desires" is inspired by a near identical line from the Shakespeare play *Macbeth* and, just like the story, the song is written in iambic pentameter. In keeping with the subterfuge of the play, it is his commentary on how an exterior of devout Christianity gives him the outward appearance of someone who's embraced the light – but behind the shining star of religious virtue lie "dark desires" – the reality of what he truly wants from life.

Herein lies the conflict for Marcus. Most religions teach that the cravings innate to being human are a barrier to achieving perfection – or even evolution – and that true spiritual enlightenment involves ridding oneself of all human desires. At the extreme end of the scale are those who live in simple conditions and fast continuously, deny themselves sex and alcohol and refuse even to bathe in their willingness to avoid the physical and focus purely on the spiritual. In religious tradition, such people are often revered for their holiness. Yet Marcus couldn't subscribe even to a tiny fraction of this commitment.

His inner compass – as seen on other songs on the album – fluctuates between first needing the structured support of a religious rulebook as a comfort blanket and then feeling angered and trapped by the same set of rules that once reassured him. Symbolic of a child gradually growing into adulthood, a parent's protection initially gives security and direction, reassurance and purpose. Yet as the child grows older, it no longer needs to cling to its mother's apron-strings and instead begins an indignant search for its own autonomy. That's when the temper tantrums and forceful door-slamming might begin. It seemed as though Marcus had entered the teenage rebellion phase in his relationship with God – and he'd grown out of the rigid doctrine that religion provided.

The Bible taught that temptation should be avoided at all costs. Yet Marcus might well ask, if temptation was so wrong, why God had engineered a world in which uncontrollable desire was so rife. He for one found it hard not to be governed by his passions. Moreover wasn't the act of tempting people and testing their faith more often associated with the Devil than with a loving God? Even on the most basic level, the Lord's Prayer – recited by millions of worshippers from every corner of the world – asks God not to lead us into temptation but to deliver us from evil.

Many of the concepts that Marcus' parents – and his brother, who had recently joined the ministry – spoke of, seemed unrelatable. Similarly the Bible seemed to discourage free will, urging followers to abandon what they wanted in order to focus more fully on what God had planned for their lives.

Therefore 'Roll Away Your Stone' sees Marcus express frustration that God is controlling him, but equally frustration that He seems so far away during the dark moments in his life. Submission to God would certainly remove his freedom, but paradoxically – if his family was to be believed – giving up freedom could ultimately make him feel freer.

Marcus was waging an inner war with himself – not least between becoming the frontman of a band, with all the promise of hedonism that this pursuit stereotypically entailed, and staying true to his religious orientation. Perhaps it was possible to strike a balance, but for many, being a famous singer and being a follower of God was an oxymoron to say the least.

Whilst he hadn't exactly sought out showbiz, that was where his musical talent seemed to be taking him. It would be hard to stay on the righteous path when continually tempted by the trappings of fame – so was it a case of following the righteous road or, a little more selfishly, a matter of following his heart?

Marcus hints at the answer when he sings that he won't give up his desires "for you" this time around. The ambiguous "you" has gone too far in his eyes and he asserts that the person has neither rhyme not reason with which to take the soul that is rightfully his.

Yet was Marcus talking to God when he says he won't allow his soul to be taken or was he saying he felt entrapped by unworthy, non-spiritual desires which controlled his thought and distanced him from purity? When he struck out against the futility of his own weakness, did he see himself as weak for giving into a relationship with God, or merely for denying it?

As Marcus had been in conflict at the time he penned the lyrics, it could have been either. Rolling away the stone could have been symbolic of letting Jesus into his life and removing the blockades that had made his soul impenetrable, or it could be a deliberate subversion of the religious metaphor, used as a form of irony. As the book of Samuel indicates that the rolling away of the stone represented a contraction of guilt, could Marcus have been saying that he no longer felt guilty for choosing a path that locked God out of his life?

For many, Christianity might seem compatible with the occasional "sin" but for unorthodox pastors such as his parents, there wasn't as much leeway as the average family might expect.

At the time, Marcus had been reading a book by the same name as the song – *Roll Away Your Stone: Living In The Power Of The Risen Christ.* The best-seller bills itself as a self-help guide filled with "life-changing Biblical truths" and challenges the reader with the words, "Are you defeated by sin? What price would you pay to remove the barriers that hold you back in life?"

One review by a pastor urged, "If you are not living like a son of God, roll away the stone… if you knew the risen Jesus, you would have such joy in your heart that nothing else could give you."

Yet for Marcus' part, he wasn't sure if it was worth the sacrifice. His friend revealed to the author, "He bought the book to give him guidance on how to be a better Christian and how to better follow the life that God had laid out for him – but reading it threw up more questions than it did answers."

The book reminded him of the obligation to give up free will. One reviewer claimed, "This book is the first one I've read that clearly explains what happened to the human race when Adam chose to follow his own will versus God's. It clearly shows what we lost and why Jesus had to go to the cross. For the first time, I see that what he gave up on the cross wasn't just his physical life, but more importantly his desire to do it any other way than the way already prescribed by the father. He nailed our self-will to the cross so that we may regain real life – spirit-led life."

Yet like the Biblical Adam, Marcus did want to take a taste from the tree of knowledge. What was more, he didn't want to give up free will – rather, he was "marking the territory" of his soul.

He also wondered whether it was sinister to ask followers to sacrifice self, surrender their individuality and march to the beat of a communal drum. Was it really God's intention for humankind or was it a means by which religious leaders could assert social control over their parishes?

'Roll Away Your Stone' seems to mark a defiant separation from God   or at least from organised religion. In the song, Marcus claims he will no longer have his freedom limited by the restrictions of man-made worship and will not be controlled through guilt, fear and convention.

While he was reconciling the inner conflict between good and evil, desire and obligation, the irony was that some early fans regarded him as their own personal God. "I don't think Mumford & Sons are believers," announced one blogger, "but anyway, how could they be? They ARE God!" She went on to describe the concert experience as being like praying to "the Mumford, the Sons and the Holy Banjo!"

While there had undoubtedly been dark moments in Marcus' relationship with God, he seems to have had a change of heart with 'Sigh No More' – a heartfelt apology for compromising his

Christianity and for the fact that he feels his heart was "never pure". This time the message is unambiguous – "Serve God".

Yet there's more to it than that. The song is heavily influenced by the Shakespeare play *Much Ado About Nothing* – a humorous story about love against a backdrop of deception, subterfuge and trickery. In fact, even the play's name is a trick, with "nothing" being a double entendre referencing the Elizabethan slang word for vagina. True to form, the storyline features murder threats, lies and infidelity – all driven by the promise of sex.

The song title 'Sigh No More' is based on the character Balthazar's rendition of the similarly named song 'Sigh No More, Ladies'. However perhaps the fictional vocalist wasn't the best performer for Marcus to model himself on – after all, his voice prompted a fellow cast member to comment in the play that he was like "a cat that sounds as if someone is killing it" and that "had he been a dog that should have howled thus, they would have hanged him".

In the lead-up to the song, Benedick – a cynical bachelor who scorns love and claims he will never marry – is believed to be secretly in love with a similarly commitment-phobic friend, Beatrice. Yet he insists he has a "hard heart" and "loves none". Despite these denials, the pair's friends and family try to convince them to confess their feelings for one another, during which Balthazar breaks into 'Sigh No More, Ladies'. This song addresses women frustrated with their partners, condemning men as the deceitful sex and philanderers who cannot be trusted. He scathingly sings that the male gender has "one foot on sea and one on shore" – a lyric that Marcus directly copies in 'Sigh No More'.

Meanwhile Benedick overhears a deliberately engineered conversation between friends, claiming that Beatrice loves him. Realising he does have feelings for her after all, he instantly exclaims, "It must be requited!" and goes on to propose marriage to her.

Benedick's conversion from heartless bachelor to loving fiancé seems to be a metaphor for a cynical Marcus' transition back into religion. When he discovers Beatrice loves him, it gives him the courage, faith and motivation to profess his previously latent feelings for her and similarly, in coming to understand that he is loved by God, it becomes easier for Marcus to bring his own drawbridge down and again open himself to faith.

However, during the song, Marcus acknowledges that "man is a giddy thing" – another line taken directly from Benedick when he explains why his stance has changed from aggressive opposition towards marriage to encouragement of it. Perhaps this is how Marcus explains his fluctuating opinions about religion – as a man, he is inherently "giddy" and, according to Balthazar in 'Sigh No More, Ladies', "never constant".

Apologising for his inconsistency, does Marcus believe that his erratic behaviour makes him unworthy of God? Balthazar's song also makes explicit references to male infidelity – could it be that Marcus is also repenting for being unfaithful to a woman?

The song lyrics also quote from a scene illustrating how love can become corrupting and twisted. In the passage that grabbed Marcus' attention, a lovesick Benedick claims, "I do love nothing in the world so well as you… come, bid me do anything!"

Beatrice instantly puts his affections to the test - by asking him to kill one of his best friends, Claudio. Her cousin Hero is married to Claudio, but a local troublemaker has accused her of cheating on him, claiming to have seen her climb from another man's bedroom window in the middle of the night. In fact, Hero has been framed and is innocent, but Claudio's reaction to the scandal has incensed Beatrice – and she wants him dead.

Clearly Benedick is desperately in love, as he reluctantly agrees to the challenge. Shortly before he prepares for battle, he learns that both Beatrice and Hero are "very ill" with grief and fear, to which he advises his woman, "Serve God, love me and mend" – the very lines Marcus uses in the song.

While the truth eventually comes out and Claudio's life is spared, could Marcus have chosen to quote from the scenes of unrest to symbolise how religion – like love – was a frequent cause of war? Outwardly, of course, the lyrics seemed to be in favour of faith, but – as the play was about trickery and sarcasm – could the song be taking that avenue too?

In this metaphor, Don Pedro, the man who falsely claims Hero is cheating to stir trouble, could represent a two-faced religious leader who seeks to exploit followers by speaking with a forked tongue. Meanwhile those affected by the unrest, who react with threats of violence, show how disputes over religion could become dangerous, deadly and – contrary to the purpose of their crusade – distinctly unholy.

However there seems to be a silver living – real love of God, when practised properly, has the potential not to enslave but to "set you free". Adding that such love will make someone become more like the man they were meant to be, Marcus seems again to be referencing the book *Roll Away Your Stone: Living In The Power Of The Risen Christ,* which advertises itself as helping followers to "become the person God made us to be" and "to walk into a new-found freedom". Finally, Marcus references Balthazar's speech in Act 5 Scene 4 of the play by copying the phrases "Live unbruised" and "We are friends".

The continual references to Shakespeare came about because, due to the age of the ancient text, usual copyright laws did not apply. "You can rip off Shakespeare all you like," Marcus would chuckle in one interview with *The Evening Standard.* "No lawyer's gonna call you up on that one!"

He wasn't the only artist to have taken advantage of the legal loophole. Bob Dylan too had regularly quoted lines from Shakespeare plays in his work. Notable examples include 'Highway 61 Revisited' (*Twelfth Night*), 'Bye And Bye' (*As You Like It*), and 'Desolation

Row', which even name-checks the characters Romeo and Ophelia. That aside, artists such as Elvis, Jeff Buckley, the Beatles and the Eagles had also referenced Shakespeare plays — but up to that point, no popular group had ever attempted to re-use lines from *Much Ado About Nothing*.

Marcus shed some light publicly on the track's meaning when he told *The Guardian*, "[It's] a deliberately spiritual thing, but deliberately not a religious thing." He added, "I think faith is something beautiful and something real and something universal, or it can be. We all have our separate views on religion, but I think faith is something to be celebrated. I have my own personal views, they're still real to me and I want to write about them."

Indeed, the spiritual theme continues with 'The Cave'. While 'Roll Away Your Stone' highlights the pitfalls of practising religion incorrectly and the exploitation that can come from it if it is misused — and 'Sigh No More' expresses a desire, in spite of lacking a "pure heart" to do it right — 'The Cave' is a statement of what true, unblemished religion really looks like.

Marcus talks of being in a dark place, but knowing his true calling once he sees "widows and orphans" through his tears — a clear Biblical reference to the book of James. That passage (James 1:27) reads, "Religion that is pure and undefiled before God, the father, is this: to visit orphans and widows in their affliction and to keep oneself unstained from the world."

Yet that purity is not always reachable — and, for Marcus, it can often feel like light years away. He talks of the "faults" and growing "fears" that have formed a barricade between his physical self and his spiritual self — faults that appear to make him too ashamed to contemplate facing his maker. Yet there is a pledge to change his ways and know his name as it's called again — another biblical reference, but this time to the Book of Revelations, which states that all believers will be given a new name.

After a struggle with the wholehearted devotion demanded by God and a fear that such a lifestyle will enslave him, Marcus seems to have changed his stance on freedom. He references Biblical teachings by Paul and Jesus asserting that freedom is found by living according to God's will – the way He intended him to be – and that only accepting Christ can truly set him free.

One of the major themes in the song is temptation and the role it plays in separating him from God. In James 1 – the same chapter from which Marcus derived his lyrics about widows and orphans – the text warns, "Blessed is the man that endureth temptation; for when he is tried, he will receive the crown of life, which the Lord hath promised to them that love him. Every man is tempted, when is drawn away of his own lust and enticed. Then when lust hath conceived, it bringeth forth sin; and sin, when it is finished, bringeth forth death. Every good gift and every perfect gift is from above."

Marcus addresses these thoughts by alluding to the Greek poem *The Odyssey* by Homer, which he studied at school and university. He claims that he will ignore the call of sirens, something which the poem's hero, Odysseus, had to battle during his 10 year long journey home after the Trojan War.

When Odysseus' boat leaves Circe's island, he encounters a group of beautiful but evil female creatures called the Sirens, which – according to popular myth – try to lure sailors to their death by distracting them with song.

Homer describes them as "sweet deluders" from whom men struggle to free themselves. Yet Odysseus is prepared for the deceptively innocent temptresses – his sailor companions have their ears plugged, while Odysseus ties himself to the mast while he listens, guaranteeing he will not be tempted by them.

Marcus references this episode by directly copying a line from the poem – "Tie me to a post and block my ears". This is a metaphor for the danger of seduction in his own life – he will beware of false prophets and temptresses disguised as angels, those who seek to lead him off his preordained path. While he is innately bound by his desires – all part and parcel of being human – he is gathering the power and resolve to resist them.

The Odyssey touched Marcus' heart because he felt it illustrated honestly the obstacles one faces on the long road home – and in his case, returning home means returning to following God. The homecoming symbolises the rebirth he spoke of in 'Roll Away Your Stone' – the resurrection of himself as a better believer and as someone who could testify that Christ's death was not in vain. This time around, the conflict which clouded his vision has cleared and Marcus has decided – as the lyrics of 'The Cave' indicate – to be reborn as a believer who is given a new name.

During the writing of this song, it seems that Marcus had found resolution – a way to follow God and be spiritual without being untrue to himself, and a way to retain free will without contradicting his spiritual beliefs. Although he might not have completed a formal degree in Right and Wrong, like his brother, it seemed that Marcus had set his own moral compass – and now that he had a more defined idea of what he believed to be good and evil, he was learning quickly which temptations to give in to and which to avoid.

Yet so many things which initially seemed innocent might be traps in disguise – how could Marcus discern between reality and well-constructed fiction? That is where the song's other metaphors come in handy.

An inspiration in this regard came from one of Marcus' favourite authors, GK Chesterton, and his biography of the deeply religious St Francis of Assisi. It was reading Chapter 5 of this book that prompted his lyrics about coming out of the cave, walking on his hands and seeing the world hanging upside down.

In recalling Francis' life, the author recalls the spiritual transformation of a man who is at his lowest ebb. In his locality, he is regarded as a coward and a fool and he becomes deeply depressed. He disappears into a "dark cavern" where he passes "the darkest hours of his life" before re-emerging a new man.

The book elaborates that, in the cave, Francis experienced "a reversal of a certain psychological kind... a profound spiritual revolution. The man who came into the cave was not the man who came out again... he looked at the world as differently from other men as if he had come out of that dark hole walking on his hands."

The conversion Francis underwent turned "complete humiliation" into "complete holiness and happiness" – something to which Marcus alludes when he talks of finding strength through pain.

The implicit suggestion is that suffering allowed Francis to truly appreciate the joys of not suffering in a way he had never known before he entered the cave. Knowing both sides – good and evil – had enriched his understanding. The author also proposes that seeing the world upside down would "emphasise dependence", a view which Marcus echoes in his own lyrics.

The author's theory is that seeing the world's fragile vulnerability gave Francis a reality check – a deeper appreciation of the need to be thankful to God for keeping us upright and intact. According to him, the fact that the word "independence" can be translated from the Latin as "hanging" "would make vivid the Scriptural text which says that God has hung the world upon nothing". In other words, He depends on nothing to keep it held up, He is all-powerful and the only person humankind is truly dependent on is Him.

The cynic might argue that natural disasters such as earthquakes and cyclones undermine the belief in God's ability – or willingness – to keep the world sheltered from harm, but for Marcus, and indeed Chesterton, the cave experience underlines the profundity of God.

Just as Marcus begs to be let at the truth to refresh his "broken mind", Chesterton writes in parallel that "he who has seen the whole world hanging on a hair of the mercy of God has seen the truth."

It was clear what Marcus was seeking – and the conversion of St Francis, who went full circle from belief to despair back to renewed and recharged belief again, was a metaphor to describe his own fluctuating and ever-developing relationship with God.

Yet St Francis wasn't his only inspiration. According to a friend with whom Marcus had studied Classics, "Plato's Allegory of The Cave was one of his biggest inspirations. When he read that, it was life-changing."

In the allegory, Plato philosophises about people who have been brought up in ignorance all their lives – those who were born and raised in a cave and chained by their limbs and head so that all they can see is the wall in front of them. To these isolated, unenlightened souls, the shadows on the wall of others passing behind them are not mere shadows but in fact a reality – the only one they have ever known. Plato then suggests that if the prisoners were released from the cave, they would perceive the shadows they'd seen on the wall to be more real than the world outside it.

Psychology talks of the Stockholm Syndrome, where – over time – imprisoned people can form an affectionate bond with their kidnappers, because there is no other option. In other words, people take comfort from the familiarity of what they know, even if what they know is far from desirable and far from normal.

Socrates commented of Plato's allegory, "In the region of the knowable, the last thing to be seen is the idea of good… the cause of all things of all that is right and beautiful."

To learn otherwise is a shock to the system. Plato's depiction of ascending into the light of the sun – after many years in the cave – and feeling pain at the light's brightness indicates that coming face to face with the truth is not always easy. Yet it is necessary. What Marcus, like Plato before him, is saying is that to know the world's truths and to understand God, one must leave the cave.

Chapter 4

The Great Depression

In a sense, the cave imagery held true not just for Marcus' relationship with spirituality, but also for his own life. When the song was first recorded for *The Cave And The Open Sea EP* earlier that year, behind the metaphors, it spoke on a personal level of the good and bad aspects that mutually existed within him. He'd wanted to defeat his demons and overcome the addictions that held him prone to self-sabotage – all the things that translated as human weakness. He'd found safety in playing the familiar role of the saboteur, but the darkness had been holding him back.

For example, Marcus relished playing the live shows but had been terrified by the idea of committing his group's "rootsy" sounds to a full-length studio album – ironically the one thing that would boost his popularity and, hopefully, give him all the more opportunities to play live.

By side-stepping the initial fear factor, he could start to secure the future of the band. Perhaps it was time to practise what he preached and step out of the safety and comfort of each dark, cocoon-like concert hall – the self-imposed cave – and take a risk on what he feared the most.

That was Marcus' mindset when he braved the calculated, self-conscious, almost anxious vibe of the studio, which had none of the freedom of being on the road. This time, there was a figure of nearly £20,000 looming in their heads – and performance anxiety didn't even begin to cover it.

Was their investor's faith in them misplaced? All four knew what was at stake and the fear of failure was the unspoken but ever-present elephant in the room.

Some tracks, of course, were slightly easier than others – especially those that had already been committed to limited edition EPs previously. One of these evoked the spirit not of an elephant, but a lion in the room – albeit an incongruously cowardly one – and the song was, naturally, 'Little Lion Man'.

The track is fuelled by anger and aggression, with a repeated expletive during the chorus. The lyrics see Marcus mercilessly belittling and criticising himself, believing he is a "little lion" who lacks bravery.

One possible literary link is the reference to a "cowardly lion" character in L. Frank Baum's *The Wonderful Wizard of Oz*. However a more fitting story is that of real-life American statesman Alexander Hamilton, who was then widely known as "the little lion of the revolution".

Born in 1755, Alexander was the illegitimate child of an aristocrat family who was first abandoned by his "father" and then orphaned due to the death of his mother. However, his chaotic childhood proved to be no barrier to a successful future – and he soon secured a job in government. More pretty than handsome, he was a slightly effeminate man of short stature, someone whose appearance belied the unlikely reputation he would later develop as a fearsome warrior. The paradox between these two aspects of Alexander saw him nicknamed "the little lion".

In keeping with the stereotypes of his effeminate appearance, he fell in love with a man – John Laurens, an aide to the government during the war – and the two were believed to have had a sexual relationship.

Unfortunately, he was contemplating intimacy with a man at a time when sodomy was a crime and the consequences could be capital punishment. He was also gay in an era before homosexuality even had a defining word to describe it. Back then, intercourse between two men was merely known as a perverse, puzzling act of "gross indecency".

As the law regarded it as secret and sinful, it was hard for heterosexuals in that era to understand why anyone would want to do it. Back then, there was no framework of knowledge to explain the compelling and possibly genetic basis for some men's attraction to the same sex. It was simply seen as anti-social, anti-family and deliberately inflammatory. There was no hope of tolerance.

In 1780, a homosexual British spy was hanged by the General – although not before Alexander had visited him in his cell. Clearly, he was skating on thin ice – but then, in a twist of courage no-one would have expected, he declared he was ready to die for his country and to protect his political beliefs. He took on political opponent Aaron Burr – the country's Vice President – and following a gun duel with him, died in action.

However his legacy lived on as a "little lion" who'd fought for freedom. His role in changing how the USA perceived same sex relationships was so prominent that he had a protest organisation named after him which aimed to prevent people in the military and government from needing to shroud their identity in secrecy.

Could Alexander have been the "little lion man" the song spoke of? If so, was Marcus' admiration purely political – or was his decision to name-check him in a song evident of some kind of latent bisexuality?

When the song lyrics sneered in self-deprecation that he'd never be what was in his heart, was Marcus referring to the futility of trying to pursue homosexual affairs against a backdrop of a conservative religious family? Was he criticising his cowardice because he wanted to keep the true nature of his desires hidden?

Undoubtedly, being bisexual in modern times did not hold the same degree of threat that it might have done in the 1700s – but for the majority of orthodox Christians, homosexuality was seen as against God's will and therefore unacceptable. It might not have invited the death penalty, but for the son of pastors, it could easily have held the same amount of stigma and shame.

As if to qualify that theory, Marcus had been notoriously non-committal when asked about the meaning of the song in interviews, merely replying, "It's a very personal story, so I won't elaborate upon it too much. Suffice to say it was a situation in my life I wasn't very happy with or proud of."

Intriguingly, he later told *The Guardian*, "The meanings, without losing the integrity of the songs, can refer to different things for you sometimes. Like sometimes people think we've written a song about something completely different – and I never correct them. They'll be like, 'Oh, this song's about a girl' and it's like, 'No, it's not about a girl – it's about a dude!'"

He laughingly retracted the statement seconds later, claiming that he'd been joking – but had he? Perhaps the song was unleashing Marcus' frustration for not having the courage to do away with convention and pursue a forbidden way of life. Either way, the track highlighted the dichotomous essence of Alexander Hamilton – like him, it was both gentle and then uncharacteristically fierce and fearsome.

Marcus would later explain, "I guess the sound of it grabs you a little bit by the balls – it's quite an aggressive song, a bit more of a punch in the face. Or at least for our stuff, anyway – a lot of our stuff isn't quite as hard-hitting as that. It felt like the right song to be the single because it represented the harder, darker side of what we do – and at the same time, the more folksy and punchy side."

Another highly charged track, 'White Blank Page', begins with Marcus struggling to express his emotion. He'd once told SESAC, "When you write a song, it's sometimes in a desperate moment when you can't really articulate it. What I love about lyrics is what T.S Eliot said, 'Good poetry is felt before it's heard.'"

Thus, the white blank page in front of him promises respite, release and catharsis – it allows him to quell the "swelling rage" he mentions in his lyrics and put the frustration he feels into words.

There are hints that this story might be told from the viewpoint of Jesus. Marcus talks about giving his heart and body to someone, yet rather than giving his heart to a woman, Jesus gave it to the church and instead of sharing his body through sex, he gave it up by dying for God.

When Marcus asks accusingly where his fault lies in simply loving someone wholeheartedly, he could be playing out Jesus' feeling of betrayal when he died on the cross and cried out, moments from crucifixion, that "My God" had forsaken him.

Yet while he lives out the anger, the song ends on a positive note, implying not only that Marcus is seeking truth, but that he will find it. In singing that if he receives the truth, he will follow its messenger with his life, he seems to be replying directly to Jesus' words in the book of John, when he says, "I am the way and the truth and the life" (John 14:6). In the same chapter, Jesus adds, "I will not leave you as orphans... I will ask the father and He will give you another advocate to help you and be with you forever – the Spirit of Truth."

This is a statement of faith on Marcus' part, asserting that even if Jesus – or anyone else – leaves him, he will never be alone because he will be guided by truth.

This ambiguous song also invites other interpretations. For example, when Marcus talks of giving up his heart and body to a mysterious "her" and then asks how he can kneel before the "King" (a metaphor for God) and subsequently say that he's clean, he might be acting out his guilt for premarital liaisons with a woman.

Perhaps he was feeling a conflict between wanting to succumb to the pleasures of sex and love with reckless abandonment and yet sensing that temptations of the flesh are derailing his virtue. The verses that follow could be addressed to God, blaming him for not saving him from the temptation.

Another possibility is that the song is addressed to God, disguising itself using the metaphor of a woman. In this theory, Marcus talks of giving himself up, body and soul, for God but is plagued with guilt as he doesn't feel worthy of Him. His past might mean he can't honestly kneel before Him and claim to be clean. Yet, as the Bible displays numerous accounts of Jesus making people "clean" again and even curing leprosy, Marcus is hoping for miraculous salvation – asking to be led to the truth so that he can follow God all of his life.

Finally, the song might echo 'Little Lion Man' in its inferences of homosexuality, told from the point of view of the lyricist's gay lover. In this theory, the song sees the man berate him for desiring his attention, but – due to religious pressures – denying his affections. There is also an angry rejection of guilt, a claim that there can be nothing wrong with merely loving someone with all his heart.

Another track inspired by anger is 'Dustbowl Dance', Marcus'enraged response to one of the most devastating moments in US history – the era of the dustbowl.

In the years that preceded it, trouble had already been brewing in America. After the First World War ended, Europe was able to support itself again and its need for grain imports reduced dramatically. Moreover, South America began to export grain at unbeatably low prices, undercutting US farmers and forcing them into poverty.

As they struggled to stay afloat, the 1929 stock market crash brought an already unstable country into total meltdown. Wages plummeted, while the one in four Americans who were unemployed had no wages at all.

In those days, there was no such thing as a welfare state and government handouts were nonexistent. Banks had lent generously to investors, hoping to boost the economy by encouraging small businesses to thrive – but when the stock market disintegrated, their plans backfired. Investors were unable to meet repayments.

In a desperate attempt to stay in business, banks – which now owned near worthless shares – foreclosed mortgages and withdrew interest rates on savings. However, it was all in vain and soon, just like the local workers, thousands of banks closed their doors and registered themselves penniless. Just a few short years previously, economic growth had been booming and now it had ground to a halt.

This era of hardship gave birth to the Great Depression. America was on its knees – and just when it seemed as though it could sink no lower, the dustbowl began. The country's farmland became ravaged by drought, the parched soil dried and turned to dust and the winds carried huge clouds of it across the country, landing as far as New York and the Atlantic Ocean. Choked by thick clouds of dust – dubbed by locals "the black blizzards" – farmers could barely see a few feet in front of them.

Yet it was more than a mere visual menace – the dustbowl destroyed over 100 million acres of prairie land. Their crops had turned to dust – and with them so had their dreams.

While heartbroken farmers – mainly centred around Texas and Oklahoma – watched aghast as their seeds and top soil from their land flew across the sky, banks stepped in to terminate their mortgages. Although small banks had been blighted by the Great Depression, larger ones such as JP Morgan and Co and Bank of America were still trading – and some felt they could afford to show some patience and compassion towards the farmers, who had been powerless to resist the force of mother nature and had lost, through no fault of their own, all which they depended upon to survive.

Texas alone is larger than France and consequently, over half a million farmers found themselves homeless. If they stayed near their home, they faced certain death by starvation and yet if they left their bleak land behind, the future was a terrifyingly ambiguous question mark.

Nationwide, there was a backdrop of fury at the actions of irresponsible bankers, wealthy aristocrats and reckless investors – all seen as the reason for the rich-poor divide – and as near-volcanic anger built, the atmosphere became riotous. There was revolution in the air but, starving and dispossessed, some farmers had no energy left to fight.

In their weakness, many were seduced by flyers which promised a more prosperous life in California. These claims sparked the largest recorded American migration in such a short period of time, seeing millions head out of the plains to start afresh and seek their fortune elsewhere. Yet along the roadside, they would often see makeshift camps set up by those returning – and they had tales of poverty almost akin to that of their homes.

California was filled with those who were unemployed already and, seeing the migrants' arrival as a threat to the chances of work, they greeted them with open hostility and sometimes violence. The farmers' desperation also left them prone to exploitation and they were forced to work for a pittance doing manual labour such as fruit picking. While they struggled on starvation wages, news filtered through about their friends back home who had saved just enough money to buy them a little more time on their farms, but had died of dust pneumonia.

Clearly the future was bleak at home, but they quickly learnt that California was no more the promised land than the plains they had left behind. Powerlessness and personal impotence prevailed, all of which inspired American author John Steinbeck to write his best-selling Pulitzer Prize winning novel *The Grapes Of Wrath*.

Time has stood still for the novel's lead character, Tom Joad, who has been serving time in jail for homicide. Released after his sentence, Tom walks straight out of one prison and into another. He returns to his childhood farm home to find it barren and deserted, its crops destroyed – and he eventually finds his family packing a truck and preparing to flee. The story traces the fictional family's journey in search of freedom and the death, poverty and violence they face along the way.

Following in the footsteps of other artists inspired by the novel and the tragic events that prompted it – notably folk legend Woody Guthrie ('The Ballad Of Tom Joad'), Bruce Springsteen ('The Ghost Of Tom Joad') and Pink Floyd ('Sorrow') – Marcus penned 'Dustbowl Dance' in memory of the era.

"Ben and I were sitting with a piano and guitar and we were working on the skeletal verse and chorus," Marcus recalled to *American Songwriter*, "and I remember he came with these chords and I said 'Alright, let's try to write something around that. Those are great chords.' And I'd just finished *The Grapes Of Wrath* and was feeling pretty wrathful… and that was it."

The die was cast and 'Dustbowl Dance' was born. Steinbeck had confessed his reason for putting pen to paper was "to put a tag of shame on the greedy bastards that are responsible for this", while 'Dustbowl Dance' – which spoke furiously of the "greed and disgrace" of banks taking from the poor and dubbed the perpetrators liars and thieves – had exactly the same purpose. Marcus speaks of a 16-year-old boy whose land has been taken and whose family has died and the lyrics follow his thirst for revenge, driving him to such extremes as meeting those who have taken from him armed with a gun. Telling his enemy that he is the only son, he prepares to deliver retribution.

While the song reflects Marcus' passion for "classical history", there are also a trademark plethora of religious inferences running through it. The tale of an orphaned man seeking vengeance against his oppressors echoes the Bible passage from Proverbs 27:10-11, which reads, "Do not encroach the fields of the fatherless, for their defender is strong. He will take up their case against you."

However the story, with its explicit references to an only son, could also play out another religious metaphor in that the injustice of the boy's fate in life mirrors Jesus' betrayal by Judas. The banks – the Judas types – broke their agreement with the character, forcing his farm into early foreclosure despite its tenants not being responsible for the tragedy, and consequently sent them to their deaths.

In Biblical times, Jesus is said to have returned to Earth to pay for the sins of humankind, giving up his own life in order to settle the scores. In the song, the character says he knows what he's doing by shooting the man responsible for his misery – and that he is ready to suffer the consequences.

Although it was carried out with justice in mind, the shooting would have been premeditated murder – and any punishment that he might later endure has a parallel with Jesus becoming a martyr for God's people and dying in their name. In the thirties in America, the death penalty would have been a real possibility for so-called wrongdoers, strengthening the Biblical link yet further.

Perhaps the orphaned teenager was willing to surrender his life to pay for the sins of the bankers, whilst hoping his demise would open people's eyes and prompt a reversal of the crimes against humanity that had now simply become part of everyday life. Perhaps even the dustbowl itself could be interpreted in religious eyes as a test of faith, to see whether the bankers could resist temptation and retain their moral judgment. They failed and the modern day Jesus figures – the Joad family in *The Grapes Of Wrath*, the fictional family in 'Dustbowl Dance' and many more besides – lost their lives amid the tragedy.

Reflecting on this highlights that there is still evil in the world and that – on a subtle level – people are still martyrs of justice every day. Yet in what might seem to the cynic to be an endless stream of negativity, there is still a polarity associated with evil and good continues to exist alongside it.

Throughout time, in a world blighted by serial killers and crimes of greed and passion, figures have existed to renew human faith – people such as Mother Teresa, perhaps the ultimate avatar of human sacrifice, and those such as Marie Curie who died of radiation poisoning in a bid to rid the world of cancer. It could be argued that acts of selflessness outweigh their polar opposites in terms of the depths of hope and inspiration they might provide.

For this reason, Marcus' intention wasn't simply to retell stories and revenge and retribution, but to deliver a more positive message for salvation, which he does in 'After The Storm'.

The lyrics here link to the final scene of *The Grapes Of Wrath*, which sees a terrified member of the Joad family – Rose o'Sharon – attempt to give birth during a torrential rain storm. The family decides not to leave her and flee but to pull together and try to build a flood wall as protection – an implication that strength lies in numbers and that evil and adversity can be conquered by staying together. As Rose screams in the agony of delivering her baby, the family looks upon its arrival as a symbol of a future. Notably the Bible also mentions a "rose of Sharon", describing Sharon as an Israeli city where the fields are fruitful and the crops are abundant. However, we hear that the baby is stillborn, a metaphor for the never-ending rut of which the family can see no way out. Circumstances have paralysed them and made them as impotent and helpless as the lifeless baby, which symbolises that their journey is now a dead end and they are now no more than the living dead.

Yet, as the heartbroken family contemplate the cold cul de sac that is now their existence, there is a twist of hope to the tale – and it turns out that Steinbeck's spiritual faith is just as strong as Marcus'. It is implied in the story that Rose o'Sharon's baby wasn't stillborn after all, but that she was told he was because the family barely had enough food to cater for themselves and they couldn't have faced the financial strain of yet another hungry mouth to feed. After all, they were now as helpless and desperate as newborn babies themselves.

John Joad, Rose's uncle, places the baby in a box and sends it down the river – an unmistakable metaphor for the birth of Moses. In the Bible, King Herod had ordered all the baby boys across the land to be slaughtered in an attempt to slay Jesus – a symbol that has similarity to the needless deaths of American farmers, which some say was caused by the merciless actions of the bankers who drove them off their land. The Bible then reveals that Moses was saved from death by being placed in a basket and sent down the river alive – just as the unnamed baby in *The Grapes Of Wrath* had been. Perhaps Uncle John had had an instinct that if the baby was sent down-river, he would have been found by someone generous and wealthier who had the means to take care of him, whereas if he had stayed with his birth mother, he would have had little chance of survival.

If the reader required any further clarification as to the baby's symbolic identity as Moses, the other clues Steinbeck shrouded in the novel seem to offer the definitive answer. Moses was like a metaphorical adoptive son of God – a prophet he'd chosen to spread His word and lead people out of the grip of evil people such as Herod and into glory. Later on in the Bible, Moses would lead God's people over the Red Sea to the Promised Land, Israel – the "land of milk and honey".

Meanwhile Rose takes her names from an Israeli place, the Plain of Sharon. Tellingly this is a real-life location, an agricultural area with long-standing allusions to fertility. The sandy soils of Sharon were used for growing fruits, vegetables and other crops – and it is the place from where the Sharon fruit gets its name. This makes it all the more fitting that it is the pregnant Rose who hails from the area.

When the storm ends, the family begins an uphill walk to higher ground – symbolic of their struggle to find a better future – and on the other side of the hill, they find a barn in which to take refuge. A starving man is nearing death inside and, as an act of humanitarian kindness, Rose offers him her breast as sustenance. In doing so, she saves his life.

Not only is this a symbol of good triumphing over evil, but it also completes the Moses/Israel metaphor. Rose breastfeeds the milk meant for her baby to a stranger, a link to Israel being a plentiful land of milk and honey, somewhere that – unlike the bleak prairie lands of the past – keeps on giving.

Rose's baby symbolises hope, renewal, rebirth, growth and a promising future – a new life not just for the arrival, but for both of them. When it turns out he is stillborn, their hearts lose hope and sink back into depression as they had pinned all their focus on the delight of the birth.

The trickery is that while they believe he's dead and that there's no hope for them, in reality there is. The members of the Joad family, in their uphill climb after the storm, are searching for their own personal Israel – a place where they can be free of pain and poverty – and Steinbeck's portrayal of the living baby boy, a tale of never-ending gloom but with powerful symbols of hope secretly shrouded inside, symbolises that they too can find the Promised Land.

The metaphors were not lost on Marcus, who – in his epilogue and the book's final scene – refers to the hill they find after the storm, urging them to see if they can find a better future on the other side. As the Bible declares to sufferers, who have lost hope or positivity, "Seek and ye shall find."

The Joads – and their real-life peers – might have felt that was easier said than done. The promise of fresh new life and opportunity had, just like the farmland, turned to dust. Yet Marcus wanted to rise above the bleak ending and replace it with a fairy-tale one, which he believed – if followers had faith and morals – was not merely a fanciful myth but a real possibility.

Like the Biblical book of Revelations, which promises "a new Heaven and a new Earth", Marcus reassures that there will come a time when there are no more tears. This mimics the Bible passage "God will wipe every tear from their eyes, there will be no more death or mourning or crying in pain, for the old order of things has passed away."

Of course it is the rebirth – the arrival of the child – that has started things afresh, just as the baby Jesus and the baby Moses sparked a new way of life. Marcus is stating that, after the storm, there will be a new Heaven, because – as Revelations says – "the first Heaven, the first Earth", symbolic of the life the Joads had enjoyed prior to the dustbowl, had "passed away". The book of Revelations continues that the "new Jerusalem" will come out of Heaven as a gift from God.

It seems certain that Marcus and John Steinbeck had both been reading the same Bible chapters – Revelations 21 and 22. Incidentally, when Rose breastfeeds the starving man, it appears to be a reference to the part of Chapter 22 when God promises that in the new Heaven, He will "give water without cost from the spring of life". In line 22, the chapter adds that, next to the river, will be the tree of life bearing fruit crops in abundance – surely a symbol of reassurance to those who lost their farms, asserting that there will be a time when their suffering and patience will be rewarded and there will be no need for fear of barren land any more.

Similarly Marcus looks forward to a time when love will not break hearts but dismiss fears – and this could be interpreted as love of God, faith that He will rescue them, arguably all that believers need to assure their safety.

Up until that time, the Joads and those like them had placed all their faith in California, which they believed was the Promised Land, one that would end all their suffering, but it had turned out to be an illusion perpetuated by the false claims of others.

However, the Bible counters that the "liars and thieves" Marcus speaks of in twin song 'Dustbowl Dance' – as well as the "false prophets" – will be "consigned to the fiery lake of burning sulfur" and left to their death, while those who believe in God will be shown the new Heaven, a place for them to prosper and find peace, safe in the conviction that their suffering has not been in vain. The book claims that they will be led to Heaven just as Moses had led God's followers to the Promised Land many centuries earlier. The story seems to suggest that by staying together as a community, finding strength in numbers, helping one another instead of acting selfishly and acting in the communal good, they too can share the rewards of God's kingdom in Heaven.

The two songs about the dustbowl work together – Marcus' fury at the patent injustice visible in American history, unleashed in 'Dustbowl Dance', is resolved with the security of faith ('After The Storm') and belief that the wheel of fortune would turn back upwards again.

However, it wasn't just *The Grapes Of Wrath* that formed the framework for the two songs – there are hints that other literature may also have been an inspiration. The orphan with a thirst for revenge to which the listener is introduced in 'Dustbowl Dance' is 16 years old – the same age that the rancher John Grady Cole was in Cormac McCarthy novel *All The Pretty Horses* when he was forced from the Texan farm he had spent all of his life on due to tragic circumstances.

While his story is slightly different – not least because it has a more modern setting and the central character flees not to California but to Mexico, it does deal with the trauma and temptations that he faces on the long journey to find his very own promised land.

Not only that but late in November 2009, Marcus blogged about the book, praising, "It's the perfect kind of book to read on tour to fill the hours of hanging around. The amber valleys of southern Texas, described with such easy triumph, become a welcome alternative to the incessant grey stream of concrete and cars on the M6 toll... I bloody loved it."

As 'Dustbowl Dance' and 'After The Storm' were both written on an early tour, previous to the studio sessions that would create the album, it seems likely that Marcus might have read the book alongside *The Grapes Of Wrath* and been inspired to write lyrics that intermingled his opinions on both works of fiction.

Of course the most poignant and action-provoking element of it for Marcus, who had a keen sense of injustice, was that the literary works were not merely the product of a feverish and overactive imagination, but referred instead to real-life historical tragedies.

Marcus, who had also openly admitted to a love of history, had had a long-standing interest in the past injustices of America, where the weak and impoverished were exploited by the wealthy and infinitely more powerful, simply "to make way for the American Dream".

Another book he'd enjoyed, which – like *The Grapes Of Wrath* – dealt with unjust displacement of people from their land, was Dee Brown's *Bury My Heart At Wounded Knee*. The book, billed as a history of the American West from 1860-1890, tells of how the US government conspired to drive the native North American Indians away from the land where they'd been born and forced them to defer to white leaders who rarely kept their promises.

The author used historical eyewitness accounts to divert from the standard, staid history textbook version and got the native point of view from those who'd directly experienced it.

Marcus blogged, "It is a tragic book and it hurts just to read it, to be honest. It becomes exhausting to read chapter after chapter of broken promises from the US government to a race of people being swept aside to make way for the American Dream... you come to hate the bureaucracy, the deception and the innumerable number of injustices done to the people who were in the way of white progress… of government-endorsed settlers moving west to claim land that wasn't theirs to claim."

He quoted an Indian chief from the book who had lamented, "The country was made without lines of demarcation and it is no man's business to divide it… the one who has the right to dispose of [the land] is the one who has created it."

Reading the book was a disquieting experience for Marcus, who'd been born in America and whose childhood holidays back in Anaheim had seen him soak up Californian culture with enthusiasm. As someone who'd been raised in the lovely idylls of suburban London, he'd also spent a lot of time outdoors in his youth playing cowboys and Indians, but he'd always thought that the cowboys – the Americans – were the "good guys" – and the book was an uncomfortable eye-opener for him.

"Too often, I think we tend to hear the winner's story more than the loser's," Marcus continued on his blog. "[But] you can tell this book has an agenda as it should have. To speak for the crushed peoples on whose destruction was built history's largest superpower. Without being melodramatic, I have grown up in a Western world so heavily influenced by America, its foreign policy and its clothing companies, its food and its late night comedy, but I have known very little about where its journey began… it was probably in the suppression of other races with the British Empire and even earlier."

This was the way of evolution – the survival of the fittest. The strongest and most dominant races usually won, so it was an evolutionary characteristic that heightened the chances of survival. Being ruthless and aggressive paid – after all, the most powerful leaders and dictators, with Stalin, Hitler and Pol Pot as just three examples, seemed cruel, callous and thirsty for dominion. They had displayed the same attitudes as the American governments, treating people not as human beings, but merely as irritating obstacles in the path of attaining their goals. The most ruthless tended to gain power and therefore perhaps the trait had spread to some degree throughout much of the human race.

It was a bitter pill for those who were questioning their faith to swallow – why had God devised a system that seemed so heavily weighted in favour of those who were evil and self-serving? Those who were defined as "weak" – inevitably the most peaceful people who were law-abiding and abhorred violence – seemed to lose and die as a result.

If the human race had evolved in such a way that the corrupt were more likely to get on in life – and studies today indicate that those in leading positions in business are more likely to have psychopathic tendencies than those who are not – did this mean that evil was a stronger force than good – and that God was weaker than the Devil?

This was one of the issues that caused Marcus to falter in his relationship with religion and what had made his life-long bond with God strain and break under the weight of knowledge. That said, Marcus still defined himself as spiritual and continued to find comfort and resonance in the reassuring religious imagery of the Bible.

Another track on the album which used this imagery was 'Thistle And Weeds'. Like 'Roll Away Your Stone' and 'Sigh No More', not only does this song use Biblical stories in its framework, but it also details the conflict involved in uncertainty about religion.

In the lyrics, Marcus seems to be having a conversation with himself, between his faith-abiding and rebellious sides. He talks of a mind clouded by confusion and asks his God-fearing alter ego to spare him harsh judgment for his disillusionment with organised religion because the conflict is ripping him apart ("tearing my seams".)

While he is on his knees in desperation and indecision, needing the structure of something to believe in but not wanting to give up his soul to an illusion rather than a reality, he criticises himself – who

A group shot at Chiswick house and Gardens, London, in July 2010 turns into a face-pulling contest for Marcus.
RICHARD YOUNG/REX FEATURES

The Mumfords get a taste of modelling when they each pose for arty black and white studio shots in Brussels, hours before taking to the stage at the Belgian capital's Club 69 on February 22, 2010. TITIA HAHNE/REDFERNS

A meeting of minds at the Telluride Bluegrass Festival, Colorado on June 20, 2010, when Marcus and Winston team up with Matt Menefee, Jerry Douglas, Sarah Jarosz and Bryan Simpson. ERIKA GOLDRING/RETNA LTD./CORBIS

Ted performs with the group at the Welsh community of Bala Cynwyd, Pennsylvania on November 9, 2010 for an intimate three-song set for Radio 104.5. SCOTT WEINER/RETNA LTD./CORBIS

The Mumfords pose in the press room to celebrate winning Best British Album at London's BRIT awards on February 15, 2011. Winston stands out from the crowd in an incongruent neon yellow baseball cap. DAVID FISHER/REX FEATURES

The group joins the Avett Brothers and Bob Dylan for a rendition of the latter's 'Maggie's Farm' at the 2011 Grammy Awards in LA. Image-conscious Hollywood music critics were bemused by the Mumfords' archetypal casual British style, comparing them to "backwoods dirt-road gas station attendants". JEFF KRAVITZ/GETTY IMAGES

Winston takes to the stage for charity when he and the Mumfords perform at the Shoreline Amphitheatre in Mountain View, California on October 22, 2011. TIM MOSENFELDER/GETTY IMAGES

The Mumfords seem surgically attached to their instruments as, together with Edward Sharpe and the Magnetic Zeroes and Old Crow Medicine Show, they launch into an impromptu offstage performance of Woody Guthrie's 'This Train is Bound For Glory' outside an Amtrak station in Austin, Texas. MYLES STANDISH PETTENGILL III 2011

A delighted Marcus performs at a state dinner hosted by US president Barack Obama at the White House in Washington D.C. on March 14, 2012. The Mumfords were the nominated guests of British prime minister David Cameron, who evidently kept *Sigh No More* on his iPod on a near continuous loop. BRENDAN HOFFMAN/GETTY IMAGES

The Mumfords return to the Hard Rock Calling Festival in London's Hyde Park, this time in 2011.
RICHARD JOHNSON/NME/ IPC MEDIA

he refers to as "you" – for allowing "riches" to corrupt him and leave his faith in shreds.

There is a Biblical proverb that suggests there is more chance of a camel passing through the eye of a needle than there is of a greedy man going to Heaven, and accordingly, here Marcus seems to berate the side of himself that craves materialism and superficial pleasure – a side that cares more about what he owns in life than the spiritual riches that the Bible implies he will gain through abstinence.

As his dark desires threaten to drown him and the water creeps up to his chest, the side of himself that possesses a niggling conscience has "begged" his rebellious, anti-God side to hear him. His urge to himself not to be covered by thistles and weeds – smothering his own spiritual growth in the process – but instead to plant his seeds on good ground, is a clear reference to Jesus' parable of the sower, found in Luke 8 in the New Testament. It talks of a farmer carelessly sowing his seed, some of which fell among thorns and was choked by them and unable to grow. However, "other seed fell on good ground. It came up and yielded a crop, a hundred times more than was sown."

Jesus then reveals in the parable that the seed is a metaphor for the words of God – and that those who heed his teachings will reap the reward with beautiful crops – in other words, a fortunate life or a place in Heaven. In contrast, he warns that those who surround themselves with ungodly distractions will take the wrong path in life and will be strangled by their bad living. This is summed up in the verse, "The seed that fell among the thorns stands for those who hear, but as they go on their way, they are choked by life's worries, riches and pleasures and they do not mature."

Marcus recognizes that there are people along the way who will try to corrupt and derail him from his preordained path. Thus he wages an internal war, begging himself to consider that there is more than mere "flesh and bones". In other words, if he takes the wrong path now, there will be consequences for his soul, perhaps in the afterlife.

When Marcus sings that he should let the dead bury their own dead, he is referring to a quote from Matthew's gospel (Matthew 8:22), which says, "Follow me and let the dead bury their own dead". He appears to mean that if others are hell-bent on self-destruction, he can be sympathetic and offer guidance but he must not allow himself to sink with them, as they are already spiritually dead – stifled and choked by thistles and weeds.

Marcus is urging the side of himself that is easily given to whim and temptation to rescue him from thistles (the thorns) and weeds and forget earthly pleasures in favour of a more spiritual life. The song seems to be a call to action for his own ears, capturing his fears that the itinerant part of him will take over and lead him towards a side of life to which he believes he shouldn't surrender.

Like so many of Marcus' lyrics, it details the struggle, the daily tug of war between the competing interests of good and evil – all that is pure measured against the seductive taste of temptation – or in simpler terms, God against the Devil. It was a war that Marcus – and doubtless other spiritually minded people like him – fought regularly.

Another song that deals with shame, guilt, grief and temptations is 'Winter Winds', this time written by Winston. According to the band members, it was a reaction to a personal experience he'd had, but exactly what happened has never been revealed.

"It was the winter," Marcus explained to *American Songwriter*, "and we were huddled around and we were aware of how Winston was feeling at the time and we stood around in this circle in Ben's kitchen and just sang together for about three hours, pretty much just [singing] that chorus over and over again... I guess there was a sense of triumph in it, mixed with the other things that he was feeling. We never even mentioned it, but sort of understood."

The song was also written to the soundtrack of 'Four Thieves Gone' by the Avett Brothers, which the group listened to relentlessly three or four times a day, every day for a week.

The lyrics seem to refer to a man seduced by superficial, outward beauty which leads him to have loveless sex. Her tactile affections momentarily distract him from his doubt, but ultimately he knows that his heart is as cold as the winter snow from which he is escaping – her arms can only offer temporary satisfaction as there is no love between them.

His logical mind tells his heart to do the "decent" thing and "let love grow", but he cannot artificially force the feeling and he must accept it for what it is – a good time.

It seems at first glance to be the account of a religious man's struggle not to feel ashamed of the weakness that led him to succumb to something he considers unChristian – the loveless carnal pleasure of a one-night stand. Some argue that those who give their bodies to strangers or casual partners are driven by low self-esteem, something which Winston hints at when he talks about the shame that sent him into her arms being the same shame that drove him away from God.

Mimicking Marcus' sentiments in 'White Blank Page', it examines a Christian's insecurities that he fails to measure up to the standards required of a devout, God-fearing man. His despair ends with the more positive message that just as snow is replaced eventually with leaves, the dark days he is experiencing will one day be no more and he will soon abandon his doubt to be "happy and wholesome" again.

The religious aspect of the song may have been Marcus and Ben's input, as the two members of the band who had a serious spiritual commitment, while a friend of Winston's indicated that the track included his concern that in the heat of the moment he had made a girl he didn't love pregnant. This rumour was never substantiated.

Meanwhile 'Awake My Soul' sees a return to angst, a battle with a lack of commitment to religion. Whilst Marcus seems at first sight to be addressing a girlfriend to whom he is reluctant to commit, this could be a smoke screen for the struggles he faces to give God priority in his life. He wants freedom to live the way he wants, knowing that to invest his love is an undertaking that means investing his whole life. He's not sure if he's willing to go through with that level of self-sacrifice. He urges that one "must" keep their soul "totally free" from entanglements and yet at the same time, he has the urge to meet his maker. Is it that he can't find truth in an expression of his dwindling faith or are his words self-criticism? Might he feel that by denying God, he is lying to himself?

Whatever the words mean, they seem to mimic those of his friends and fellow folkies Noah and the Whale as the group's song 'Rocks And Daggers' contains similar lyrics about someone who is surprised to find truth in lies.

'I Gave You All' is another tale of dissatisfaction, when Marcus seems to express that he has been duped, lied to and betrayed. When he says he gave his all to someone who simply ripped it from his hands, it could again be an indication of how he feels about the ever-complicated relationship he shares with his creator. He feels he trustingly, wholeheartedly and unquestioningly gave himself – mind, body and soul – with reckless abandon to God, with the kind of all-consuming devotion common to a passionate love affair.

Yet he finds himself disappointed and disenchanted by life's curveballs and when his heart is blighted by sorrow, he seems to wonder how a loving God could cause him suffering and take away everything he holds dear. While Marcus didn't elucidate on exactly what was ripped from his hands, tragedy is common to all human beings – whether through bereavement, the end of a love affair or other personal woe. In times of despair, Marcus might have felt God had betrayed him by not protecting him from grief – although he had been a believer and followed Him devoutly – and then started to feel daunted.

The outlet for his feelings, given his love of Shakespeare, might well have been the play *King Lear*. The major themes of the story are greed, lust, war and corruption, and bloodthirsty fights are both frequent and casually provoked. When King Lear announces that whichever one of his three daughters loves him the most will win the largest share of his inheritance, two of them make false declarations of how much they owe, driven purely by financial greed. The honest daughter, who genuinely loves him but decides not to be saccharine sweet, is ousted from Lear's home with nothing, while the other two openly talk between themselves of their contempt for him.

Similarly Marcus feels he has given his all to someone who has betrayed him and drawn him in under false pretences. His reference to a blind man sleeping in a doorway could be a wry look at the rose-tinted glasses often worn by someone in love, causing him or her to be oblivious to their lover's betrayal. In Lear's case, his blindness to the lies he is told leads him to be kicked out of his own home, staggering helplessly in the doorway, a scene to which Marcus may well have alluded deliberately. Other references to loss of sight – and with it, sensibility – come when the character Gloucester has his eyes ripped out.

The play also details needless war and violence, which Marcus discusses in the song too, without a hint to the perils of religious conflict. His talk of ripping the earth in two and subsequent mention of "brass wires" seem to point to bombings – perhaps the 2005 London tube train bombings, by which he has claimed to have been deeply affected.

He then asks how anyone could say that their truth is better than someone else's. Perhaps this is a reflection on how people are born into their religion rather than consciously choosing it and how, although there are alternative belief systems they could adopt, they are often prepared to go to war and kill others to defend something which is merely the product of their upbringing. Are there so-called holy wars authentically in the name of religion or are they actually territorial turf wars about one man's desire for power over another, and for his self-serving way of life to be publicly acknowledged as the correct one?

After all, as discussed earlier, evolution promotes survival of the fittest – those who can dispense with their rivals. And, with most religious books teaching peacefulness and non-confrontation and urging people not to take things into their own hands but to turn the other cheek, surely religious wars were nothing but holy.

As Marcus was raised in a Christian country, the song's allusions to war could have focused on the Irish War of Independence – somewhere close to home – but could just as easily have been a commentary on Israel and Palestine or the myriad of other countries engaged in so-called religious feuds. Marcus highlights that these conflicts might not be as God-orientated as they profess to be when he comments that all that he has is ripped apart, merely so that someone else can say that they've won.

Finally, 'Timshel', which takes its name from the Hebrew word for "Thou mayest", was inspired by Marcus' favourite book of all time, *East Of Eden*. The book was set in the author's hometown, the tranquil Salinas Valley in California, amongst the mountains – somewhere that Marcus had seen for himself. He would later tell *Q* magazine, "Steinbeck is my favourite American author – I've even made a pilgrimage to his house."

Following in the doorsteps of Anna Nalick ('Drink Me'), Meg and Dia ('Monster') and Bruce Springsteen ('Adam Raised A Cain'), Marcus was keen to pay homage to *East Of Eden* with a song.

Influenced by Genesis 4 in the Bible – where Cain kills his brother Abel – the book centres around the jealousy and rivalry between brothers and the sometimes deadly consequences that can ensue. Cathy, a selfish, cold-hearted and self-centred woman, first attempts to abort her children and then, when that fails, abandons them, leaving both sons emotionally damaged for the rest of their lives.

Unbeknown to them, she assumes a new identity and secretly becomes the manager of a brothel with a sadomasochistic theme – a fitting match for her penchant for indiscriminate cruelty.

Meanwhile at home, her estranged sons – Cal and Aron – are struggling with the magnitude of her betrayal. Little knowing whether she is dead or alive, they look to their father, Adam, for comfort, hoping he can offer the parental love of which they had been starved by Cathy.

However he favours Aron, praising his efforts in life while belittling his brother. Feeling like a worthless spare part forsaken by both of his parents, Cal's bitterness, anger and resentment build.

In the Genesis story of Cain and Abel, Cain decides to kill his brother after his father favours Abel's gift of meat more than his own present of fruit from the orchard. Likewise in *East Of Eden*, the jealousy finally reaches a climax with a cold-blooded murder – but the process is a little more subtle; learning where his mother is living, Cal takes an unsuspecting Aron to see her. Recognising her instantly, Aron recoils with disgust and, just as his brother had hoped, is shaken. Racked with self-hatred, her conscience – formerly as abandoned as her sons – finally comes into play, and Cathy commits suicide to end the pain. Aron, meanwhile, shakes aside his grief by joining the army, where he is killed in battle.

Adam – who, in a similar twist of fate, was once almost murdered by his own brother Charles in a fit of jealousy – has a stroke due to the shock. While he lies paralysed in a hospital bed, furious with Cal for seemingly driving his favourite son to his death, his friend Lee urges him to show forgiveness and compassion to Cal, telling him that he has a choice and to do the right thing – "Thou mayest". His words try to persuade Adam not to carry his anger to the grave.

'Timshel', meanwhile, is littered with references to both *East Of Eden* and a sprinkling of the group's own artistic licence. The song begins by lamenting freezing cold water, a jokey nod to the time that the group travelled to Stornaway on Scotland's Isle of Lewis and accidentally fell into the river on a teeth-chatteringly cold day.

Things take a more serious tone when Marcus sings that death is at someone's doorstep and that – while it threatens to steal a person's innocence – it cannot take their substance. "Death" is used as a euphemism for sin and is a clear reference to Genesis 4:7 when God tells Cain just before he murders his brother, "Sin is crouching at your door, it desires to have you, but you must master it."

In other words, the Biblical message is that sin may always be a temptation and is part of being human, but that God has created the human race with a default setting of "Good" and it is only through misusing the free will he has bestowed upon them that they submit to crimes of passion. Even after doing so, they still retain the soul they were given by their creator – their "substance", as Marcus describes it – which has the potential to balance out their sin. Allegedly, all someone needs to do is make the choice to put sin behind them.

Cain may endure punishment for his actions, but when he cries that he will be hidden from God's presence due to his misdemeanours, God replies "Not so", adding, "Anyone who kills Cain will suffer vengeance seven times over."

Even after murder, he still has the chance to start over because the human race will always have a choice – "Thou mayest." This message, that he is still one of God's children, highlights the major themes, both Biblically and in *East Of Eden* and 'Timshel', of forgiveness.

It is the over-riding theme of Lee's impassioned speech to Adam on his deathbed, urging him to forgive Cal. Lee claims, "The Hebrew word, the word Timshel – 'Thou mayest' – that gives us a choice. It might be the most important word in the world. That says the way is open. That throws it right back on a man. For if 'thou mayest', it is also true that 'thou mayest not'. Don't you see?"

Marcus sings that there are choices and that they are what makes a man great, providing his ladder to the stars – again, a clear reference to Lee's speech, which continues, "Millions... feel predestination in 'Thou shalt'. Nothing they do can interfere with what will be. But 'thou mayest', why, that makes a man great, that gives him a stature with the Gods, for in his weakness and his filth and his murder of his brother, he has still the great choice. He can choose his course and fight it through and win... this is a ladder to climb to the stars."

Perhaps describing his belief that the human soul always has the choice to return to the path it was made for, he later adds, "It is a lovely and unique thing in the universe. It is always attacked, but never destroyed – because thou mayest."

Humanity might be inherently flawed, but – according to Lee's theory, even in cases of extreme evil, there can never be a point of no return. Even Cain was not exiled for his crimes and, similarly, mercy is even extended to the seemingly irredeemable Cathy. Marcus implicitly mentions her when he talks first of brothers and then of a mother of a "baby child" who still has her choices.

In fact, "thou mayest" had been the subject of some contention. It had originally been translated as "thou shalt", until a group of Chinese scholars had claimed otherwise, offering the true meaning of "Timshel" as "Thou mayest".

This distinction between the two turned out to be meaningful for Marcus and perhaps symbolic of the shift in his thinking in how to – and whether to – best include God in his life.

"Thou mayest" implied taking an active role in the outcome of one's own life based on the choices one made about whether to allow evil or good in their actions. The distinction between "Thou shalt" and "Thou mayest" – and the possibility of reverting to the latter – offered an opportunity to decide one's own fate without blindly giving in to predestination. This was of particular interest to Marcus at a time when he had been questioning his reluctance to give all of himself to God and risk losing his free will as a result of that level of devotion.

Traditionally, most of the world's major religions have implied that human beings are passive vehicles of God's will, victims of a pre-assigned fate at birth or condemned by their subsequent actions to punishment in hell. Depictions of such punishments can be seen in temples, shrines, mosques and churches worldwide. Meanwhile Christians typically say, "What will be will be" and Muslims have a stock phrase, "Insha'allah" or "God willing" – in other words, an acknowledgment that what they plan or wish for will only happen if God allows it.

The concept of "Thou mayest", on the other hand, suggests that humans can be absolved from sin and change their fate, that they are not condemned to eternal misery for the mistakes they have made. More importantly than that for Marcus however, it represented a green card to take control of one's own life, rather than sitting back for God to mould the path ahead. It was liberating – an opportunity to embrace the freedom of following his own moral code, instead of accepting the rulebook handed down to him. It offered the previously unthinkable prospect of retaining his autonomy and singlemindedness without contradicting his Christianity.

Perhaps it would give Marcus the courage to veer off the present path every now and then in the name of exploration, driven by the safety of believing he was one of God's children regardless of his actions. After all – as Marcus had perhaps been afraid of – humans can sometimes be capable of unwittingly committing evil, without realising the consequences or intending to hurt anybody.

Evidence of this comes from another Steinbeck novel, *Of Mice And Men*, which is set, like *The Grapes Of Wrath*, in the era of the Great Depression. The tragic central character, Lenny, is an unemployed manual labourer blighted by severe learning difficulties which see him taunted for being ignorant and simple. He is heavily built, but a gentle giant who at times is unaware of his own strength. It turns out to be a deadly combination.

He accidentally strangles a woman while he tries innocently to stroke her hair. It's unintentional manslaughter, but the woman's friends and family might not see it that way – in fact, the only person who truly understands Lenny and his haplessness is his close ally, George. When he discovers what his friend has done, he comforts Lenny, assures him everything will be OK, and then silently shoots him in the back of the head.

The murder was a mercy killing, to protect him from being tortured by an angry lynch mob for his actions. Knowing that his death was inevitable as the others would have taken justice into their own hands, the grief-stricken George killed his friend quickly to save the prolonged pain of a beating.

The story again introduces the complex themes of mercy and forgiveness, which are far from black and white but rather shades of grey. Additionally, can George be held accountable for his actions – taking another man's life – or is the intention behind his actions, born out of kindness, more important in deciding his spiritual fate?

Further evidence that Marcus may have been inspired by *Of Mice And Men* as well as *East Of Eden* comes from the reference to cold water. After someone dares him, Lenny is depicted jumping into a cold water creek and almost drowns, while Marcus and his bandmates – who had a similar experience in Stornaway – discuss the perils of cold water in the lyrics of 'Timshel'.

Looking below the surface, the assertion that water freezes an already cold mind is perhaps a warning not to drown in sin or self-doubt, but to make the right decisions. The placement of this verse, just before declaring that death – sin – is at someone's doorstep, is no accident. Just as God urged Cain when he was on the verge of killing Abel to resist the calling of the sin, Marcus is saying that there are two choices and that true freedom is achieved by wakening a mind that is frozen by evil and mastering or conquering the undesirable urge for sin.

There are other clues that both Steinbeck novels are linked to the song – for instance, the lyric when Marcus says he will whisper, "Lose your sight". Lenny is blindfolded by George just before he kills him to protect him from the trauma of what he is about to do.

Similarly in *East Of Eden*, Lee urges Adam to turn a blind eye to what Cal has done in the name of forgiveness – both powerful metaphors involving the loss of sight. However, perhaps the strongest link to the 'Timshel' lyric is a Biblical one, as Corinthians 2:5-7 reads, "For we live by faith, not by sight". This refers to having faith in redemption, and following the teachings of God that all that is needed to save oneself is belief.

Another Bible passage describes a sick boy being cured by Jesus, purely because he has faith in him. After curing him, Jesus runs to the Apostles and explains, "If you have faith the size of a mustard seed, you will say to this mountain, 'Move from here to there and it will move. Nothing will be impossible for you."

Marcus then adds in 'Timshel' that although he can urge someone to lose their sight and revert to faith, he cannot move the mountains for them – that can only happen if belief has been internalised, which is a process they must work through by themselves. If someone has faith, he feels, they will be able to move their own mountains.

When Lenny trusts George and submits to him for an unknown fate – his death – he places his faith in his friend and in God and, in doing so, discovers the pleasure of letting go of fear and inhibition. By trusting George, his fate is not a gory death – instead he is released to a more gentle one which is over in seconds and of which he is blissfully unaware. When he allows himself to be blindfolded, he is losing his sight – just as Marcus mentioned in the song – and as a result, he bypasses suffering altogether.

In the seconds before he fires the fatal gunshot, George delights Lenny by telling a familiar and comforting story he has told to his friend so many times before. It satisfies his longing to live a rural existence in the mountains with George and keep rabbits – something he had always hoped to do.

The continual references to mountains are more than mere metaphors about faith – and, in the scene from *Of Mice And Men*, idealism and Heaven – moving up into the afterlife – for they are also a reference to the ongoing war waged between the dual forces of good and evil. The backdrop to the Salinas Valley, where *The Grapes Of Wrath* is set, had been two mountain ranges, one on each side of the valley. These too represented good and evil – both were powerful and both were ever-present.

Yet for someone questioning the boundaries of their religion, as Marcus had been, the imagery was as disturbing as it was comforting. By choosing evil, he would be enslaved by sin – but by choosing good, did that bind him, making him a slave to God?

As the rousing chords of 'Timshel' ring out, perhaps the listener can picture Marcus, Ted, Ben and Winston staring into the infinity of those mountains in their mind's eye, and contemplating the unknown – all that lies in the gaping chasm between the two.

Chapter 5

Blind Belief Put To The Test

The album had finally come to fruition – but was it good enough? Unlike the EPs they'd experimented with in the past, this time the foursome were driven by pressure – their agenda was to convince record executives that they were ready to take the next step.

It wasn't that fame, fortune and five-star reviews were at the forefront of the Mumfords' minds – far from it – but wagering a deal with a record label was a golden ticket to the one thing they did care about – playing live.

When it came to the all-important tracklist, the band knew they had to include songs not only that they were proud of, but that were exactly representative of the future of their sound. Their best tracks would be the ones that allowed them to impress corporate listeners whilst staying true to themselves at the same time – a difficult combination. Consequently, there was fierce debate about which tracks were truly worthy of inclusion on the album. The wrong material risked alienating potential investors and, if it hadn't been for the insistence of Winston, 'Little Lion Man' – one of their biggest hits to be – would never have made the cut.

"We weren't going to put it on the album," Marcus would later confirm wryly to *Entertainment Weekly*, "but Winston was the real champion – 'We've just got to!' I was very reluctant especially, but he was right!"

As the final tracklist fell into place, the stress of agonising over it melted away. Whilst it might have been momentarily nerve-racking to record an album without any concrete promise of a deal, there were plus points to the decision – for one thing, there hadn't been an A&R executive breathing down their necks.

As Ted would later reveal, "The sound you hear is exactly the sound that we wanted to make – without reference to anyone else."

Their authentic, uncontrived approach to making music helped them attract representation that was on their wavelength. Louis Bloom of Island shared the same values as the group, assigning merit not to financial rewards or superficial hype but to artistic quality. For him, jumping on the bandwagon to sign the latest cookie-cutter trend was in the realm of the cliché – it was more important to release an album he could be proud of.

"I would never sign a band just on the back of the hits they had on Myspace," he would later claim. Ignoring the YouTube viewing figures, Louis was looking for longevity in his artists – bands whose music would attract genuine, committed, long-term fans rather than those merely trying to keep up with the in-crowd.

He was passionate enough about music not to have lost his heady idealism, his commitment to making music that sold for more reasons than shock value. He yearned to attract listeners that sought something more heart-warming than a soulless processed beat – and after hearing the album, which he dubbed "music for the thinking man", he was convinced that Mumford & Sons fit that category.

Although he'd faltered prior to the studio recordings, by June 2009, he was no longer dragging his feet – he was ready to make an offer.

Yet there was much for the foursome to consider. Due to Louis' background, his love of rootsy music had at first seemed counterintuitive. Not only had he worked in his youth as a record scout for Simon Cowell – the enemy of many a pioneer of 'real' music – but he'd also been responsible for bringing pop puppets such as Mika, McFly and Busted onto the music scene.

Yet while McFly seemed a saccharine sweet pop group, with the type of insipid ballads, boyish good looks and bare-chested pin-up status that reliably sent the young teen mass market into raptures, there was a little more to them than met the eye – they also played their own instruments.

This was a priority for Louis, who'd also worked with Keane and made bids – albeit unsuccessful ones – for bands like Kasabian and the Arctic Monkeys. Inescapably, Louis had a lack of experience with groups such as Mumford & Sons – not least because his label barely had any to its name – but one thing he didn't lack was enthusiasm.

One of the executive's qualities that would prove particularly seductive to the Mumfords was his willingness to look beyond mere profits. His favourite album of all time to work on had not been the biggest *Billboard* hit, but an understated recording with songwriter and Nick Drake sound-alike Scott Matthews. It was unsuccessful in terms of sales, "but we made a beautiful record".

For the Mumfords, to whom integrity meant more than dollar signs, having someone behind them with that attitude was both rare and extremely desirable. "I admire musicians who just do what they do and don't try to be anything else," Ben would later state. "Whether or not what they do is successful commercially, they are the real winners in the end – and often write better music because of it."

The message was clear: the band's role models were those who were not slaves to communication or material trappings and didn't allow the pursuit of those goals to shape their work. They didn't write purely with the public in mind, calculating every song for catchiness – they wrote for themselves. If the choice was between a tiny basement bar loving them for who they were, or an entire stadium cheering them on under an illusion of something they were not, there would be no contest. That way, they might or might not make it big, but regardless, they'd managed to keep their integrity.

They knew what they wanted, but – increasingly – signing with Louis didn't seem to be a barrier to their ambitions. Recognising their restlessness in the studio and knowing that on stage was where the magic was, Louis promised a significant spend on tour support and vowed to market them as a live band, should he earn the chance to work with them.

Yet they remained cautious. Hailing from wealthy, well-heeled backgrounds had given all four a self-confidence, a surefootedness and, as they weren't money hungry, it gave them the privilege of being able to focus on the music and how they came across rather than grasping in desperation at the first offer that came along. They didn't just want an opportunity, but the right opportunity. "We could have made the album earlier, or signed a deal earlier," Marcus would later tell Australia's *Herald Sun*, "but we wanted to be patient."

The calm and collected demeanour soon paid off. Before long the four had resolved to make negotiations on their own terms – by forming their own record label. While Ben explained, "We wanted to maintain control and ownership," Ted added, "It gets diluted the more other parties are involved."

They were well-equipped to take the plunge. After all, Ben was no stranger to owning his own music-related company, while Winston had his father on hand to dole out business advice. Thus, Gentlemen Of The Road was born.

The label was christened in honour of the 2007 Michael Chabon book of the same name. According to the book's back cover, it promises a world of "wicked cunning, outrageous daring and foolhardy bravado" as these self-proclaimed gentlemen of the road embark on a revolution to help a young prince reclaim his lost throne.

"It was AWESOME," Marcus would later gush on his book blog. "I always felt I was supposed to be a highway man and the one remaining hope I have is the existence of reincarnation and time travel, as I would love to be reborn at least as one of the Scarlet Pimpernel's homeboys, if maybe not as one of the dudes that ended up swinging at Tibbet's Corner in SW19."

He added of the book's plot, "It's basically a brilliant, well-written story of his unlikely best friends who go on tour... it follows their adventures to reinstate an overthrown teenager from the made-up Jewish kingdom of Khazaria... they're torn between their mobility and their morality, as their whole nomadic meaning of life is challenged when this kid shows up and needs their help... a really colourful tale of honour, faith and friendship."

Like any good adventure, sword duels, evil and eccentric emperors and elephant-back warriors are all part of the furniture. While the Mumfords' business venture wasn't quite as colourful – for a start, and perhaps to the relief of their audiences, there were no raucous elephants – it involved another type of trumpeting that was equally exciting. With a now distinctive and well-established trademark of slow, sentimental verses and rousing folk-rock choruses, Marcus, Ben, Winston and Ted were on a mission – to bring ukuleles, banjos and the like firmly back into fashion.

First however, there were a few loose ends to tie. For example, what type of deal could they strike with Louis?

A licensing deal would see Island paying a set fee to purchase the rights from Gentlemen Of The Road to distribute the album. They would take on sole financial responsibility for manufacturing, distributing and promoting their music, but – aside from the original licensing fee – would give up none of the profits to the group.

On the other hand, if they opted for a distribution deal, they would receive no money in advance and would have to pay for promotion and distribution themselves. However, they would not need to share their profits.

There were countless advantages associated with a licensing deal. Firstly, it would take the minutiae of selling an album out of the group's hands, while there'd be no need to hire new and experienced staff to run the business from day to day – a necessity if it was to survive.

Licensing would also allow Gentlemen Of The Road, a virgin label a matter of a few days old, to place marketing into the hands of well-established labels, who'd already built up beneficial relationships with advertisers, radio stations, media sources and most importantly of all, the shops that might stock the album. These kinds of long-standing relationships would help propel the group into the public eye – a far safer prospect for the newcomer than going it alone.

However, the biggest reason to accept a licensing deal was money. Admittedly all four in the band came from affluent backgrounds – but their parents hadn't spoilt them with infinite disposable incomes. After all, even for the momentous and potentially life-changing occasion of recording their first studio album, not everyone had the correct instruments. Ted had even pleaded poverty when faced with buying a new bass.

Taking a huge leap into the unknown would be made possible by a licensing agreement as it required no money upfront and offered an advance. While a distribution deal allowed the Mumfords to keep all that they earned, their profits might be zero – and if they made a loss, they would be responsible for repaying it.

As tempting as total control might have been, the group had endured their fair share of risk-taking already, recording their entire album before a single piece of paperwork had been signed. Leaving their fate in the hands of a precarious distribution deal was probably one risk too many.

After a group meeting, the boys opted for the more cautious option of a licensing deal, signing to Louis' record company, Island, in the UK and sublicensing the album to Glassnote Records in the USA, Cooperative Records in Europe and Due Process in Australia.

Once they'd signed on the dotted line, things began to move rapidly. Yet they were not hurtling along the "pop band conveyor belt" that Marcus and his adopted sons despised so much – they were adding the finishing touches to the album on their own terms.

"There's a danger with labels that they can mess things up," Ben warned darkly to *Clash*. "We spent almost a year coming to a deal with Island and fortunately we didn't have to change the album."

It wasn't that the band drove a hard bargain – rather that they knew what they wanted – and selling their souls for commercial success was the antithesis of their goals.

"Working with Chess Club got us into the habit of working with nice people," Ben reminisced. "We were friends before we worked with them. I think that's continuing – and if you don't look after your sound, how can you maintain your integrity? It's at the heart of everything."

In a world that valued shock tactics and controversy as a means of attracting the attention of large audiences, Island's approach was both surprising and refreshing. With TV shows like *Big Brother* and *The X-Factor* all the rage, gimmicks and spoofs seemed to be an integral part of the modern era – and it was one that could be hostile or indifferent to those who relied on talent alone.

The foursome didn't have pneumatic breasts, tales of sordid love triangles, Russell Brand-style sexploits or reality show-worthy meltdowns to offer. In fact, complete with ruffled hair and bohemian waistcoats, aside from the giveaway iPhones poking out of their pockets, they didn't even look as though they belonged in the modern era. Yet they had their music – and, according to predictions by Island, their honesty, rawness and authenticity was about to make them global stars.

To their relief, when it came time to mix the album, the group was able to ensure these qualities shone through. "Mumford & Sons are a very straightforward, organic band," mix engineer Ruadhri Cushnan – who'd previously worked with Markus Dravs on one of the group's favourite albums, *Wall Of Arms* by the Maccabees, confirmed. He added, "The album is very truthful. It wasn't over-produced, it was really a case of Markus and Francois [Chevallier, engineer] capturing the band's live energy… they are the way they are and they play the way they play, so let's just try to get that across and make sure that the excitement of their live performances translates into the recording. That was the most important thing. They managed to do that without many tricks and were confident enough to simply let the band's natural sound through."

In line with that goal, the group made sure they asserted their rights when it came to the subtleties of the sound. "One of the biggest talking points during the mix was the banjo and how much it should feature," Ruadhri clarified. "The band were adamant that the banjo is very critical and important to their sound and trying to make it cut through and giving it the dynamic punch that it needed, without it completely overpowering everything and it becoming a banjo record, was a delicate balance."

Perhaps asserting creative control and refusing to compromise until they had exactly the right sound wouldn't have been possible if the group hadn't had the luxury of their own record label – and all of the independence that entailed. But equally perhaps Island sensed that they weren't a band that could be justifiably manufactured and were happy to let them shape their own sound.

After all, the notoriously single-minded Amy Winehouse – who'd split from her first management company, 19, for controlling her, and who'd mainly spent her time with them publicly ridiculing her bosses, insisting they couldn't "fuck with" her and mocking Simon Cowell's "dodgy hair" and "perma-tan" – had also signed to Island. It seemed that the freedom it offered was a perfect match for feisty artists.

The band had an equally strong view about the backing vocals – according to them, they should emulate Fleet Foxes. Ruadhri explained, "Quite often, being able to reference another track is more effective than somebody waxing lyrical about what sound they want."

Meanwhile the lead vocals and acoustic guitar played a central role – and in contrast to most albums, they were mixed prior to the drums.

With pop bands, the framework of a song is its rhythm, with vocals being added later – and a catchy beat is conceived almost universally to make it a hit. Ruadhri's decision to mix the song the opposite way round emphasised the dominance of an organic, instrument-based, self-made sound. What was more, it set the Mumfords sharply apart from counterparts that relied on processed beats.

As sessions drew to a close, all were happy with the way they'd been portrayed. That said, the Mumfords couldn't have everything their own way – and the record label drew a line at profanities on live radio. 'Little Lion Man', a song of which Marcus had once been so ashamed he'd attempted to banish it from the album, was Island's idea of a perfect debut single. There was just one problem – the chorus' relentless use of the word "fucked".

The label made desperate attempts to compromise, but Marcus was unyielding. "There were people asking, 'Is there any way you can write a different word? We'll do anything!'" he laughed later to *Entertainment Weekly*. "We were like, 'No, there's no other word, we tried it and it was just horrible, it didn't work at all.'"

In fact, he felt so strongly about it that even his staunchly religious mother got involved in the campaign. "I now have my parents agreeing with me as well!" he added. "My mum's justifying it to other people – 'There's no other word that fits, it has to be that one!'"

So the expletives stayed on the album – but, grudgingly realising that it was akin to career suicide to sabotage their chances of getting airplay on family-friendly radio, the band agreed to have the word bleeped out or supplemented with "messed" for the radio edit version.

Giving in quickly paid off – with the help of veteran radio plugger Guillermo Ramos – an employee from outside the label, due to Island's inexperience with the folk genre – the track was soon all over the radio airwaves like a rash. "In times when radio is dominated by dance, urban music and loads of US pop," reasoned Louis Bloom, "to get a band with banjos and rootsy music played is an amazing result."

It wasn't just played – it was celebrated. What was more, it transcended the usual genre boundaries. Zane Lowe, a TV and radio presenter who specialised in alternative and heavy rock, cast aside his penchant for pigeon-holing and labelled 'Little Lion Man' the Hottest Record in the World – just a couple of weeks before its release.

Plus there were some surprises in store for those awaiting the sale of the single. Its bonus track, 'To Darkness', ensured listeners an eclectic mix. Confessing his weaknesses and bemoaning a flawed heart, Marcus sings out his pleas not to be consigned to darkness, while its fury-fuelled predecessor, with its expletive-based chorus, set a very different tone.

"It's not like we love swearing," Ted would announce playfully, "but we did write a song with 'fuck' in the chorus, I guess!" It was an early sign that Mumford & Sons would be anything but predictable.

Fans' curiosities were duly piqued and by August 11, the day the track hit the shops, it had exploded. While it narrowly missed the Top 20 in the UK, it made the Top 5 in Belgium and in Australia – incidentally, Zane Lowe's home country – it sailed to a triumphant number three.

Meanwhile Aussie radio station Triple J conducted the largest music poll in the world – with over 800,000 votes cast – to narrow down the Hottest 100 tracks. Arguably, due to the popularity of illegal downloads and YouTube plays, listener polls were more representative of musical tastes than the charts – and 'Little Lion Man' emerged at number one. The track hit the top spot by the largest margin ever recorded in the competition.

Even in the notoriously insular USA – where the charts were overwhelmingly filled with home-grown talents – Mumford & Sons made the number one spot in the *Billboard* Alternative Songs chart. The song would go on to sell over one million digital copies.

'Little Lion Man' was an indisputable success. Yet while other artists might merely have revelled in the glory and cracked open the first of many bottles of champagne, a worried Marcus, on the other hand, was panicking.

He grumbled to *Adelaide Now*, "It's pointless, people plucking a song from an album they think can get played on the radio. That's not a good test of a record, it's just cherry picking."

"We don't consider ourselves a singles band," he would also agonise in memory of the success, "but an album band – a gig band really. We didn't want to put too much attention on 'Little Lion Man' – we want to move on from it."

Some of the band's peers found their awkwardness comical. "They didn't know what to do with themselves!" Laura Marling would screech of the quartet's reaction to their newfound success. "It was hilarious!"

And while the group was collectively squirming in discomfort and trying to ignore friends' titters, Paul Piticco of Australian label Due Process was delighted. According to him, "It restored my faith in the concept of a song just unifying people and a moment."

In spite of the group's unease, there would soon be time to prove themselves as an all-round act. The album closely followed

'Little Lion Man' on October 2 – and three days later, a concert took place to celebrate the launch. In keeping with their down to earth image, there was no glitzy venue, no VIP bars, no champagne popping and certainly no Playboy bunnies. Instead, blanketed by the faint aroma of horse manure, the band and their instruments were surrounded by straw.

Undeterred by the lack of glamour – and now very much in his comfort zone – a triumphant Marcus' first words were simply, "How sick is this barn?"

He'd first had the idea for the unconventional concert while passing through the Isle of Islay – a tiny Hebridean island with a plentiful number of whisky distilleries, but more geese than people.

Islay held an annual festival by the name of Malt and Music, characterised by whisky-tasting, bagpiping and folk dancing in honour of the isle's Gaelic roots. To Marcus, for whom the Scottish Highlands and islands had been a mainstay of childhood farm holidays – it might just be the perfect place to perform.

However, the isle was largely undiscovered by mainstream tourism, no doubt due to a punishing two-hour ferry ride over choppy water from an equally remote port being the only method of transport. As much as he romanticised the island, it was unlikely to be teeming with Mumford & Sons fans. Similarly, on one of the island's nearest neighbours, Jura, deer outnumbered people by 33 to one.

Although he was taken aback by the islands' remote beauty, Marcus knew it was time for Plan B – and that meant booking the Lordship Farm in Standon, Hertfordshire, instead. Even getting to this venue wasn't without ardour – bewildered urbanites in London were piled onto coaches, braving implausibly heavy traffic to reach the farm-side idyll.

"What we did was to take 500 people on buses from the centre of London to an hour out of London to a barn," Ben enthused to *Faster Louder.* "But they all met at Kings Cross, at the international train station. No-one really knew each other before that, they were all just told to meet there, and we didn't even know what was going to happen. But everyone showed up, and we had 10 double-decker buses to drive them!"

As Mumford enthusiasts packed into the straw-lined barn, in anticipation of what Marcus would proudly declare a "countryside barn dance", it was clear they were in for a justifiably special night.

Never a band to be predictable, the foursome combined the expected rendition of album tracks with a couple that never made the cut. 'Feel The Tide' was one of those that narrowly missed a place on the tracklist, but which was warmly received by fans at the show. The lyrics depicted a grief-stricken priest who laments his talent for perceiving evil, undertaking a fast that has become not just God-honouring but masochistically self-punishing, and a heart that seemingly cannot heal. The chorus contradicts the bleak tale of depression by insisting that, with a little insight, it's possible to feel the tide turning.

'Where Is My Heart?', a rather more light-hearted track centring around a lovesick man whose emotions send him spiralling out of control, was also on the tracklist.

The band was joined onstage by fellow folk friends such as Pete Roe and King Charles for a selection of cover songs too. 'Whisper In The Dark' was a Christian rock track originally recorded by Skillet in 2006, while the group also made the unusual choice of performing 'Mary, Don't You Weep', a spiritual song traditionally performed by African slaves prior to the days of the American Civil War.

The song tells the story of the Biblical character Mary of Bethany and her dialogue with Jesus as she begs for her brother Lazarus to be raised from the dead. Loaded with symbolism, the lyrics include themes of racism and liberation, and consequently the song became a signature anthem of the fifties and sixties American Civil Rights movement. This era symbolised a change in fortune for black people, who were then seen as second class citizens, segregated in all aspects of public life, sent to race-specific schools with little teaching, appalling conditions and even denied seats on public transport.

Rosa Parks has often been credited in the history books with sparking a revolution when, in 1954, she refused to give up her seat on a bus for a white "superior". This was just one memorable event that sparked a vociferous chain reaction – something which was predicted in 'Mary, Don't Weep'. The song carried references to Moses and the Rainbow Covenant God had with them, which was symbolic of a time of peace and universal tolerance. Tragically, the song's writer would never live long enough to see this achieved.

With its connotations of slavery it might have seemed an unusual, if not controversial, track for a group of white British men to perform, but it had previously been covered by the folk singer Pete Seeger and, subsequently, Bruce Springsteen.

They were not alone in their choice to cover Dolly Parton's 'Jolene' either – it had already been performed by the White Stripes and the Sisters of Mercy. For this rendition, however, the group recruited Laura Marling to join them onstage.

Anyone who discerned a flicker of chemistry between Laura and Marcus as they combined their harmonies wouldn't have been mistaken. Laura, who had ended her romance with Noah and The Whale singer, guitarist and songwriter Charlie Finch the previous year, had recently decided to take her long-standing friendship with Marcus to the next level.

The rapport between them as friends had long been evident – yet how compatible were they as lovers? The pair were both privately educated, both God-fearing and both had a passion for a selection of literature that included Gothic romance and ancient Greek myths. Yet outwardly, that was where the similarities seemed to end.

Laura had the type of attitude to life that implied she'd stepped straight out of a Jane Austen novel, inherited a time-travel machine, pressed the wrong button and accidentally been delivered, dazed and confused, into the 21st century. She would tell bemused interviewers that year that her laptop "troubled" her and that she shunned social networking websites because "there's nothing elegant and romantic about Twitter".

One of a near nonexistent number of teenagers who couldn't be found on Facebook, elegance was very important to Laura. She was prim, proper and combined all the moral virtue and painstakingly fastidious etiquette expected of the average Victorian housewife.

She would describe herself as "prudish" – albeit "not in an extreme way" – and had a liking for anything that was "polite and elegant". She didn't seem particularly forgiving about anything that failed to fall into that category – for example, one imagines, a group of sweaty, dishevelled boys on a tour bus – so perhaps it was little surprise that Charlie Fink marvelled with some relief on his subsequent breakup-inspired album, *The First Days Of Spring*, how quickly he'd been "set free".

Laura was a home-loving girl and a fan of the countryside and was, by her own admission, happiest when knee deep in manure and surrounded by sheep. No stranger to "living off the land" – which included culling sheep, personally skinning and then eating them – she would fit in perfectly at the Mumford & Sons barn concert, although it had to be said that where the aforementioned elegance was concerned, Twitter probably had the edge over slaughtering rabbits.

However there were certain skeletons in her closet that might have seemed a little more irrational. Laura would alternately describe herself in interviews as "incredibly neurotic", "a control freak", "quite a recluse" and "extremely withdrawn". Plus while the average teenager might have had a few fears or insecurities, Laura's manifested as a pathological and relentless phobia of death. Other concerns on her agenda included "the depreciation of the individual".

Marcus might also have had to embrace himself for a long string of evenings in. Not someone who socialised with ease, she felt unable to relate to the "frivolous" lifestyles of people her own age. She claimed that she'd "never been particularly wild" and that her definition of a perfect day involved letting loose with "a nice café and a crossword". Painfully shy, Laura had even refused to wear a trace of make-up when it came to promoting her album, wiping her make-up artist's efforts off surreptitiously seconds before she was due to hit the TV studio or stage.

Oddly, one of her press commitments had involved an appearance on Russell Brand's Radio 2 show. Quite what she might have made of the scruffy, unkempt, torridly promiscuous and gratuitously vulgar Russell – who had a penchant for decidedly inelegant jokes – would be hard to imagine.

Yet Marcus? Although he was conservative and far from a party animal, he had a penchant – like many adult males – for a beer and a rowdy night out. In contrast, Laura's commitment to an unorthodox lifestyle – at least, by the standards of her era – may have made her an acquired taste. Plus Marcus might have found it challenging to live up to her stringent ideals. That said, he shared her love of romanticism.

Despite the slightly eyebrow-raising nature of the pair's partnership, pictures that later surfaced would leave the viewer in no doubt about their affection for each other. In one, Marcus clasped her face in his hands while she gazed back at him in adoration, in another she lay stretched out on a brick wall while he cradled her head in his lap, while a third showed a grinning Laura hitching a piggyback ride from her beau up some stairs. Subsequent candid photographs captured the pair smoking, singing, laughing and taking a ride on a bicycle. It looked as though Marcus might just have cured a little of her reclusiveness.

The concert – which ended with the "21st century barn dance" group Cut A Shine leading some spirited traditional folk dances – was one of the first public appearances Laura and Marcus would make as a couple. While onlookers might have seen them as an unlikely match, there was one thing the pair undeniably did have in common. Like Laura – who, during gigs, barely spoke a word between songs – Marcus was awkward when it came to self-promotion. What was more, his bandmates usually felt the same.

While they'd refused media training, many might have argued that they needed some. A PR rep's worst nightmare, every time the band opened their mouths, it was for self-deprecation. Many groups' media interviews were consumed by defensive comments, holding back wounded expressions as they laughed off yet another catty remark or accusation. However Mumford & Sons didn't need any enemies in the music world – the worst criticism they'd face came from themselves.

With every casually self-deprecating comment, they seemed to be taking a step closer to the edge of the cliff of career suicide. Meanwhile their management were watching helplessly behind the scenes, their mouths gaping wide open in horror.

"I don't think we're special," Marcus would remark to one journalist. "We're just fucking lucky." "We're not a cut above the rest," Ben would concur. "We never have been."

Meanwhile, when asked what was special about where they'd grown up – a district that had been home to a thriving music community, in a suburb of London that attracted only the affluent and well-heeled, the band responded simply, "Nothing. It just happens to be where we live."

Whilst Marcus had made a "pilgrimage" to his idol John Steinbeck's house, his nonchalant dismissal of his home town was unlikely to inspire his own fans to do the same.

The band's responses were often painfully self-conscious – and totally uncalculated. When asked retrospectively whether they'd ever busked, the answer was not "No" but "Not yet!"

To the observer, they seemed to imply that if their career crashed and burned, they'd happily play in the street to get their fix. What was more, to them, longevity wasn't a calculated plan, but simply a bonus. They'd realised that it was "a really strange thought" that they might be doing the same thing in a year's time. "[We don't] feel like we have any secure future," Ben told *Clash* in just one of a series of similar comments. "It's surreal to think that we could be doing this for a while. We just love playing music."

The group seemed like starry-eyed teenagers, scarcely able to believe that their favourite hobby could actually generate an income.

In one interview, Marcus was asked why listeners should choose Mumford & Sons above the vast array of other groups competing for their attention – a perfect opportunity for him to highlight all of the reasons why their music stood out. Yet, rather than giving a carefully rehearsed speech focused on increasing sales, his response – shockingly – was "Nothing". "We don't feel that we're the best band," he continued. "There's plenty of good music out there – listen to all of it."

Perhaps this was the diplomatic response – after all, Ben's Communion club nights saw him promote dozens of artists, while the group intended to sign others to their Gentlemen Of The Road label. Perhaps this was a way of generously placing themselves on equal footing with their – as yet still unsung – musical comrades, instead of attempting to lord it up above them. However, it seemed more probable that the boys simply weren't given to ego massages, preferring to let the music speak for itself. That way, rather than judging them by well-worn marketing clichés, listeners could make up their own minds.

"We feel like gigs are the places we can really justify ourselves a little bit more," Marcus clarified. "We don't understand radio promo, we don't understand the press and definitely don't understand charts – but we definitely understand gigs. That's where we feel we can earn [the praise]."

All four shied away from self-analysis, despising what they interpreted as self-indulgent navel-gazing. Having expressed surprise that anyone would want to listen to a "fat bastard" like him, Marcus was downright uncomfortable with the notion of asking audiences to buy his album. "I cringe at marketing these days," he would continue. "I hate the idea of forcing things down people's throats."

Understandably the band's distributor and PR company were less than thrilled with Marcus' ideal of a casual "word of mouth" strategy that might be successful in a small town, they reasoned, but – with thousands of up and coming bands struggling to find their footing on London's music scene alone – it was far from reliable.

All the statistics indicated that it was those bands signed to major labels with large marketing budgets that usually made the biggest impact. Whilst YouTube videos and the like could send an artist viral before they'd even been signed – acts like Conor Maynard, Justin Bieber and Jessie J being prime examples – soliciting hits on the internet still involved a marketing campaign (albeit a self-led one).

One of the biggest factors in success – arguably even more important than talent – was the opportunity for music enthusiasts to hear a band in the first place. While getting a record deal usually indicated a level of talent or market value, was this in itself enough? A good band could go by without impact if they couldn't make themselves known to those likely to appreciate them, whilst a less talented rival might take off, given the right amount of exposure.

For example, the controversial erotic novel *50 Shades Of Grey*, which mainly featured softcore S&M, was dismissed by hundreds of reviewers as "trashy", "badly written", "repetitive", "asexual" and "not worth the paper it was written on". Nonetheless, the novel turned its author into an overnight millionaire, probably aided in no small part by an aggressive, widespread marketing campaign. Regardless of talent or lack thereof, with billboards, TV, radio, magazines and the internet all saturated with a dizzying array of "must buy" items at any one time, the challenge was attracting the public's attention in the first place. Music fans could only choose from what, to their knowledge, was available.

In spite of the risks involved in dismissing marketing, Marcus was resolute. He would attend interviews and fulfil his contractual commitments, but to him PR was merely a necessary evil – something to be endured with gritted teeth if it meant a chance to continue playing his music.

"I didn't want to be a marketed band, a billboard band," he would later explain to the *Herald Sun*. "I know these things are necessary eventually. I feel OK about it. We're only selling what we are, not selling something we're not."

Perhaps the air of desperation of a billboard campaign was, in Marcus' eyes, akin to losing his pride, dignity and credibility. That was aside from the fact that he found the idea of seeing his face emblazoned on a poster awkward and almost irredeemably embarrassing. It wasn't in keeping with his unassuming, incognito image – and in any case, he was adamant that word of mouth popularity was more credible on the basis that it couldn't be bought or sold.

"Due Process have hardly spent a penny on marketing," he would reveal triumphantly of the group's record label. The hype that followed would offer strong support for Marcus' anti-marketing theory. Not only had the first single made it to third place in the charts, but his first concert on Australian soil, in Brisbane, Queensland, was a roaring success. "It was the biggest gig we'd ever played, 6,000 people going crazy," Marcus would later reveal. "They knew all the songs. I don't have a box to put that in in my head."

Another success would rear its head in Australia when the album made it to number one in the country's charts. In one interview, his guard let down by the joy of unprecedented success, Marcus swallowed his shyness for once, opening up about what might have made Mumford & Sons so special to the band's listeners.

Intriguingly his answer suggested he might have had more in common with Laura Marling than onlookers would previously have thought. "People are reacting to the way things have been going over the last 10 or 15 years. We're in a day and age when so many relationships are done over the internet or through technology," he would assert. "People are responding to the idea you can come to a gig and engage with a band. They want to downsize."

While he hadn't taken his convictions as far as Laura by banishing all social media from his life – on the contrary, he was a regular on Facebook – Marcus did nevertheless feel that there was a calling for earthier, more back to basics living.

In an era of synthetic, over-produced, Auto-Tuned electronica, Mumford & Sons were offering a slice of the lost art of authenticity – real instruments and songs written by the same people who were singing them. What was more, rather than relying on the crackly, tinny sound of digital downloads on their MP3 players, listeners would know from word of mouth that the best way to experience the band would be to see one of their live shows.

Yet while enthusiasm for the gigs was becoming increasingly contagious, there was still room for improvement in the group's relationship with the media. The group had once revealed that they played music not only because it was their passion, but "because we can do nothing else". Their choice of words was unfortunate, broadcasting an image not of accomplished musicians, but of hapless simpletons who'd stumbled into their line of work as a result of having no other option. Had they taken the concept of modesty too far?

On the contrary, at second glance, even that seemed to be weighted in their favour. The band members were modest and humble and, measured against the ego-driven, paparazzi-whoring stereotype that surrounded the stars of modern music, they stuck out like a sore thumb. Perhaps it was this outwardly self-assassinating brand of humility that gave them the patience they needed to win fans over, one small town at a time.

No location prompted a cooler-than-thou attitude and no bar was too small to play. It didn't matter whether there were 2,000, 200 or even just two fans in front of them because, with an ever-present smile on their faces, Mumford & Sons would reliably put on a show. As Ted would later tell *The National,* "We've said yes to every gig we've been offered."

According to Will Hodgkinson, head music critic at *The Times,* this was exactly why they had survived in America where so many other British bands had failed. "They've been instilled with old-fashioned upper-middle-class British values of politeness, respect for others and hard work," he observed. "These values are the bedrock of American culture, but they're not the bedrock of British culture: they're an arcane aspect of British culture that has somehow survived in the States... what tends to happen is, the Americans get excited about a British act – let's say it's Arctic Monkeys – and expect them to do what American bands would: appear on the local radio, do the local press, meet and greets, promotions. Big British bands hate this. They think it's cheesy and demeaning. Arctic Monkeys refused to do it and they've gotten nowhere in America. But Mumford & Sons did play the game, as did Coldplay, as did Pink Floyd – all of whom are upper-middle-class and well-educated."

It was a controversial claim to make – but could there be some truth in it? Regardless of whether or not the stereotype of the archetypal quiet, polite, British public school boy held true, it was indisputable that the Mumfords lacked pride – and parallel to that, their album was making a meteoric rise up the charts.

They'd also kept a realistic grip on their expectations and weren't commanding instant fame. Rather than indulging in shameless rock star behaviour such as stamping their feet and demanding to play nothing less than sold-out arenas they had no delusions of grandeur.

Although some would-be celebrities might seek to get into character straight away, screaming, "Don't you know who I am?" before their first CD had even entered the shops, the Mumford boys were more likely to be seen having a chat with fans in the bar after a show – maintaining a slightly bewildered expression that they'd managed to draw in a decent audience at all.

In a showbiz world where some stars insisted on several dozen red roses in every hotel room and water at a carefully controlled temperature – and where rider requests were becoming ever more ludicrous – the group's abstinence from the usual clichés was refreshing. They'd refused to let a record deal go to their heads.

However that didn't stop the rumour mill from turning – and it was up to Marcus to set the record straight. "How do rumours like that start?" he laughed incredulously to the *Herald Sun*. "I love the idea someone thinks I have my own area with polar bear rugs on the floor, drapes made out of Persian girls' hair, white lilies, M&Ms with all the purple ones removed and people can't make eye contact with me."

Dissolving all of the fun yet fabricated myths, he added, "It's a stinky bus with stinky boys."

While their refusal to succumb to arrogance had stood them in good stead for success, it was that same lack of ego that left them with little protection when it came to hearing acid-tongued reactions to their work.

Generally, being part of a band was almost an open invitation to be annihilated by the media. Number one albums, sell-out gigs and adoration by the public did little to protect an artist from scorn if their professional critics disagreed. Celebrity skin was meant to be rhinoceros-thick and impenetrable by even the cruellest of taunts – an illusion not dispelled much by singers such as Kanye West, who viewed conversations with the media as an opportunity to introduce the super-sized ego he sang about.

Yet while Kanye could fan the flames of indignation with assertions like, "I am the tree and the people are the leaves" and "I believe that I am the greatest", Marcus, on the other hand, wasn't feeling so confident. He was painfully sensitive and, by his own admission, found the faintest hint of criticism hard to handle. In fact, by the time he'd read a couple of newspapers' album reviews, he was reduced to tears.

"I cried," Marcus grimaced. "I hated it. I thought, 'Fuck, that's pretty bad.'" While more ego-driven artists might dismiss all the negativity with a disbelieving smirk before using the offending article as toilet paper, on Marcus, it had a lasting impact – and he resolved never to read another review again. "It's just that they picked up on things that I was insecure about," he would later explain, "and commented on things that I knew were weaknesses. It was brutal for me."

The media certainly had a lot to say – but just how much of it was truly negative? *Pop Matters* raved that the band seemed to have "a master's level education in American roots music traditions", which – to Marcus, who was still being ribbed by friends and fans for dropping out of university – was quite a coup.

The online music magazine added, "They can whip up a brainstorming hoe down like it's nobody's business. Therein lies a major part of their appeal… they treat the banjo like a Stratocaster."

Ted had already confirmed that in an interview with the *Herald Sun*. "It's not like electric instruments where you don't have to work too hard to make it loud," he'd commented. "With acoustic instruments you really have to beat the shit out of them." And, he'd assured, "We do."

Meanwhile the praise was equally forthcoming from *Music OMH*, which claimed, "They succeed by virtue of their sheer, unabashed wholeheartedness."

Then there were heart-swelling, pride-inducing references to idols they'd never thought would become peers – bands such as Kings Of Leon and Arcade Fire. Some reviewers felt the album "inspires evangelism through sheer force of will" and according to the BBC, "hell hath no fury like a folkie scorned".

All Music added a further generous helping of praise with the words, "The group's heady blend of Biblical imagery, pastoral introspection and raucous pub-soaked heartache may be earnest to a fault, but when the wildly imperfect *Sigh No More* is firing on all cylinders, as is the case with stand-out cuts like 'The Cave', 'Winter Winds' and 'Little Lion Man', it's hard not to get swept up in the rapture."

Finally, as testament to their genre-defying mass appeal, even the steadfastly pop-oriented *Now* magazine recommended it, branding the album "earnest" and "alluring".

Yet if only the media claim that it was "Teflon-coated against criticism" had been true. Reviews ranged from an almost flawless 9.5 out of 10 to a dismal 2. While some magazines were raving about the band's authenticity, others disagreed on the grounds that Marcus just wasn't authentic enough to realistically play the role of a killer.

Pitchfork Media, true to its name, sneered, "'I'll go out back and I'll get my gun', Marcus sings, like a man who had never handled a firearm in his life." He might brandish aggressive words and a chorus with an F-bomb, they seemed to reason, but who had he shot lately – if the bizarre complaint that he wasn't the type to brandish firearms was the worst criticism the group could face, they were surely untouchable.

Yet, regrettably, it was just the beginning. *Drowned In Sound* would leave no stone unturned in its annihilation attempts when it claimed, "It's limp, it lacks character and... despite any popularity that may come their way, what Mumford & Sons have produced in *Sigh No More* is nothing more than the empty skull of a half-decent record."

The notoriously unforgiving *NME* stuck its knife in too, side-stepping the religious and literary references with which 'The Cave' was resplendent, to dismiss it as a meaningless student lament about a one-night-stand. "'The Cave' sounds like it should be played through a veil of freshers' week tears after a drunken grope failed to make the earth move," the reviewer castigated. "Not to put too fine a point on it, but at times they need to man the fuck up."

So much for the album being Teflon-coated against criticism – and, true to the *NME*'s words about his lack of manly stoicism, two of the reviews in particular had left Marcus in floods of tears.

Yet negative reviews were no barrier to success. *Pitchfork Media*, which had made its feelings about *Sigh No More* only too clear, had famously rubbished Amy Winehouse's debut album, *Frank,* too, denigrating it in the harshest of terms. Yet it would later go on to become an award-winning, multi-million selling chart-topper. Even so, it was difficult for the soft-centred group – and it wasn't just the sections of the media that were patrolled by music critics where they'd find insults either. Ex-Oasis member Liam Gallagher would later make entertainment headlines when he claimed the four piece looked like "Amish people".

"They look like fucking Amish people – you know them ones with the big sideys that don't use electricity?" he'd sneered during an interview with *Shortlist*. "Growing their own food and putting barns up… I need music to be a bit more sexy, played by people who look a bit fucking dangerous."

Ironically, his brother Noel – whose huge feud with Liam had ripped apart Oasis – stepped out to reveal it wasn't just personal differences the pair disagreed on. In Noel's eyes, 'The Cave' was one of the best songs he'd heard in a long time. "I haven't heard anything that sounds as good as that," he'd tell *Rolling Stone*. "A lot of people fucking hate them in England. I think it's the waistcoat and facial hair. I don't mind them. I think that guy's got a good voice… I wish I had written that song. That's the biggest compliment I can pay whoever wrote that."

Was it mere sibling rivalry that had prompted Noel to publicly condemn his brother's views just two months after he'd heard them?

Or could Mumford & Sons really count the notoriously outspoken Gallagher among their fans? Either way, it was all part of an era that a stunned Winston would describe as "surreal" – and his bandmates would echo him in agreement.

While the vintage clothes that had invited Liam to ridicule them so much – interspersed with a few incongruous symbols of modernity such as Winston's Reebok trainers and the now perpetually bleeping iPhones owned by all four – were staple wardrobe items, they insisted it wasn't part of a calculated image.

Was what they wore even important to them? "Nope!" Marcus would fire back, with cheerful indifference. "That's [just] what we wear. We don't sit down and map out those types of things."

Yet the style they sported, combined with their distinctive sound, gave birth to another irksome stereotype – this one even more irritating to them than the claim that they looked Amish – that they were exclusively a folk band. "We certainly weren't trying to be a folk band," Ben countered to *Pollstar,* "and I still don't think we are. We were just massively influenced by simple songwriting. I suppose out of all the genres, that's what folk takes pride in most – the joyous simplicity of the songs."

The next criticism the group would face regarded their authenticity. The media would repeatedly question why Marcus sang "in an American accent" about tragic events from a country in which he hadn't been raised and from an era in which he hadn't been alive. Was it patronising – insulting, even – for a man of wealth and privilege, who'd never experienced war, poverty or displacement in his life, to assume understanding of such things? What had he been through in his life that could compare? Why would the public believe that Marcus, as a songwriter, was singing from the heart, given his lack of personal experience of the era, when it all seemed to be an elaborate role-play?

While he'd claimed that frequent holidays and dual nationality led him to identify more with America than the average Brit, those claims were ringing hollow in the ears of many who'd been both born and bred in the US. They would cry indignantly, "He isn't even American!" To them, he was turning tragedies like the Dustbowl or the Great Depression – of which US nationals remained sensitive and aware – into a song for the purpose of profit, and all without having paid his dues and worn the T-shirt.

It had been a similar story with Amy Winehouse. Why, her detractors raged, was a skinny white Jewish girl from North London singing with a soul voice more often associated with the black soul sisters of the sixties? They claimed that her Motown persona was a cheap cabaret act, an unworthy fake. To them, she was simply illegitimately taking the place of someone who was truly a child of the era – a black woman – and more specifically, a black American woman.

There was a belief in certain circles that her success was a symbol of racism, oppression and inequality, that her white skin and slim figure opened automatic doors for her, while her chocolate-coloured, more voluptuous counterparts were out of luck. It didn't matter to some how much talent Amy demonstrated – to them, she was still a thieving fraud.

And it was exactly the same criticism that was levelled at Marcus. He was well-spoken, educated and articulate – all that was needed to skilfully put the horror of the American tragedy into words. In his detractors' eyes, these qualities made him a perfect – albeit undeserving – candidate to be packaged for British audiences. The fact that he was raised in England would inspire patriotic support from fans at home, while his portrayal of American events might earn him some attention stateside.

Yet it was all calculated for maximum effect, furious protestors accused, and the only people who could justifiably write about American tragedies were American lyricists and authors. To believe otherwise was to facilitate the oppression of "genuine" Americans, some of whom – a generation or two on – were as downtrodden and ignored now as they had been during the time of the Dustbowl, and were left unable to vocalise their experiences themselves.

All extreme claims to make, but nonetheless unrelenting ones. Whether it was an American gossip forum or a British broadsheet, the criticism was widespread and coming thick and fast. Marcus had been singing during the making of 'Dustbowl Dance', 'After The Storm' and it now seemed that his critics were equally so – in fact, all four were lodging a near daily shower of bullets with their names on.

While he might not have lived through the eras he spoke about, events had a knack of capturing his imagination and bringing forth his inherent empathy. Interviews for Marcus would later imply that the anger he'd felt reading *The Grapes Of Wrath* had been as all-consuming as it might have been had there been a personal entanglement.

While Mumford & Sons had braved being the first British band to tackle these all-American issues, they had seemed to do so with the prerequisite amount of tact and compassion. They'd also grown up with the sounds of Dustbowl survivors such as Woody Guthrie – and all four were his enthusiastic cheerleaders. He'd inspired Bob Dylan, who in turn had inspired Marcus and his fabled sons – and he'd been a regular soundtrack in the past during Mumford recording sessions.

Moreover, in spite of insistence that everything about them – from the folk and bluegrass tinges in their sound to the controversial topics in their lyrics – was an audacious and unjust emulation of American culture, Marcus argued that to sing about matters that were important rather than light-hearted and insipid was crucial to Mumford & Sons' very ethos. "If we were singing about wearing Reebok trainers in a certain area," Marcus offered by way of example, "I'm not saying it'd bad, I love songs that do that, I love the Arctic Monkeys, but I personally can't do it."

He also hit back that – to him, at least – the tracks were honest. "I find it easier to sing songs over and over if they feel honest, if we feel passionate about them," he insisted. "That's an important thing – we need to be able to feel what we sing every night and believe it."

Claiming that they could feel and believe with absolute honesty songs about a farmer who was ruthlessly thrown off his land – when they were residents of mansions in southwest London's leafy Wimbledon Village – seemed to be inviting offers to tear them to pieces, but no matter, the Mumfords stood strong and soon others stepped out in support of them.

"Mumford's understanding comes from novels; the fact that he sings with an American accent doesn't help his case," cautioned Abu Dhabi's *The National*, "but for every critic who points out that the posh London boys have no business singing songs rooted in the American Midwest, there are legions of fans who are happy to get swept up in Mumford & Sons' old-fashioned fantasy world."

Meanwhile one piece of glowing praise offered arguably more weight than any defensive retort the band could have made themselves – and it came from music critic and former judge at the annual Mercury Music Prize David Smyth. "Whether you think it's authentic or not, there's authenticity about it," he asserted, with a tone that warned against further argument. "It certainly feels authentic within the context of the charts, which are full of Auto-Tuned vocals and super-produced R&B songs."

However the stream of criticism remained constant – and they didn't always have music industry experts on hand to fight their battles. Another complaint – one that has been levelled at many a group raised in plentitude – was that they had bought their way to fame; musical hopefuls in particular turned on them, seeing them as products of an unfair culture, balanced now more than ever in favour of the wealthy.

Just as the characters in Mumford & Sons songs had fallen prey financially to the Great Depression, the modern music world had been sent into a spin by the recession. As the financial state of the Western world plunged to new and unexpected lows, something which had once been every child's right – an education in music – was now considered a wasteful luxury.

As purse-strings tightened, schools began to drastically reduce funding for music. While in 1990, local authorities spent a total of £100 million a year on teaching music in schools, that figure by 2012 had declined to little more than a third of that amount. Now each year, just over £1 per child was allocated to music and it was feared that subsequent spending cuts would wipe out that altogether. Even something as simple as strumming a few chords on the guitar had become symbolic of the distinction between the "haves" and "have nots" in life.

The inequality had measurably taken its toll – whilst statistics show that 60% of chart acts today were privately educated, that figure was just 1% a couple of decades before.

The BRIT School still existed to give talented children a free education in the performing arts, but spaces were limited and often logistically were only accessible to Londoners. While the charts had once been filled with bands like Blur and Oasis, who were out and proud about their working class roots, they had now been replaced with their classier contemporaries – the likes of Coldplay, Pixie Lott and La Roux.

Consequently – and inadvertently – the four seemingly innocent men that were Mumford & Sons had become the poster boys of every inequality that the lower and middle classes despised. They were in the firing line merely by association.

When they weren't fielding resentment from struggling musicians and their supporters who hadn't had the same musical facilities growing up, they were being ridiculed by authors who found their elongated vocals and polished cut-glass Queen's English accents comical. They were dismissed as otherworldly nerds who interrupted their studies only for "arrrrfternoon tea" and scones and spoke Latin for fun. One blogger remarked, "Indie wouldn't even exist were it not for sensitive kids who like books, of that there is no doubt; it is middle-class through and through. Tunes, indeed, for wankers who use semi-colons – and words like indeed."

Subjected to endless jibes about their privileged background, should Mumford & Sons, like others before them, attempt to play down their upper-class roots to make them more accessible and relatable to the mainstream?

After all, those with impoverished childhoods such as Cheryl Cole – who'd somehow managed to scrape together the cash for ballet lessons (for which she was relentlessly teased) but had otherwise grown up on a violent, crime-stricken council estate where passing round heroin was commonplace – were often more popular than their privileged rivals. Cheryl was testament to the public's fantasies that anyone, anywhere, regardless of their background, could achieve anything. She represented their hopes that dreams, however wildly improbable against their setting, really could come true.

Public school graduates, on the other hand, merely taunted the working class, unintentionally, by dangling before their eyes everything that had never been available to them. So if the market for wealthy artists wasn't the poor, who was it? Arguably those with more promising futures, who'd been dealt a more fortunate hand of cards, were comparatively few and far between and were usually self-confident enough not to require idols or buy into avatars of success.

So while black rappers under fittingly titled record labels like Young Money spoke to those who'd been racially oppressed, implying that they – just like them – could turn the tables and break the poverty-blighted mould with which their forefathers had been cursed, and those who'd overcome adversity in any way symbolised hope for others to do the same, where did Mumford & Sons belong in the complex and twisted psychology of the music marketplace?

Perhaps it was little wonder that Lily Allen, who'd attended renowned private school Bedales, which attracted fees of up to almost £10,000 per term, had emphasised a faux Cockney accent in her songs. The effects of the total immersion of boarding school clearly seemed at odds with her singing voice. Yet it wasn't even necessarily a cunning marketing ploy, but perhaps more a chance to be liked before being stereotyped.

Jim Morrison before her – who at that time had been in the minority due to his dual status as both privileged and a famous musician – had told the media his parents were dead, rather than dare to publicly acknowledge that his father was a high ranking officer in the US Navy. Most likely, he sensed that he'd be ridiculed – or perhaps he simply wanted to be judged on his music alone, rather than risk the public's perception being distorted by any stereotypes they might have held about anyone hailing from his background.

The same pattern can be observed even outside of the music scene. Ben Westwood, the son of famous fashion designer Vivienne and someone who called punk star Malcolm McLaren "dad" might be a prime example. He disguised his private boarding school roots, often insisting that his parents had never been of privilege and that his mother had struggled financially at the time he'd been in private schooling. He would, as an adult, move to a one-bedroom flat on a rundown Clapham council estate, work in charity shops and regularly wear second-hand clothes that were falling to bits, building his image on a bedrock of bohemian shabby chic that was at odds with both his mother's profession and his schooling.

While it was fashionable – pardon the pun – to outright deny one's connections to privilege, Mumford & Sons wouldn't fall prey to the same disguise, or fret over what their image was. As a four piece, they felt they knew exactly what they stood for – and they didn't feel they needed to change it.

They were all about faith, love, emotion, honesty and communicating the difficulty of being spiritual in a modern world just as loaded with temptation and travesty as the past on which they reminisced. They were telling a story of the pains of being pure at heart, communicated through a framework of not only the Bible, but some of the world's best known literary classics. Just as they urged their listeners, they could sigh no more because their job was done.

They'd survived the veritable obstacle course that was the music industry while staying true to themselves and their instincts. Their detractors could sneer all they liked, but at least they – and any fans worth having – knew who they were.

As for reading bad reviews, Marcus found that the agony had been cured by the wonder drug that was music. "I was playing a gig and by the end of the gig I thought, 'Well, we're still doing what we want to be doing and we're really proud of the work we've done,'" Marcus rationalised.

He'd also found a resolution. "Now we've made a decision as a band not to send reviews to each other – if one of the band wants to google us, that's up to them, but they can't share it, because in all seriousness, it can affect how you feel."

Wise words – after all, wasn't faith blind?

Chapter 6

Bridging The Gap

By the time 'Winter Winds' was released as a single, on December 7, 2009, the band was thousands of miles away – and metaphorically, a few million further. As a promotional video was broadcast around the world, featuring the foursome shivering on an open road while bitterly cold snow rained down around them, in reality, they were on the outskirts of Delhi, India, enjoying the baking hot sun.

Perhaps it was just as well that they weren't around to see the fruits of their labour, because lip-syncing at the camera for hours on end, posing shamelessly in a corn field and pretending to shiver in fake snow on a mild autumn day were experiences the band counted among the most embarrassing of their lives.

"We had a shameful moment of making that music video which has really sort of changed my life in a number of ways," Marcus would later tell *American Songwriter*, shuddering at the memory. "I mean, like, I never want to sing into a camera ever again!"

The single, which featured the trusty and faith-affirming additional track 'Hold On To What You Believe', would peak at number 44 in the UK charts and wouldn't register in India at all – but the purpose of the band's visit there transcended chart positions. They were on a mission to create music which promoted world peace.

Dharohar was an eight-piece group of musicians, taking their name from the Sanskrit word for "legacy". The group's members were both Hindu and Muslim, struggling to co-exist in a country paralysed by violence and unrest between the two. There was a culture of religious disharmony and Dharohar's goal was to match on musical harmonies instead.

The band was a veritable melting pot of six men and two women, seven Indians and one Brit, all with different cultures and religious beliefs, but united momentarily through music. In the UK this group and everything it represented might have been intriguing, but far from surprising. To some more conservative Indians however, it was akin to hearing that the leader of the BNP had enjoyed an orgy with a room full of African women in the Houses of Parliament – completely improbable. These were some of the attitudes the musicians were forced to face, with religious tension and disapproval rife.

To Mumford & Sons, while they might have been born into different castes and cultures, all of them believed in a God and had vowed to do good with their lives – and that was all they needed to know. Thus the boys found themselves holed up in a makeshift recording studio – a semi-abandoned arts and culture school in the hinterlands of the city – over the winter season.

The two groups were working to create an East-West fusion EP, delivering a nod to both the UK and India's musical traditions simultaneously. They soon found common ground in their mutual passion for literature, with Dharohar introducing Mumford & Sons to the works of the mystic poet Kabir. Hanging back shyly in the background while the conversation raged on was none other than Laura Marling, who completed the picture for the collaboration.

Her track, 'Devil's Spoke' – also the opener on her award-winning second album, *I Speak Because I Can* – was intermingled with Dharohar track 'Sneh Ko Marg', while Mumford B-side 'To Darkness' met 'Kripa', resulting in a triumphant marriage of banjos and sitars. 'Devil's Spoke' had been nothing like the quiet acoustic number Laura had originally intended – first it was livened up by the insistent strums of Marcus' banjo and the growl of his voice on additional vocals, then the uniquely Asian interpretation of folk joined the party to carry the tune into another dimension.

Meanwhile 'To Darkness' benefitted from new lyrics and an uncharacteristically energetic chorus. Laura and the Mumfords would then join Dharohar tracks 'Anmol Rishtey' and 'Mehendi Rachi'. The latter, featuring guest vocals from Laura, was perhaps a fitting tribute to her self-confessed desire to one day flee the trappings of the music industry and spend the rest of her days living an uncomplicated lifestyle as a stay-at-home mother. The lyrics spoke of becoming a bird, flying away and giving everything in her life up to pursue something simple – a life she was hoping might be open to her and Marcus one day.

These four tracks would form the first recording, although – unbeknown to fans – the following year, there would be additions to come. During the making of the tracks, a multi-national collective had been formed and they'd had much to learn from each other's cultures. In fact, even for artists such as Mumford & Sons, who'd made a name for themselves based on being deeply spiritual, it was still a culture shock to learn how their Indian bandmates started each jam.

"They started by invoking the [Hindu] elephant God [Ganesha] to help them come and play music," Winston told the *NME* later. "They start every music session like that!"

Aside from exchanging cultural traditions, Dharohar would also translate Indian songs into English for Laura and the Mumfords to work their magic on. The nature of the collaboration was reminiscent of the time that the Beatles first travelled to India, indulging in transcendental meditation with maharajas while recording more than a full album's worth of new songs in one trip alone. Albums like *Revolver* proved to be unmistakably influenced by Indian music, while George Harrison – whose passion for the sitar was well-known – would also return for solo work. The Beatles' journey had marked the start of an intercontinental love affair.

Interestingly, the fusion of Eastern and Western music wasn't the only similarity between Mumford & Sons and the Beatles – who were outwardly poles apart. While 'I Gave You All' carried references to the Shakespeare play *King Lear*, John Lennon had liked the story so much that he'd even included a BBC Radio broadcast of it on the song 'I Am The Walrus' as a bizarre form of background vocals.

Several months later, Ben would take the comparisons a step further, declaring on a *Live On Letterman* performance in New York that he and the band were a "poor man's version of the Beatles". When he made the comment, he was at the Ed Sullivan Theater, named after a presenter whose show had allegedly been the very location where Beatlemania in America began. Yet, according to MTV, instead of being greeted by thousands of hysterical teenage girls, Mumford & Sons had inspired mania in their own way – they'd been followed by a group of autograph-hunting "dudes with beards".

While the boys, like the Beatles before them, had enjoyed their stint in the studio in India, there was another reason that had prompted their visit. In modern times, the decision for a chart-topping group to collaborate with an almost unknown one, in a country where the public knew very little of either, was an unusual one. However, the unlikely trio – Mumford & Sons, Dharohar and Laura Marling – were about to put their invisibility to rights by touring the country together.

Their concert in Delhi would be a roaring success, although in other, perhaps more conservative cities, they weren't so lucky. "In Hyderabad we had to resort to being a trip-hop band as we couldn't hire any instruments we needed," Ted later revealed to *The Sun*. "Ben was there with a little Casio keyboard like the ones kids play on. It was literally toy instruments. Only 15 people turned up – and they were all English anyway."

"The infrastructure just wasn't there for touring," Ben added by way of explanation. "One night in Calcutta, a woman was shouting at us to go home."

Ted wrote off the entire tour as "awful shows we won't want to repeat", but the time they'd spent on the East-West fusion project was the icing that transformed an otherwise inedible cake – it had made the journey worthwhile.

They'd also made use of their prolonged stay in an exotic location to liven up the video shoot for forthcoming single 'The Cave'. The foursome were filmed biking across a dirt track in rural Goa before meeting a traditional Indian marching band handing them the instruments from their backs. "All right, lads?" they would ask. "We heard you looking for these."

The marching band, wearing red feathers in their caps and decked out in elaborate uniform – think cartoon character Paddington Bear with an unusually colourful military theme – moved to the tune, while the Mumfords sang in smart suits. It was a step up from the "cheesy" 'Winter Winds' video shoot and its unrealistic fake snow, the like of which the whole band had been hoping never to repeat. They'd all regarded the "poseur" image of video shoots as a necessary evil – but one that they could at least have a little fun with in the process.

On their return from India, Marcus and Laura struggled to adjust to their separation – they'd gone from spending every day both working and playing together to a hectic promo schedule that sent them in different directions. In fact, on Laura's birthday in February, she and Marcus were at opposite ends of the world. While she was holed up in an LA hotel room giving a seemingly endless string of interviews, her beau was thousands of miles away touring in Australia. Yet these were the types of sacrifices that success in showbiz was all about – and, according to Marcus, the two of them were "very patient" people.

That month, the Mumfords would also make a flying visit back to London to take part in the *Later With Jools Holland* show – complete with a twist no-one could have anticipated. They had vehemently denied mutterings that they were bringing folk music back into fashion by none too subtly dismissing the reports as "fucking bullshit".

"I think it's fair to say that we're not folk," Ben would tell one interviewer in as diplomatic a manner as he could muster. "Folk music, to me, is Crosby, Stills, Dylan, Neil Young and it would be a bit embarrassing to be put in the same bracket – if I was them, and saw myself lumped in with us, and Noah, and Laura then I'd be wondering to myself just how broad this 'folk' genre was! Nobody likes to be pigeonholed."

The group stressed time and time again that they weren't exclusively a folk band, but their efforts to convince the public of that seemed to be in vain. Some had a penchant for pigeonholes – and the media would respond to their denials by merely giving them a "not folk folk band" tag.

Yet if their collaboration with a collective of Indian musicians hadn't been convincing enough to prove to onlookers that there was more to them than being the face of a folk revival scene, their surprise collaboration with none other than Kinks frontman Ray Davies might help to spell it out.

Those who'd written them off as insipid, soulless, financially privileged but musically impotent public school boys would watch open-mouthed as the quartet lived up to their promise that they were anything but predictable. They performed a medley of two Kinks songs – 'Days' and 'This Time Tomorrow' – with Ray by their side. In their day, the Kinks had been an electrifying rock group who, like the Mumfords, had often been considered to be at their best live.

Yet there was more to the story than a one-off live show. As it turned out, Ray – who'd already hit the studio to record a version of Kinks song 'Better Things' with Bruce Springsteen and a version of 'Celluloid Heroes' with Jon Bon Jovi – had been looking for fresh blood to work with him on his forthcoming album *See My friends*. Every song on the album would be a collaboration: some of the Kinks' most celebrated hits reworked with special guest singers.

While some collaborations were far from surprising – such as work with Frank Black of the Pixies, Metallica and Billy Corgan of the Smashing Pumpkins – could Mumford & Sons claim a place on that rock-dominated list?

Ray's approach to them spoke for itself. After hearing that he was keen to work with them, the Mumfords had proactively made a phone call to get the ball rolling and, to their delight, he had responded positively. "He had mentioned that he'd like to include us," Ben recalled to XFM, "so we jumped on it and chased it up!"

Excitement didn't even begin to describe how the band was feeling when Ray gave the collaboration the green light. Marcus would later gush, "I am more excited about that than I have ever been about anything before in my life!"

In his eyes, the experience was set to eclipse the recording of the Mumfords' own chart-topping album – before it had even begun. At first the "shell-shocked" and starstruck group hadn't expected Ray to be present, thinking they'd record their vocals separately before submitting them electronically to the Kinks frontman for his approval.

Yet when they arrived at North London's Konk Studios, they were proved wrong. "We figured that he's such a big name that maybe he wouldn't even be there," Ted clarified. "Maybe it'd just be an executive producer on the mic saying, 'Do it better!' But sure enough, he was there and he is such a creative guy."

"We love love love the Kinks!" Marcus added to *Entertainment Weekly*. "[Ray] was amazing. He just walked in and delivered his vocal – one take. The engineer said, 'Ray, do you want to hear that back?' and he said, 'No, I heard it whilst I was recording it!'"

Marcus instantly went into teenage fan mode, burning with questions he wanted to ask about the Kinks. Yet he inadvertently put his foot in his mouth – and momentarily turned the atmosphere ice cold – when he tapped into a long-standing feud Ray had with a former partner in music, his brother. "He mentions his brother a lot [although] they don't really speak," Marcus later revealed. "We made the mistake of saying 'Strangers' was our favourite Kinks song, we got all ready to play it and all excited and I guess the guy who was producing it knew, but Ray finally told us, 'My brother wrote that song.'"

However the awkward moment wouldn't sour his affection for the foursome. He would later tell *Virgin*, "I bonded really well with Mumford & Sons. There is a great acceptance with their band, they are intuitive players – a real band's band. We built up a mutual admiration."

The mutuality might have been news to Marcus, who'd looked up to Ray in a role of near hero worship. While he was the fledgling singer with just one album to his name, Ray was the "teacher" with years of experience. "Ray Davies is like the headmaster knocking on the door," Marcus had announced to the *Herald Sun*, "and you open the door."

Perhaps even more surprising than the news that Ray "loved" their album was hearing that, in this game of musical opposites, he felt the group reminded him of himself in his younger days. "It was great to me to be amongst a bunch of musicians who have not been put together by a record company or some talent show," Ray would explain. "They're a bunch of people who knew one another and had similar tastes and ambitions with their music, so I found that really liberating. They reminded me very much of the Kinks in that period when we were doing the *Village Green* and *Something Else* albums."

The rock collaboration gave the band the confidence to make their own genre to describe their sound – folk 'n' roll. "You have no idea how happy I would be if one day I walked into a record store and saw 'folk 'n' roll' as a genre," Ben would muse after the recording session. "Rocking out, boys will be boys – but with banjos and accordions, and mandolins, and double-bass. What's wrong with that? It's part bluegrass, but if we said we were bluegrass we'd get shot. That conjures up a whole other world of association that you may or may not want to be lumped in with... for us, it's like musical heresy. What I love about bluegrass is that it's hearts on sleeves, and getting everyone involved, and rocking out. But unfortunately in the UK people think of rednecks, and hillbillies. We wouldn't ever call ourselves bluegrass, but there's a lot about bluegrass that's just fun, and inclusive, and dancing music. So 'folk 'n' roll' is the dream genre."

Meanwhile, parallel to Ray's glowing praise, the band was also beginning to make a name for itself in America. On February 16, *Sigh No More* was officially released in the USA and Canada, and the following day – just five days after the performance with Ray – they would make their first public appearance on US TV. They would play 'Little Lion Man' – with the expletives bleeped out – to a home audience that reached into its millions for CBS' *The Late Show With David Letterman*.

Then, on February 26, they'd make their second appearance on US soil for *The Late Late Show With Craig Ferguson* to perform 'The Cave', a single which was released worldwide the same day. They were now moving fast – just a couple of years earlier, they'd still been playing basement bars, with a handful of drunken revellers their sole audience. Now, with the exception of the disastrous shows in India, people were finally sitting up and taking notice. Perhaps their newfound fame had given them added confidence as they'd also developed unique ways to laugh off any criticism.

While Marcus was still ignoring it, Ben had decided to tackle the problem head on, with a dose of his trademark humour. On one of his secret Google searches – shrouded from more sensitive band members in case it hurt them – he had discovered a Facebook group with the none-too-subtle title "Mumford & Sons Suck Ass".

He could have resorted to indignation, outrage, embarrassment or despair – but in the face of his recent success, Ben simply found it funny. Together with the support of a group of friends and on-tour colleagues, he made a total mockery of the trolls.

As metaphorical fists flew – with insults including references to the band as "fucking hillbillies" who had "ruined rock 'n' roll" – Ben proved that the pen was mightier than the sword by jokily retorting, "I'd have to second that… and today should be the international Beat Down A Mumford Band Member Day."

One of Ben's friends joked in reference to the online group's paltry membership, "If there are only 92 people on the entirety of Facebook that think these semen stains suck ass, it's no wonder the world is in the predicament that it is!", while another added, "and half of them are in said band".

A co-writer chipped in, "I just want to say that I work with the band and even I think they are a bunch of twats – fucking hate those guys!" After the band's own personal army flooded Facebook, the online group's shamefaced founder closed it down. While the insults probably hadn't dented Ben's pride too much, the victory was nonetheless a satisfying one.

That said, there were more discerning things on which to focus online. The group had recently been given free rein on their website mumfordandsons.com to build their own personalised sections, which they hoped would allow their fans to get to know each of them in their own right. No longer merely Marcus the singer-songwriter, he'd introduced fans to another dimension of his personality with a book club blog. While he knew the pressures of touring meant he'd struggle to update it more than a few times a year, it was a way of keeping in contact now and then to recommend his latest novels of choice.

While Marcus was a keen reader on the tour bus, Ben saw himself as a part-time master chef and delighted in blogging about his favourite on-tour recipes. It was hardly a rock 'n' roll on-road pursuit, but the Mumfords had always been keen to distance themselves from the "cocaine and prostitutes" clichés of fame, which to them, never went beyond being the subject of jokes – in fact, they'd even told one interviewer that they "didn't have sex".

Meanwhile Ted was passionate about photography and would post pictures of wherever the band's tour took them. In fact, the only Mumford member conspicuous by his absence, who didn't have his own section, was Winston. "Well observed," he would tell the interviewer who'd cottoned on, before breaking a golden PR rule and confessing to what he believed to be a personal ineptitude for his craft.

"The original idea was to get banjo lessons, but unfortunately I'm really not good enough to do that," he'd told *The LAist*. "Then the next idea was to get out the video camera and talk about the cities we visited on tour – I did one in Delhi and one in Los Angeles. I lost my flip-cam, so that was the extent of it."

In fact, Winston's appetite for novels rivalled Marcus' and he'd proved himself to be a voracious reader when he'd packed 10 books for a tour, finished them and then picked up "another 10 or 15" before returning home. His tip was, "If you ever come across a book that you think you'll read in the next 25 years, buy it."

In spite of that, writing book reviews didn't appeal – not least because he wanted an area all of his own to specialise in, and Marcus was already competition in that department – but Winston did reveal that he'd like to see a future for himself in comedy. "I very much consider myself to be a comedian," he added, "because I'm bloody funny. Actually, the first modern day banjo player turned comedian was Billy Connolly. He started in the Humblebums with Gerry Rafferty, who went on to write 'Baker Street'. So Billy was in the band and they took so long tuning and stuff between songs that he started doing comedy – and that's how the comedy career began… I'm very much the Billy Connolly of the now."

Who would have thought that an elderly yet spunky Glaswegian with a penchant for politically incorrect spoofs and scant regard for manners could be Winston's role model? He'd even emulated his idol's move into travel TV presenting when he'd made him own flip-cam recordings, but on this occasion, Ted cut into his fantasy by contradicting, "I believe Billy Connolly is still the Billy Connolly of the now." "True," Winston had shot back begrudgingly. "Maybe I could be his apprentice!"

He'd started to put his sense of humour to the test during live shows too, with one of his favourite onstage jokes being, "Why is it rubbish being an egg? Because you only get smashed once, laid once and the only person that sits on your face is your mother."

Meanwhile a part of their website that all four band members could contribute to was the Recommendations section, where both old inspirations and new finds in the music world were revealed to fans. They would enthusiastically squeeze in blogging between gigs on what would be the most demanding tour thus far. There were some hiccups – for example, they'd appointed a less than experienced merchandiser – one of Marcus' friends from university – and consequently by the time they reached Europe, they were £5,000 down.

"Marcus and I were at Edinburgh together before he packed in his studies to pursue music," revealed the offender himself, Thomas Gray. "'Good luck with that one pal!' I said to myself snidely. 'Think I'll stick to my history degree, thanks!' It goes without saying that I now regret the arrogant assumption implied by these thoughts.

Anyway, a few years later and after months of unemployment and crying I was asked to come along and sell merchandise for the band in Europe and America; T-shirts, CDs, vinyl and so on. Very foolish decision. 'It'll be easy,' said Marcus – but it was way out of my league and I knew it."

His lack of confidence wasn't down to the demands of the job – rather, it was the absence of sufficient musical credibility. "The last CD I'd bought was, I think, Aqualung's 'Dr Jones', which – though a great tune – did leave me feeling somewhat lacking when it came to touring with an actual band that played their own instruments and sang Shakespeare and stuff. So I bought a waistcoat, a petrol station discount copy of Bob Dylan's greatest hits and tried to get by undetected. I failed miserably."

As it turned out, being able to feign a musical education or rival Marcus and the three new buddies that accompanied him in the vintage clothes department was the least of his worries. Within weeks, he'd made the biggest faux pas possible for a merchandiser – waking up in Denmark £5,000 worth of T-shirts lighter and realising he'd left them in another country with no hope of retrieving the stash. As he groaned in shame and agony, feeling his alcohol-ravaged head pound against the pillow, reality set in fast.

"'You plonker!' I muttered to myself repeatedly and into a tear stained pillow. 'PLONKER! PLONKER! PLONKER!'" Thomas continued. "After crying and reciting these words of penitence all morning I finally plucked up the courage to tell the lads what I'd done. To my surprise they were very understanding, probably recognising that they were in part to blame given the frankly ridiculous level of responsibility they'd heaped on my shoulders so early on."

Referencing the children's novel *The Chronicles Of Narnia*, he added, "I felt like Edmund [a 10-year-old boy] in front of Aslan [a strong but kindly fictional lion] – forgiven – and resolved never to let them down again. Which of course I did – almost immediately."

Needless to say, the well-meaning but hapless – and less than business-savvy-Thomas was swiftly removed from merchandising duties. Yet in spite of the disaster, Marcus was in high spirits at the Copenhagen concert the following evening – even reportedly seeming "choked up" that 'White Blank Page' was being sung along to by "a bunch of Vikings".

Affirming that the financial implications of losing the T-shirts were but a drop in the ocean, Marcus joked, "We've got towels on stage these days – and when you have towels, you know everything is going to be all right as a band!"

Yet of course it was more than just towels that had changed for the band – in stark contrast to the year before, the band could now finally afford their own instruments. What's more, they had the foresight to buy everything they needed in advance – in all probability, the humiliation of being forced to play on children's toy instruments in India had made sure of that.

For Marcus' part, as the profits from the album started to trickle slowly in, he ploughed his earnings back into the band and embarked on a musical spending spree. "I just bought a hundred-year-old harmonium," he would tell the *Illinois Entertainer*, barely able to contain his excitement. "And I've got a vintage drum kit that I really love. I actually bought two Martin guitars that are brand new, just for touring purposes. But for recording purposes, we use old amps, an old Gibson, and an amazing grand piano that's so old I can't even remember the name of it. We work with whatever we can, whatever isn't broken at the time."

For the time being, however, recording was a long way off – and it was back to the open road. The quartet were booked for no less than 27 summer festivals across the globe and before that they would be embarking on a sold-out American tour. To top it all off, Marcus was struggling with a bad bout of tonsillitis.

By May, as the North American tour raged on, Ben had found an axe to grind – those who bought their tickets specifically to sell them on for profit. "The thing that's annoying me, especially on this tour, is what you guys call scalpers," Ben would reveal to *Loveshack Baby* with barely disguised irritation. "It's really frustrating when you meet lovely people outside venues who are fans of the band and they can't get tickets and scalpers go and sell them."

One such scalper felt the full force of Ben's rage when he caught him red-handed. "This guy in Montreal," he spat indignantly, "tried to sell me a ticket to my own gig! He had no idea [who I was] and I was on the edge... I was just angry... I mean, he wasn't a fan and it ultimately takes away from musical creativity and it makes it impossible [to continue doing what we do]."

That said, the majority of North Americans they would encounter were genuine and – a far cry from their earliest concerts in the States as a support act when enamoured audience members started up chants of "What's your name?" – everyone at the shows knew who they were.

As summer set in and saw them make transatlantic hops from the US to the UK to Australia and back, a feeling of jubilation set in. When asked about the never-ending stream of festivals at which they'd been playing, Ben had promised, "[We'll] get back to basics, be a bit feral and we'll get to see lots of great bands. Beirut, the Strokes, Stevie Wonder; we're going to tear up Glastonbury!"

He hadn't been exaggerating – they were overcome by the size of the monumental Park Stage, the largest they'd ever played. Confronted with fans screaming along in unison as far as the eye could see, Marcus' main response was, "Woah! Where the fuck did you come from?"

Another highlight was the Green Man Festival, at which they were delighted to lose a bet with their manager about just how many revellers would turn up. "I had a bet with our tour manager that there wouldn't be 100 people there," Marcus told *Performing Musician*.

"We were playing in this tent and somehow we filled it. That was probably the most special gig so far. There were like 2,500 people and playing in front of that number of people is a huge responsibility, because they're all looking at you and you can't really fuck up or make a shit gag."

Perhaps the latter would have been more of a challenge for the perpetually joke-cracking Winston – but that day, facing a mixture of nerves and thrill, even he had been silenced.

Sandwiched right in the middle of the European festival season was something completely different, something to remind fans of just why Mumford & Sons were unpredictable. They'd been performing a couple of shows in the UK with Dharohar – having been invited to play on the home turf the previous year, as disastrous as it may have been, the Mumfords now wanted to return the favour.

The highlight of the mini-tour was the concert at the Camden Roundhouse in gritty North London on July 7. Performing as part of the iTunes Festival, the show was recorded for a limited edition live EP known as *The Dharohar Project*. As well as the four tracks they'd worked on in Delhi, live versions of 'The Cave' and 'Roll Away Your Stone' as well as fusion versions of two more of Dharohar's songs – namely 'Mala Ramaniya' and 'Sakhiri Maha' – completed the eight-track project.

Very few copies were made available to the public – it was almost a secret side-project – but the EP was nonetheless picked up by a couple of prominent sources in the media. *Rolling Stone* would note approvingly that the fusion of East and West sounded "like a pub band crashing an Indian wedding" and advise, "The next logical step in Mumford & Sons' career? Sitar lessons!"

Meanwhile the BBC would commend the "shared understanding of each other's music", adding, "The recordings colourfully culminate in a mass jam session of colliding cultures, rhythms and harmonies – mercifully without a rent-a-religion, new age 'omm' in earshot.

Ben stands behind his keyboard at the RockNess Festival in Inverness, Scotland on June 8, 2012. Mumford and Sons headlined the event on the main stage. PHOTOSHOT

Group shot at RockNess 2012. Closely following a performance by fellow folkies Noah and the Whale, the Mumfords played to a crowd of 35,000 Scots. PHOTOSHOT

As part of the SBSW Festival on March 17, 2012, the boys perform 'The Cave' at the University of Texas with a little help from the Austin High School Marching Band. ANDY SHEPPARD/REDFERNS VIA GETTY IMAGES

Marcus takes to the stage in Huddersfield for the first leg of the group's very own self-funded Gentlemen of the Road Stopover Festival on June 2, 2012. TONY WOOLLISCROFT/WIREIMAGE

A sheepish-looking Marcus dodges the paparazzi who catch him hand-in-hand with his wife Carey Mulligan on August 2, 2012 in the SoHo district of New York. ALO CEBALLOS/FILMMAGIC

The group joins American singer-songwriter Emmy Lou Harris in the CMT TV studio in Nashville, Tennessee. The country and folk star joined the Mumfords live on stage for a 2012 episode of *Crossroads*. RICK DIAMOND/GETTY IMAGES FOR CMT

Marcus and Alexander Ebert, lead singer of Edward Sharpe and the Magnetic Zeroes harmonise together for the first show of the Railroad Revival tour, in Oakland, California. MYLES STANDISH PETTENGILL III 2012

Marcus takes to the drum kit backstage in the jam car of the band's personalised train. MYLES STANDISH PETTENGILL III 2012

Winston enjoys a candid moment jamming backstage on the Railroad Revival Tour. MYLES STANDISH PETTENGILL III 2012

Continuing their tradition of playing small and obscure venues just as readily as large-scale arenas, the Mumfords perform at London's Rough Trade East on September 25, 2012. ANDY SHEPPARD/REDFERNS VIA GETTY IMAGES

The Mumfords pose alongside a giant poster of their official Gentlemen of the Road avatar to mark yet another successful tour. ANDREW WHITTON/NME/IPC MEDIA

Instead there's a clattering, driving energy that unites the musicians in a passionate, stomping hoedown and results in infectious grins all round."

The very idea that Indian music could even be placed in the same sentence as the word "hoedown" was an achievement on its own and testament to the successful blending of two distinct sounds. Meanwhile the BBC review would continue, "All initial fears of patronising, multi-cultural do-gooding, faux hippie culture-stealing and misguided Beatles homages are unfounded, as any hint of tweeness is blown away by a vibrant cacophony of Anglo-Indian joy. This… triumphant experiment… is an uplifting, celebrating piece of music in its own right."

The verdict, then, was that it was an authentic match indeed. A successful affair, perhaps, but not one that was built to last. Inevitably this marriage of musical frenzy ended in separation – Dharohar returned to India and Mumford & Sons – with a jubilance and renewed sense of purpose – got back on the road.

The month of July also saw them go back to basics and join an eclectic line-up of acoustic performers – including Ray Davies, Pete Doherty, Laura Marling and Bob Dylan – at the Hop Farm Festival in Kent. Here, they introduced the public to new track 'Nothing Is Written' – which had previously been performed in its early stages as 'Untitled' and would finally become 'I Will Wait'. The group had been writing furiously on tour and road-testing new songs almost immediately, and others outed during the summer festival season included 'Whispers In The Dark', 'Lover Of The Light' and 'Below My Feet'.

The band, who couldn't stand being confined to a set list, would regularly shake things up – and that summer proved they could rely on the audience to do the same. At Reading Festival, for example, on August 27, 2010, their tunes transformed a muddy field into a mosh pit. "People [were] pummelling each other," Winston enthused to *The LAist*. "Fists flying! That was the best day of my life."

It certainly compensated for the disappointing reaction to the single 'Roll Away Your Stone'. Since its release on June 3, complete with an instrumental of the Irish jig 'Merrily Kissed The Quaker' at the start of the song, it failed to ignite sales. Even a bonus track of 'White Blank Page', live from London's Shepherd Bush Empire, which captured the energy of the group at their best, hadn't persuaded listeners to make a purchase. While it had been popular in the US, achieving a Top 10 spot on the Alternative Songs chart and briefly appearing at number 11 on the *Billboard* Rock Songs chart, in the UK it had peaked at a measly number 141, making it their worst performing single to date.

Their spirits picked up when they were shortlisted for the Mercury Music Prize on the strength of *Sigh No More*, but even that was fraught with disaster – it would bring Marcus head to head with Laura Marling, putting the pair in direct competition with each other for the first time in their lives.

Just when it seemed as though things couldn't get any more awkward, the two lovebirds had been assigned to one table at the ceremony, while Laura's ex Charlie Finch – who'd also been to school with Winston – was sitting conspicuously close by. What was more, his latest album with Noah and the Whale just so happened to be filled with tracks about his troubled relationship with Laura and the agony of the breakup.

That night, the close-knit nature of the music industry proved hard to bear – Laura and Charlie smiled politely at one another, while Marcus – who could have been forgiven for hoping the ground would swallow him up in the midst of this musically incestuous scene – was able to busy himself by focusing on a live performance of 'The Cave'. In the end, neither Laura nor Mumford & Sons won the award – and the £20,000 prize money was eventually allocated to the xx.

Meanwhile, amazingly for a band that didn't see themselves as natural recording artists, October 1 saw the low-key release of yet another EP, *The First Dance*, their third in just a couple of years. Marketed under the alter-ego the Wedding Band, the four-track mini album was a collaboration between Mumford & Sons and their musical allies, featuring vocals from no fewer than nine artists. Marcus signed over percussion duties to Jesse Quin, a member of both Keane and their Communion-supported side project Mt Desolation. Meanwhile Nick Etwell, Ben's former music teacher from his school days, played trumpet, musician friends Callum Lindsay and David Williamson played the fiddle and the trombone respectively and Adam Stockdale – the band's guitar tech and sometime support act in the group Albatross – played lap steel.

"I had been learning lap steel for a while when the time came around," Adam recalled to the author, "and when I got a call saying, 'Do you wanna play on an EP with the lads?', obviously I said yes. It was a great opportunity for me to do some playing, and I got to work with Ethan Johns, which was awesome."

Ethan was a renowned producer in the industry, who'd worked on *Aha Shake Heartbreak, Youth And Young Manhood* and *Holly Roller Novocaine* for Kings of Leon, *A Creature I Don't Know* and *I Speak Because I Can* for Laura Marling and *Future Is Medieval/Start The Future Without Me* for the Kaiser Chiefs. Among his other production credits was an album for the Vaccines, *Come of Age*, which reached number 1 in the UK chart. As he was associated with a number of Mumford-approved groups, he was an obvious choice for production and engineering and, along with fellow producer Dom Monks, was said to have understood the album's vibe perfectly.

That was just as well as the EP was as diverse as the guests on it, it could perhaps best be described as a country-influenced collection with a twist. As a reflection of the atmosphere in the studio – that of camaraderie between a large gathering of friends – gone were the maudlin Bible passages and the Shakespearean tragedies. It was all washed away by light-hearted love songs instead.

'I Take Your Hand' was a trombone-heavy declaration of love; 'Susie' was the tale of a man's crush on an Irish girl and his preparation to track her down at the airport with a rose in his hand; and 'Thumper' promised unconditional love to a woman who doesn't need to give up her body to hold her partner's attention, against the backdrop of an uptempo country fiddle.

Only 'She Said Yes', with its unmistakable nod to Marcus' idols Old Crow Medicine Show, offered a hint of darkness. In the track, a man is delighted when the woman he loves accepts his wedding proposal, but he soon gets a reality check that strips him of all dignity when his lover's father kicks him to the kerb. According to Marcus' lyrics, he's now the loneliest he'll ever be.

Yet while Mumford & Sons had a penchant for writing *Romeo And Juliet* style tragedies that ended in lonesome despair, the reality for the band couldn't have been more different. In fact, the contrast only elucidated a talent for imaginative story-telling, for – as they ploughed through a UK tour – they were amongst friends, and not just the audiences that sang along faithfully to every word.

On October 4, the date of their homecoming show at Hammersmith Apollo, a very special friend would join them on stage – Ray Davies. Marcus jokingly introduced him to the public that night as "a new member of the band", before breaking into a rendition of 'Days/This Time Tomorrow'. Winston then poked fun at those who stereotyped the band as folk artists and believed their musical preferences didn't extend beyond that genre, by threatening to cover a song by Blink 182. "We've had the privilege of seeing some great bands in this venue over the years like Alice Cooper and Blink 182," he announced, "so we want to pay tribute to them. Any Blink 182 songs we could play?"

More surprises were in store later that month with the release of the self-titled *Mt Desolation* album on October 18. The CD, a side-project of Keane members Tim Rice-Oxley and Jesse Quin, included special guests such as the Killers' drummer Ronnie Vannucci and, of course, Winston, who made an appearance on the album's debut single, 'Departure – State Of Our Affairs'. Mischievous Winston would also appear on the song's promo video as the naked musician, his modesty preserved only by a strategically placed banjo.

The group had been working tirelessly on collaborations, with recording sessions chaotically sandwiched between tours, but the work ethic was clearly paying off, because the remainder of October saw them net two awards in a matter of days.

First of all, on October 24, they won the Best New Act category at London's Q Awards and then, just three days later, they scooped Most Popular International Artist at the ARIA Awards in Australia. Astonishingly, they beat off competition from fellow nominees Lady Gaga, Katy Perry, Taylor Swift and Michael Bublé – all of whom were heavily marketed mainstream pop acts. Just don't make the mistake of telling the Mumfords that they'd made folk fashionable – by this point, their response might be unprintable.

It had been the most successful year of the group's career so far – but, as the winter winds of December set in, Marcus looked set to experience a tragic ending. December 7 would see the *Dharohar Project* album get a USA release via iTunes, but – by a cruel twist of fate – it would be the last public appearance Laura and Marcus would ever make together as a couple. By Christmas, the pair had split permanently.

The Sun reported their breakup the following year, making the slightly incendiary claim that Marcus had been unfaithful, but both parties bit their tongues and maintained a dignified silence, leaving the report neither confirmed nor denied.

The reality was that, regardless of the reason behind the split, Marcus had struggled to fit love into his life – and their romance had primarily been lived out through snatched international phone calls and late night Skype chats. As someone who dismissed all things electronic as "inelegant", it wasn't hard to see that a long-distance relationship was far from satisfactory for Laura. Yet Marcus' refusal to lose musical focus had yielded undeniable rewards and, while he was crushed and conflicted by losing his love, the events of the next few months would prove that the only way was up.

Chapter 7

The Antithesis Of Celebrity

"I got out of bed, ran outside and jumped around like a mad man!" exclaimed Marcus Mumford.

It wasn't that he was suffering from a bad case of Tourette's or even that the band had just scooped two Grammy nominations – which, in itself, might have been reason enough – but rather hearing the news that he'd be taking to the stage on the night of the ceremony with his number one childhood idol, Bob Dylan. This was the same singer-songwriter who'd made him want to pick up a pen and paper in the first place – and he was, understandably, elated. "You can imagine the reaction of someone who probably wouldn't have been playing music at all if it wasn't for Dylan," he'd told *Rolling Stone*, as if to rationalise his outburst.

In his mind, he'd transformed right back into the wide-eyed child foot-tapping along to his mother's 1979 vinyl copy of *Slow Train Coming*. He was no longer Marcus Mumford, the frontman of a band with a chart-topping album who could sell out gigs from Austria to Australia – in his awe, he was reduced to a nameless groupie, delirious with excitement at the prospect of sharing the same room with his idol – but it could have been much worse.

Despite appearing alongside an unsettling list of bubblegum pop artists such as Justin Bieber – the mere sight of whom could make Ted cringe – for weeks, the Grammys' organisers hadn't been able to tell them who the mystery guest was that they'd be collaborating with on the night.

"It could have been Lady Gaga!" Ben had spluttered to *Entertainment Weekly*. "Not to say Lady Gaga isn't great in her own right, but as a marrying of two musical styles, it probably wouldn't work! But they said, 'Trust us, you won't be disappointed.' They were right."

Later organisers had tentatively suggested the Avett Brothers, a group the Mumfords regarded as "legendary", but nothing could have beaten the final announcement.

One day, after rehearsals at LA's Staples Center, the group became trapped in an elevator with Justin Bieber – not to mention a four-person entourage who worked overtime to protect him from overzealous female fans. While they nodded a polite greeting, the Mumfords were breathing subtle sighs of relief that it hadn't been Justin they'd been asked to perform alongside. While it was a highly improbable match, this was LA, where anything was possible.

The final rehearsal highlighted that. Dylan, a veteran performer way beyond stage fright, had a well-deserved reputation for attempting to change the key or arrangement of a song seconds before they were due onstage.

"That was a definite moment!" Winston recalled to *The National*. "I can't promise you we wouldn't have fucked the whole thing up just out of sheer nerves. Luckily even members of the band were like, 'Come on, boss, let's just leave it like it is.' I get the feeling Dylan is pulling that shit all the time."

Fortunately for them, the no-nonsense producer T-Bone Burnett had been appointed the musical director of the show – and there would be no last-minute dramas on his watch. "He was the one getting everyone into shape and making sure things ran smoothly and telling Bob he couldn't change the song five minutes before we went on national TV," Ben later recalled to *The Daily Record*.

The Mumfords began the performance with a rendition of 'The Cave', complete with a three-piece brass section to back them up, before surrendering the stage to the Avett Brothers for their track of choice, 'Head Full Of Doubt, Road Full Of Promise'. Then both groups joined Dylan for the main event – a multi-instrumental version of 'Maggie's Farm', where singing was free-for-all. The tension was etched across Marcus' face, but during the triumphant choruses, each frenetic strum on his guitar seemed almost cathartic, like an orgasm for the soul.

Meanwhile American critics had their own unique take on the band's penchant for vintage clothes and hillbilly chic, with *Taste Of Country* commenting that "a couple of them were dressed as backwoods dirt road gas station attendants". However, in spite of the snide remarks, the webzine couldn't fault the show, adding that "they all threw themselves into the music with such abandon that the keyboard player seemed to hurt his wrist mid-performance".

Yet the Mumfords – who had built up a turbulent relationship with the media to say the least – hadn't come this far to rely solely on the views of their critics. Indeed, within hours, the American public had made up their own minds.

That week, *Sigh No More* hurtled to number two in the *Billboard* chart, with 49,000 sales. They narrowly took the lead over Justin Bieber, whose album *My World 2.0* – also distributed by Island – had sailed into third position with 48,000 purchases.

The group might have felt a little out of place among a line-up of all-American artists in the Top 5 albums list as they beat both rapper Nicki Minaj (47,000 sales) and soft-rock singer Pink (41,000 sales) but the public's purses had spoken. The only artist they couldn't beat in the popularity stakes was the unassailable Lady Gaga, who'd sold 448,000 downloads of her single 'Born This Way' on Sunday alone.

However, the down to earth Mumfords were unlikely to care. "I'm a musician and a romantic who loves the road," Marcus had told *The National* unapologetically, "[and] if we have a belief, it's that we can make music and not be part of the machine – showbiz or whatever you want to call it. We live in a mad time where everyone thinks 'celebrity' rules everything. It doesn't. Having a showbiz career is not important. You can connect with a room of 50 people and it can be the greatest feeling in the world. I don't want anything more than that."

As if to punctuate that point, he added, "I don't see anyone like a preacher man or Bono when I look in the bathroom mirror. I see a man who needs to play some football to stave off getting another chin."

Thus they shunned clothes with built-in fireworks à la Gaga and stuck to the simple pleasures of foot-thumping acoustic sessions – the ones their fans knew and loved. They rejected the culture for its own sake and knew that, in a city that had spawned Paris Hilton and her infamous sex tape, one where thousands were selling their bodies and souls every day to make it in music or on the silver screen, they were going to need to avoid the seductions of Sin City and keep their feet firmly on the ground.

"We are glad we didn't leave our hearts there," he assured. "It was fun but it's not really us. LA is not us. Awards are not us. We are from England. We like the road and we like the pub. We don't want celebrity. We don't feel good at the awards dinner table. It's not where music happens, is it?"

What was more, in their hearts, they'd been secretly longing for a more authentic interaction with Dylan, one far away from the screaming crowd and the glaring spotlight; one that placed the two acts alone together in a room to simply talk music. That, for the Mumfords, was where the real magic happened.

In a moment of honesty that would see one journalist rage that he wanted to give him "a bit of a metaphorical slap", Ben had told *The Daily Record* of the Grammys, "Very few words were exchanged and there was a lot of people running around with headsets. It was terrifying and the experience was quite contrived. It wasn't natural or us hanging out playing music. I'll remember it till the day I die, but it wasn't like we were just jamming traditional songs on guitars and banjos and singing songs back to each other. Maybe one day. That's the real dream, proper musical interaction instead of a pairing for a show."

While they waited for that moment, a string of seemingly endless appearances at award shows was, at least, not a bad consolation prize. Although they hadn't won either of the Grammys for which they'd been nominated – Best New Artist and Best Rock Song for 'Little Lion Man' – they had received a European Border Breakers Award the same month for international success. And, as US sales doubled – increasing by 99% in the period that followed the Grammys – the boys made their way to their UK equivalent, the Brits.

Sidestepping competition from a line-up including Plan B, Tinie Tempah, the xx – who'd beaten them to the Mercury Music Prize a matter of months before – and the world-renowned veteran pop act Take That, the Mumfords won the Mastercard-sponsored Best British Album of the Year award.

This was the moment when – for one night only – the group caved in to temptation and began to party in a way that was finally synonymous with a group of showbiz stars. *The Mirror*, which had caught them having a rowdy celebratory drink or 10 each, published a column about it in the next day's paper sporting the slightly inflammatory opening line, "Take two toffs, hand them a Brit, point them at the free champagne, then watch them lark about like public school boys on helium."

The *3am* celebrity gossip page of the tabloid was probably the last place the Mumfords had expected to find themselves. The daily double-page spread was a true exercise of *Schadenfreude* – one where undercover journalists took great pleasure in watching and of course reporting celebrities' darkest hours. Whether they were exchanging blows on the dance floor, stumbling drunkenly out of nightclubs when they thought they might have gone undetected – and in some people's cases, popping into the toilets for a spot of nose candy to get them through the night – there'd be paparazzi waiting to document it. All too often, they would be indulging in something their PR department would prefer not to know about – but *The Mirror* would be only too happy to oblige in informing them. Plus, in order to avoid strongly worded letters from lawyers, they usually made sure to capture every incriminating exploit on camera. There was little escape from the watchful eye of the journalists but, in the Mumfords' case, they had escaped with a damning reference to one of the boys vomiting profusely into a flowerpot.

They'd been chauffeur-driven to the Savoy, where Take That and Universal were co-hosting a lavish after-party, with almost half a million pounds' worth of alcohol behind the bar. It was a recipe for disaster for anyone with an addictive personality – and even for those who kept it in moderation.

The Mumfords, who'd told a number of interviewers that they "didn't really drink", were now guzzling champagne and whisky in celebration of what was, to be fair, a once in a lifetime moment – their very first Brit.

"Clearly on a mission to have a night to remember, they were seen barrelling around the place, knocking into guests, and fighting off a few girls all keen to take one of them home to meet Mum," the paper had reported. "No wonder rumours reached my ears that one of the boys was violently sick into a decorative flower feature."

The piece concluded, "The VIP goody bag Marcus was clutching was heaving with other freebies (watches, chocolates, All Saints clothes, a Nintendo 3DS, a bottle of gin and some Jimmy Choo perfume, in case you're interested) but sadly no Anadin, which is a shame, because I bet these Little Lion Men had roaring heads the next day..."

Yet it seemed they'd learnt their lesson when, a few months later, they'd announce incredulously that they didn't know how classic rock bands legendary for their heavy partying had managed to keep it together. "I don't understand how those old bands did it," Winston mused to *The Independent*. "We worked out that if we did three gigs in a row and went out afterwards, we'd lose our voices. We know our limits."

The Brits performance, which had seen all four on form playing 'Timshel', proved that they hadn't reached their limits just yet. In any case, Ben had work to do. Communion had gone stateside and he'd just launched a monthly residency at Public Assembly in Williamsburg, New York.

In a bid to stamp out musical elitism and put a stop to the elevated prices of the music scene in the USA's informal capital, Ben and his team would organise half a dozen acts each month – hand-picked themselves to fit the Communion mould – and charge just $15 a time to see them. It gave new bands a voice in an environment that wouldn't price out their potential fans.

"Williamsburg is a bit of a New York cliché at this point," Ben told the *NY Daily News*. "We'll see if we can show people a real scene instead of a fake one."

The venue he'd chosen for the nights – Public Assembly – embodied that vibe. It was anti-celebrity, unpretentious and shamelessly unglamorous. "It's the exact equivalent of the Notting Hill Arts club," he would reveal. "It's slightly industrial – you can see the air conditioning vents and the wires. No glitz, no glamour… it's about showing how sharing music can create a real, live community."

His quest to make music accessible and affordable, in a format that exploited neither artists nor listeners, had even cut into his time in Mumford & Sons – he'd tracked down the venue whilst touring New York with his bandmates the previous year.

Ben's commitment to building his community was impressive, even seeing him state that while Mumford & Sons was his hobby, Communion was his work, and he planned to remain dedicated to it for a long time to come.

Similarly, Marcus' highlight of February hadn't been performing at the Grammys or even winning a Brit – it had been an inconspicuous secret basement gig in Nashville, with dozens of his friends surrounding him. This was the low-key hoedown that the band had longed to have with Dylan and was at the heart of the Mumford & Sons philosophy – a few beers in the company of like-minded friends and a night of relentless music. Unlike the Brit Awards and all the obligatory pomp and pageantry that it entailed, these private, multi-instrumental jams were where real music took place, in a location that set their creative spirits on fire.

Yet admittedly the show – which saw Marcus join his good friend and guitarist Mike Harris with his band the Apache Relay in the basement of his home – was special for more reasons than one. His childhood friend, actress Carey Mulligan, was there and that night old flames began to reignite.

They'd attended church together in their younger days and had always been fond of one another but had drifted apart and lost touch, meeting again for the first time at a concert in Nashville a few months before. Now Marcus had returned to the city and Carey – who'd arrived with her *Brothers* co-star Jake Gyllenhaal – was looking blushingly into his eyes from the front row of the tiny audience.

Physically, Carey was just Marcus' type. Her tomboyish looks were emphasised by a blonde pixie hairdo and she was slim, delicate and baby-faced – a dead ringer, in fact, for his ex, Laura Marling. She wasn't the type to wear much make-up and had a down to earth nature and a simplicity that Marcus – who once claimed he must have been a farm boy in another life – found very appealing.

That wasn't where the similarities with Laura ended, either – Carey had made her acting debut as Kitty Bennet in a film adaptation of Jane Austen novel *Pride And Prejudice*. The part originally hadn't involved much acting, as Carey had the same type of old-world grace and elegance peculiar in someone of Marcus' era.

Her other film roles, on the other hand, had been more diverse. She'd also played the orphan Ada in Charles Dickens story *Bleak House*, followed by a school girl in the 2010 film *An Education*, a performance which netted her an Oscar nomination. She'd even appeared in TV series *Dr Who* and *Waking The Dead*.

Like Marcus, she was a high achiever, but she had modesty with it – and he quickly found himself falling in love with all the qualities that had first attracted him to his ex. That said, although they'd parted ways a matter of a couple of months previously, and Carey had split with fellow actor Shia LaBoeuf equally recently, both felt there was something more to their attraction than a rebound relationship.

After the concert in Mike's basement, the pair – along with around 50 friends – had piled into an upstairs bedroom for an epic all-night party that wouldn't slow until 4am. While Jake Gyllenhaal, Marcus and several others strummed on guitars, Carey would join Marcus on vocals for an impromptu rendition of 'Amazing Grace' and Old Crow Medicine Show's 'Wagon Wheel'.

Days later at the Brit Awards, it seemed as though that night might have been forgotten, as Marcus flirted with and fawned over female vocalist Ellie Goulding, calling her "beautiful" and echoing the band's jokey assertions that she was their "only friend" at the event. To make matters even more complicated, Ellie had been shortlisted for the same award as Laura Marling – Best British Female – and had ultimately lost out to her, too. Yet the relationship between the Mumfords and Ellie was purely one of friendship – Ben had produced her track 'Your Song' – the debut single from her re-released album *Bright Lights*, originally written and recorded by Elton John. Ben had even sung on a version of her track, while Ellie would later cover 'The Cave' at a number of live shows and voice her desire to tour with the group. Ellie would perform 'Your Song' at Kate Middleton and Prince Harry's wedding reception, something which was special for Ben even though he hadn't been present. Meanwhile Marcus' heart lay not with Ellie, award ceremonies or the much-publicised Royal Wedding – instead, his sights were set on Carey, someone he believed might be the one.

Meanwhile, March saw the Mumfords move across the UK, beginning with an eight-day tour of the Scottish Highlands – Tobermory, Stornaway, Ullapool, Kirkwall, Lerwick, Fort William, Inverness and Forres.

Despite album sales by now having hit the two million mark worldwide, it was clear the group didn't consider themselves above playing small and rustic locations. In fact, with its rich tradition of roots music, the Highlands was where they would pick up some of their most devoted fans. Yet some of the smaller locations rarely saw groups from outside the country at all.

By March 18, the day after St Patrick's Day, the band had moved to Ireland for a show at the Dublin Olympia. Yet, before they played their gig, the four were on a mission – to find the O'Donoghue's Pub they'd spoken about in the song 'Susie' – the first place ever to play host to famous folk group the Dubliners back in the sixties.

They'd end the afternoon sipping Guinness while sitting by the city's landmark Ha'Penny Bridge. Yet Marcus was flagging fast – suffering from a throat infection and overexertion of his voice, he had no choice but to smile through the pain and force his way on to the stage. "I just focused on these two girls in the front row, who knew all the words," Marcus would tell *Spin* magazine later. "Sometimes the crowd carries you through it – them and the codeine."

Yet the next month brought not only better health but emotional support from girlfriend Carey, who joined the group on board the

Railroad Revival Tour. It was an epic journey across the American Southwest the vintage way – in antique railcars that hailed from the fifties and sixties. Throughout the 2,000 mile journey, they'd be eating, sleeping and socialising exclusively within the train, stopping off only to play shows at six locations along the way.

Understandably, some of the band members became a little claustrophobic, getting their exercise by pacing up and down the train – but their saving grace was the music car. Kitted out with an open bar and free-flowing drinks at all times, there were plenty of instruments on hand – including a grand piano to entertain them.

What's more, they weren't alone – the 15-car, 1,500ft long train would be shared by two other bands, Edward Sharpe and the Magnetic Zeros and their beloved Old Crow Medicine Show. Besides that, the train was bustling with photographers, journalists, tour crew members and of course friends and family – this was far from a solitary trip. Also in tow was a documentary film-maker, Emmett Malloy, on hand to capture every moment of the tour from the show themselves to the Mumfords' jams with the other bands behind the scenes – for an on-the-road reality show to screen at a later date.

Emmett, who'd also produced videos for Metallica and Blink 182, had previously filmed *The White Stripes Under Great White Northern Lights*, a 2007 documentary on the American rock group's one of a kind tour, featuring performances in buses, in bowling alleys and even in front of Indian tribal elders – not to mention an infamous one-note show. The documentary he was about to make with the Mumfords would, likewise, capture the group as they'd never been seen before.

Capturing the open road by rail was an American musical tradition. Folk artist Woody Guthrie had trailed migrant workers from Oklahoma during the era of the Great Depression to learn more about the largely unrecognised folk and blues culture that got desperately poor farmers through tough times – and he'd been astonished at what he'd seen. These migrants were people with nothing to live for – their entire lives and everything in them had been dissolved into dust, so what reason was there for them to continue? They'd trudged countless footsteps with a wrenching hunger in the pits of their stomachs, until every last vestige of hope seemed, before their very eyes, to fade away.

They weakened not merely from exhaustion, but from the perpetual cloud of dust and tears that threatened to choke them up. They no longer knew where they were going, or what they might find when they arrived. Every corner they turned seemed to echo their worldview of a parched, fruitless desert dustbowl, all of the things that might sustain human life were now absent – they lacked food, money and work – and most of all they lacked hope. Life had become purposeless.

Yet one thing cut through their dark cloud of depression – and that was the healing power of music, the only saviour that still had the potential to give them pleasure. Guthrie discovered a rich musical culture at the migrants' fingertips – one which was spirit-lifting and community building and which prevailed even to the point of near-starvation. Even something as simple as singing together, or playing on the cheap wooden instruments they'd salvaged from their farms, had uplifting powers that painted a glimmer of hope across migrants' hearts. There was a reason to stay alive one more day.

Touched by the arresting imagery he'd seen, Guthrie would later become politically active, adorning his guitar with a sticker that read, "This machine kills fascists". This was a symbol of how music could triumph over both adversity and evil. In recognition of the bravery and determination he'd seen, he recorded the track 'This Train Is Bound For Glory'. He would go on to play at charity gigs, organised by the John Steinbeck Committee To Aid Farm Workers, aimed at raising money for the dispossessed migrants his music honoured. It was hardly surprising he'd earned himself the nickname the Dustbowl Troubador.

However he'd learnt about more than just music – his travels had awakened in Guthrie a hunger for the allure of the open road.

It was an unusual but deeply traditional way for touring musicians to traverse America's southwest – and the Mumfords were thrilled. "To misquote the great Woody Guthrie, this train is bound for disgrace!" Winston would cheerily announce for a press release. "Glorious disgrace, Woody rode with his fellow drifters around North America – we get to do it with a bunch of other musicians from different corners of the world. A dream come true to be on tour with them, a privilege we get to do it on a tram – one of Britain's greatest inventions, by the way."

On April 24 – Easter Sunday – the group arrived in Marfa, Texas, a town so small it had but one ATM and a population of just 2,100. "Marfa, your good reputation knows no bounds," Marcus announced, taking over Winston's role as the joker. "You have a marvellous town, or should I say Marfalous?"

The chuckling audience turned out to be bigger than the town's actual population. Next to crack a joke was Ted, who lost a couple of bass strings during the performance. "The west Texan sun melted my bass," he exclaimed in mock indignation. Yet when Old Crow Medicine Show stepped in to lend him one of their own, he replied with an Easter-themed message – "She's back! She's been resurrected!"

If, in the words of Depeche Mode, the music was his own personal Jesus, then it had proved a very fruitful Easter indeed.

Another unconventional gig location was a shipping yard in San Pedro, California, where actor Jake Gyllenhaal jumped on board to join Carey and the others without so much as a change of clothes. It was evidently a week of "anything goes", with Winston even making his live debut on drums when he joined in with Josh Collazo of Edward Sharpe and the Magnetic Zeros.

In Arizona, they'd take a trip to the state's very own Railroad Museum, with Winston stubbornly reminding everybody that the train had been a British invention – by the Scotsman James Watt, in 1765. He might have received a better reception reminding punters of that on the band's Scottish Highlands tour the month before.

Yet each show culminated in an experience that bonded both audience and bands alike, as some 30 musicians across all three acts packed the stage, joining in for an encore of the Woody Guthrie classic 'This Train Is Bound For Glory'. The Mumfords were doing a good job of matching that song's sentiments off the stage too – as the show rolled in at its final destination of New Orleans, the band's trumpet section broke into a triumphant rendition of American gospel classic 'When The Saints Go Marching In'.

The most surreal moment of the tour might have been discovering that tickets had sold out faster than for one of Lady Gaga's shows. Yet somehow the group had managed to do success – even at this level – on their own terms. Their live act emphasised their values of faith and spirituality, literary sensitivity and traditionalism. Yet while all of that would see *Spin* magazine typecast them as a group that looked like extras in a screenplay of *The Grapes Of Wrath*, the taunts concerned them about as much as water off a duck's back. It was simply all part of the territory.

The shows had seen sleepy towns pull in up to 10,000 people, often a figure bigger than their location's population count. These were euphoric times, indulging the band in their desire for total immersion in music – they'd go straight from the stage back to the music car and jam with their fellow acts until the early hours.

Yet they had to eventually emerge from the railroad bubble. Marcus' girlfriend, Carey, would leave for New York, where she'd start a stint on the Broadway show *Through A Glass, Darkly*, while the Mumfords would return to a life of planes, hotels and cross-town traffic as they continued the tour.

May would also see the boys take time out to write some new songs. They'd received an invitation to contribute work to a film adaptation of classic 1800s novel *Wuthering Heights*, directed by Andrea Arnold. The band dropped into a secret screening and apparently emerged "very inspired". The two songs that would result were 'Home' and 'The Enemy'.

Both songs were a commentary on the relationship between the novel's leading characters, Catherine and Heathcliff – a complex, twisted one that was doomed to fail.

'The Enemy' captures the moment when, consumed with guilt, Heathcliff goes into mourning over Cathy's death and Marcus captures this with lyrics that beg not to be told of heartbreak. The lyrics span a gauntlet of emotions, from humility and quiet indignation to incandescent, unchecked fury, driven both by Catherine's perceived weakness and refusal to follow her heart and his own impotence in life, bound by society's stereotypes and prejudices.

Meanwhile 'Home' spans even darker emotions, telling the story of a pair in their youth whose love was torn apart by greedy hands. It scorns society's obsession with wealth and status, lamenting the pressure to conform that drove Catherine away from Heathcliff and into the arms of another man.

The frustration and sense of injustice were palpable – and, according to a friend of the group named Joe, it encouraged them to pen their darkest song yet. "The film screening they saw started with Heathcliff smashing his head repeatedly off a wall that had Catherine's name carved into it," he revealed to the author, "and that was just the opening scene! The whole film had a kind of desperate emotion running through it and they knew they'd have to come up with something really gutsy to match that frustration. It was a creative challenge for them – they loved it. Past Mumford songs have always had an element of hope and faith in them or a silver lining somewhere. With *Wuthering Heights* though, they had to look at someone whose life had been so bleak and unjust, they'd never seen a silver living before and didn't know what one was, didn't know what hope was. The band all knew that this was going to be an opportunity to get their imagination going and create their darkest song yet."

If that was their ambition, they didn't disappoint. Plus, although the Andrea Arnold version of the story ended with Catherine's death from a broken heart, the novel had an extended ending not featured on screen. Heathcliff would be plunged into grief and then, 12 years later, would start to see visions of his dead lover before retreating, inconsolable, to the room that she died in to pass away himself.

That was the scene that the band had in mind in 'Home', when Marcus sings that the water will lead him home and he'd soon see his lover again. In Greek mythology – something which had featured heavily in Marcus' Classics course at university – water is commonly used as a metaphor for death.

Hermes, the Greek god of travel, would traditionally pass over those about to be deceased to the boatman Charon, who would lead them over the river Acheron – also known as the "river of woe". This river separated the earth from the afterlife – it was a place that any soul could enter, but from which no-one could return.

In the novel, a distraught Heathcliff starved himself to death and likewise in the song, it also implies that the character is contemplating suicide. His longing for death to take away the pain echoes the desperation seen in 'The Enemy', where he pleads to be buried alongside his lover.

Both songs captured the agony of bereavement and loss, but it was 'The Enemy' that was chosen for the film; the track would play alongside the closing scene.

Admiring the band's new-found intensity, *The Independent* would later laud Marcus as "the new Kate Bush". Meanwhile, inspired by their flirtations with tragedy, they would promise *NME* that their second album would be full of "gloom folk" – a cross between the notoriously noir Nick Drake and the heavy rock group Black Sabbath.

Ironically, against this backdrop of doom and gloom, things were looking better than ever for the group. On May 30, in a moment of personal victory for Ben, Communion Records would release one of its biggest EPs yet – *The Flowerpot Sessions*.

Mimicking the Mumfords' early experiences in showbiz, the recordings had seen 23 aspiring artists cram into a tiny North London pub, the Flowerpot, for a pressure-free, week-long jam. Artists included Mt Desolation, Matthew and the Atlas, Marcus Foster and Michael Kiwanuka to name but a few. Ultimately the week saw not so much competing musicians reluctantly sharing a venue with their rivals as one large supergroup, where cross-collaborations and mutual writing sessions abounded.

That summer would also see the breakout success of another of Communion's protégés, Gotye. Although he'd been in the music industry for almost a decade, Gotye had never achieved widespread commercial success, charting almost exclusively in his home territory of Australia. Yet just a matter of weeks after Ben struck a deal to release his EP *Easy Way Out* on vinyl, his single 'Somebody That I Used To Know' stormed the charts.

After its July 5 release, it rocketed to the number one spot in 27 countries and became one of the best-selling singles of all time. By the point that Communion had got a piece of the action – *Easy Way Out* would be released on December 5 – Gotye was no longer a well-kept secret but a household name. What was more, Ben had been one of the first to discover him.

Having now built a credible reputation as a talent scout, the future for Communion was looking promising and, as if to highlight that, the label would soon celebrate its first ever US tour.

There'd been enormous demand for the UK shows, with music lovers travelling from as far afield as West Coast America – and that was all the persuasion Ben had needed to set up a full-length tour stateside too. The tour, featuring Mumford friends such as Matthew and the Atlas, would run from October 18 to November 11.

While the Communion acts were in the midst of a "three-day party" in scenic Big Sur, California, the Mumfords were in the very same state, performing at a charity gig hosted by Neil Young. A veteran rocker famous for cutting an idiosyncratic swath through the music industry and doing precisely what he – as opposed to others – wanted, Young was a Mumford & Sons favourite. It wasn't their first meeting with the man they regarded as a "legend" – in fact, they'd joined him at the Bonaroo Festival, an event set on a 700-acre farm in rural Tennessee, just a few months previously. They'd even hitched a ride in his Cadillac Eldorado – a car which he'd bragged had contained "the best sound system ever".

Neil was notoriously particular about the sound quality of music and, in a world saturated by electronically generated pop, that was something that he felt set the Mumfords apart from their contemporaries. Favouring a raw, old-school sound over tracks that were heavily produced, he'd once raged that "modern music makes me angry" and claimed that the average MP3 file only retained 5% of its original sound.

The Mumfords, he argued, were different – and it was exactly that sentiment that meant they found themselves on stage at all his all-acoustic annual charity show, alongside other approved musical veterans such as Tony Bennett, Foo Fighters and Arcade Fire. This year, the show celebrated the 25th anniversary of the Bridge School, an institute Neil had founded in honour of his disabled son, Ben.

The school gave a specialised education to children with speech impairments and physical disabilities and profits from the annual benefit show helped to keep it in business. In an era crippled by recession, special needs schools were closing their doors in droves, making the concert all the more poignant. The Mumfords chose to cover Neil's track 'Dance Dance Dance' – one which they'd also recorded in 2010 as part of a live session in Edinburgh – and they then joined the other acts at the end of the night, including Neil himself, for a rendition of the Youngbloods' 'Let's Get Together'.

The following month, the Mumfords would be performing in honour of yet another 25th anniversary – this time to celebrate Sir Alex Ferguson's 25th year in charge of Manchester United FC. Boasting joint billing along with the Script, the group performed to 600 VIP guests at the Old Trafford Cricket Ground. One member of the group however, who could rarely be seen without his signature Reebok trainers, was a little more star-struck than the others. "This was a massive deal for me and Winston, both being United fans," Adam Stockdale told the author. "Our childhood team was there!"

By this point, the Mumfords' popularity in elite circles was no surprise – after all, they'd just emerged as the first independent group ever to hit the one million mark on digital sales. They'd also end 2011 by succeeding where almost all other British bands before them had failed – with the elusive feat of conquering America.

Just two artists had previously managed to sell a million digital albums in the States – Adele and Eminem. Naturally there were reasons why the Mumfords might appeal to a country that largely excluded British music from the top of its charts. The group's combination of folk, bluegrass and stadium-filler style soft rock tapped into a long-standing love of and tradition for that sound stateside, while their lyrics consistently showed an empathy for tragic events in American history. The cynic might say that the group's focus on the USA, as one of the world's biggest musical influences, was no accident. Nonetheless, for the Mumfords, their success was surreal – and the next private show to which they were summoned would leave them open-mouthed.

On March 14, 2012, they would find themselves at the White House, staring back into an audience that included US president Barack

Obama and British prime minister David Cameron. That day, the two leaders would face hours of intense conversation on war-torn countries such as Afghanistan and Syria, as well as face debate on the economic recession, followed by a joint press conference – their evening of dinner and entertainment would be their only interlude. While Cameron – also a fan of the Smiths – had admitted to continually playing *Sigh No More* on his iPod, music savvy Obama might have proved harder to impress. Just a month previously, he'd duetted with blues giant BB King on his track 'Sweet Home Chicago', while getting into the spirit of things at a White House blues evening. The month before that, he'd broken into an impromptu rendition of Al Green's 'Let's Get Together' to underscore the message of unity in a New York speech he was delivering. He'd even shared a stage with Bruce Springsteen.

Yet the group had the perfect antidote to ward off performance anxiety – a total disinterest in politics. "I have no idea about British politics," Ben would reveal. "I know Cameron is not a popular character [but] I have no idea what he stands for."

While it had been an ego-rush to be appreciated by the world's most powerful leaders for the evening, he added, "It would be stupid as a band to align yourself to a political party. We need to be aware that politics can change. We don't want to put ourselves down to one prime minister or one candidate. It's dangerous territory."

The following month, all four Mumfords would be about as far away from a political summit as it was possible to get – they would be gathered at an intimate location to witness Marcus' marriage to sweetheart Carey. Taking his cue from the vintage American novels that had captured his imagination, Marcus had decided to host his big day on a 250-acre farm. On April 22, he'd find himself at the secluded Stream Farm in Bridgwater, Somerset for a ceremony that represented the very antithesis of VIP celebrity culture.

High up in the valley and surrounded by free-roaming cattle, the farm produced organic beef, chicken and lamb and stream-fed rainbow trout – and even its own mineral water. They prided themselves on being entirely self-sufficient and had made a name for themselves by selling produce directly to those who would eat it instead of entering the supermarket chains. To help with this project, Marcus had ordered a giant buffet of organic-only food sourced directly from the farm for his guests.

The freedom of the simple life, along with the independence that living off the land provided, appealed to Marcus' secret desire to give it all up one day and toil on a farm himself. "I really want to study agriculture," he would tell an astonished Q journalist, "because I'd really like to know how to work on a farm. I just find it so amazing, so fascinating."

It was something that his more modern bandmates would goad and taunt him about. "Marcus wants to be a farmer," Winston would jeer jokingly to *The Big Issue*. "He's always down on the farm, isn't he, with his Biblical farmer bullshit. I'm not interested!" Laughing hysterically, Ben would add that Marcus could often be found "with a Bible in his left hand, a lamb under the other".

The good-natured ribbing of the other Mumfords did little to dissuade Marcus from pursuing the dream, however – and Carey felt likewise, getting into the spirit of farm life for her wedding by appearing in bright pink Wellington boots. She seemed devoid of ego or self-consciousness – but for a glamorous bride such as Carey, who was no stranger to red carpet events, the rustic style did have its limits – and she paired her wellies with custom-made Prada.

There were also celebrities in attendance, including Sienna Miller, Jake Gyllenhaal and Colin Firth, who made a speech. The party was serenaded by Adele, who made a rare appearance following a touch-and-go throat operation, while Marcus' father took on vicar duties to formally pronounce the couple man and wife.

While grief-stricken breakup tracks such as 'Someone Like You' and 'Rolling In The Deep' might not have seemed like the best omen to welcome a couple into married life, Carey and Marcus both loved Adele – and the feeling was mutual.

"Mumford & Sons? I adore them!" she would gush to *The New York Post*. "Whenever I hear Marcus Mumford's voice, it goes right through me, literally goes into my chest and beats me up and makes me completely fearless."

She would also reveal that *Sigh No More* was the inspiration for her multi-platinum selling second album, *21*. "That Mumford record was me and my ex's album," she explained. "If it wasn't for that album I don't think I'd have been able to write this album... I've got to be a bit thankful really, because it's doing really well!"

Marcus reciprocated her praise, claiming he'd like to collaborate with her not just on one song but an entire country album. Not only were they impressed with each other, but both artists had conquered America and were almost ever-present in the US charts. A collaboration between the two of them might be the biggest hit known to either party yet.

The Mumfords then had another victory when they were finally able to match Obama's boast that he'd shared a stage with Bruce Springsteen. The rock 'n' roll veteran headlined the Pinkpop Festival in Holland on May 28 and, during his encore, invited the band to sing onstage with him.

"It was the best fucking day of my life," Marcus enthused to *The Sunday Times*, dispelling any potential rumours that he might have valued the pomp and pageantry of the White House dinner any more highly. "Unbelievable! The Boss had watched our show, which I didn't know until the penultimate song, when I turned round and saw him in his Ray-Bans, nodding!"

Yet the best was still to come. "We watched his set from behind the monitor desk, then halfway through 'Hungry Heart', he nodded at us and waved us onstage," Marcus continued. "He grabbed me round the neck and shoved the microphone in my face! Have I watched the YouTube footage? Absolutely, from every single angle. I never watch our band but I'll never stop watching that!"

Caught up in the moment, maracas in hand, Marcus had also danced live on the stage for the first time in his career. "I'd never really danced before [but] I couldn't stop myself!" he'd told *The Big Issue*. "What are you gonna do? Try and look cool? Fuck it, it's the Boss!"

A mere few days later, the Mumfords were no longer in a crowded arena with thousands of fans in front of them – instead they were meeting success on their own terms in a series of small towns off the beaten track.

The Gentlemen of the Road Stopover Tour was a way for the group to play in places that bands rarely visited and that the majority of their fanbase barely knew existed. In doing so, they were promoting local music venues and nightclubs and experiencing an authentic slice of small-town culture.

They'd been inspired by festivals such as Ullapool's Loopallu, an event so popular that it attracted a crowd larger than the village itself. The festival had been created by the American rock-grass band Hayseed Dixie (one of the groups that had inspired Winston to start playing music), who'd persevered despite being warned that placing a music festival in a remote village 60 miles from the nearest town was doomed to fail.

With Loopallu in mind, the Mumfords had set out to make their own tailor-made tour, where they chose the venues, the ticket prices and the line-up, using a combination of musically talented friends and those they'd admired in the industry. On the tour's website, the group even posted mini travel guides, recommending activities and must-see attractions for those coming to town especially for the festival. Their personalised suggestions, written in a chatty, informal style – and promises that they'd be checking out the local nightlife themselves and hoped to meet fans there – created an intimate feel.

The group's voice was not lost in a sea of sales speak or PR jargon – instead fans and band were communicating directly. Marcus might urge fans to take a cruise or visit a brewery, while Winston would tip off readers about the hotspots of country music tourism.

The tour, tantalsiingly billed by the Mumfords as a "Victorian travelling circus", started out in the unlikely location of Huddersfield on June 2. Sharing the bill with them on the main stage was the Communion-signed Michael Kiwanuka, a singer who'd since stormed the media and had been tipped by the BBC as the sound of 2012.

Yet the Mumfords urged fans to look beyond the hype to his musical longevity, insisting that he was not merely another manufactured act. "He means so much more than polls and charts and competitions and contests," they asserted. "He is simply classic!"

Another artist closely involved with Communion, whom Marcus had known since his stint living in Denver in 2006, was Nathaniel Rateliff. According to the group, Nathaniel "creates moments so beautiful and intimate in his songs and then breaks out into euphoric, relentless rock 'n' roll!" Ted's former bandmates, the Moulettes, also performed.

Taking the second stage were the Correspondents, a mixture of "sixties jive swing with everything between dubstep and drum and bass"; Slow Club, a group with whom they'd shared stages earlier in their career; and folk-pop sensation Willy Mason, whom the Mumfords believed was criminally underrated.

"Willy is a serious sickhead!" they'd marvelled. "Is it weird to have a man crush on him? Short answer? NO. He's one of the great songwriters of our generation. We remember watching the video to his song 'Oxygen' as a young, impressionable teenager and thinking, 'If one day we're half as cool as this guy, then we will definitely be cool dudes!' We still live in hope."

Finally, looking for a local flavour, the band had also recruited homegrown Huddersfield talents the Rag Tags, a genre-defying mix of modern hip-hop and traditional folk expressed via banjo, acoustic fiddle and mandolin. They'd recently been given the seal of approval after winning Huddersfield University's Battle of the Bands competition, but – again – for the Mumfords it wasn't about the accolades or the hype, but about how the bands made them feel – and in their eyes, everyone on the line-up fitted the bill.

A week later, they'd moved to Galway, Ireland, when they'd performed with Nathaniel Rateliff again and their close friends the Vaccines – "without a doubt the sickest rock 'n' roll band touring at the moment". The group would even claim, "We've listened to their album so many times that the CD has literally melted in our Discman!"

While their friendship with frontman Jay Jay Pistolet had been a long-standing one, they'd also taken a chance on newcomers Zulu Winter, claiming, "These lads have seen a lot of the world for a band that's only a year old."

Gracing Galway's second stage was flamboyant glam rocker King Charles – a lookalike of the Cure's Robert Smith and another close friend of the band dating back to their schooldays. Doing little to dispel the rumours of homosexuality that the release of 'Little Lion Man' had dredged up, Marcus would cheekily assure concert-goers that, should King Charles – nicknamed by the group "His Royal Disgrace" – decide to "kick a beer out of your mouth for 'King and country music'", that they had his personal permission to "spank his tight little leotard arse!"

Two very successful shows later, disaster struck. The band had been due to make an appearance at Denmark's Northside Festival on January 15 and Sweden's Hultsfred Festival the day after that, but – following a drunken incident that left his hand broken in two places – Marcus was paralysed. Doctors inserted metal wiring into his hand to set the bones back in place, before bandaging him and ordering him not to remove the cast for six weeks.

For an active musician, it was a metaphorical death sentence. Not only was he in agony, reduced to tears by a pain that only super-strength medicine could silence, he could no longer play the guitar or drum sequences that were a vital part of a Mumfords show. Frustrated by his sudden musical impotence, a shamefaced Marcus blamed himself, telling interviewers he'd been "an idiot". Quoting Coldplay, he would add that his injury "hurt like Heaven".

Substituting Hell for Heaven in the well-known phrase was symbolic of the group's unswerving, unrelenting optimism. "When it happened, obviously the spirit on the bus was like, 'Fuck, you know, this is really bad,'" Ben recalled, "but we have this spirit that's just uncrushable. Everyone just mans up and everyone just gets on with it. We just work out how we're going to do it and make the best of a bad situation and I think that's why we've continued to get along well. There's no-one here who is defeatist. Whenever challenges occur, everyone starts to dive at it."

Fortunately the silver lining came when Sweden's Peace and Love Festival stepped in to save the day, transferring the band's show to their stage instead and offering visitors of the June 28 event free entry on presentation of a ticket for Hultsfred.

While Marcus could only fulfil his singing role, the Mumford ethos had been built around celebrating their fellow musicians instead of competing with them – and that approach guaranteed them plenty of supporters to help instrumentally. Winston's former bandmate Harry Cargill would step in on guitar, while Ben's Hot Rocket bandmate Chris Maas would play drums, enabling the group to go forward with a show that was "sonically as close as possible to what you would expect from a Mumford & Sons gig".

Marcus was shuddering in anticipation of the day the wiring in his hand would inevitably need to be "pulled out with pliers", but nonetheless he was back on top form for the Open Air St Gallen Festival in Switzerland, which took place on July 1. The boys would close the three-day party in style with a rendition of the Band's 'The Weight', together with fellow artists Wolf Mother, Paolo Nutini and the Kooks.

The following month would see the release of the Disney Pixar film *Brave*, featuring 'Learn Me Right', a song written, arranged and produced solely by the group. At first glance, the Mumfords were hardly a match for the kitsch, intentionally juvenile Disney generation – but they had the baby-faced teenager Birdy joining them on vocals, a valuable asset in bridging the gap between themselves and the children's market.

However Birdy – real name Jasmine van den Bogaerde – was no ordinary teenager. She'd learnt to play the piano at seven, was writing her own music at the tender age of eight and had beaten 10,000 competitors to victory when she won the Open Mic UK contest aged 12.

With a professional concert pianist for a mother, Birdy could easily argue that music was in her blood – and as if to prove it, she'd broken records to gain a Top 20 song in the UK charts aged just 14.

'Learn Me Right' would be a collaboration between Birdy and the band, with the Mumfords joining in on harmonies. The soundtrack's composer, Patrick Doyle, would set the tone of the song. The film had been set in the Scottish Highlands and consequently there were bagpipes, flutes and Celtic harps in abundance, alongside traditional Scottish dance rhythms such as reels, jigs and strathspeys.

The film itself, which saw an August 17 release, was filled with the type of wildly implausible fantasy that Disney kids knew and loved. Lead character Merida colludes with a witch to transform her unsuspecting mother into a giant bear and her brothers into cubs. When it emerges that the spell has a time limit to be reversed before it becomes permanent, Merida starts a race against the clock to repair her family's tapestry.

A classic children's tale of action and adventure, sorcery and subterfuge, it was sprinkled with a couple of adult metaphors, but concluded with the obligatory fairy tale ending, with members of the cast happily riding horses into the sunset.

According to Pixar insider Katherine Safarian, the Mumfords captured the spirit of the film perfectly. "'Learn Me Right' is an amazing song," she asserted. "I feel something every time I hear it. Mumford & Sons stitched out a piece that would do justice to the culminating moment of the movie, in underscoring the emotion, heart and the lessons learned between mother and daughter. They really found that moment of truth in the story we were trying to tell and it takes the movie to a new level at the end."

As ludicrous as it might sound to suggest that the Mumfords had happened upon the right musical formula as a backdrop to an apology for turning one's mother into an animal, perhaps that wasn't quite the scenario the group had in mind when penning the lyrics. After all, they would reuse many of them for their subsequent track 'Not With Haste'.

"We liked the idea of having an orchestra in the background," Marcus would later affirm, "and having a girl like Birdy sing – it's been quite liberating."

The day after the film's release, the Mumfords would embark on the first of their American stopover dates. They'd already tried their hand at the formula in the UK but, according to guitar technician Adam Stockdale, it worked best stateside. Due to the vast size of the country, they were more easily able to find remote, untouched corners with hidden historical value. In other words, it was an authentic journey through the wilds and backwoods of undiscovered America.

"I really respect the idea of what they are trying to uphold," Adam told the author. "Good music, low ticket prices and specifically they picked very small towns and only wanted local vendors, to make the town part of the event rather than just playing a gig in a town."

The Mumfords' online travel tips and involvement of almost every pub or club in the vicinity made sure of that. It was a team effort – band and town working together – and that extended to the other groups on the set list too.

Indeed, the shows were a way for Mumford & Sons to introduce audiences to their wider extended family. The line-up was packed full of extra surrogate "sons" that their fans might never otherwise have encountered. They were sharing their own personal iPod playlist publicly and showing altruism to fellow musicians that were struggling to get a foot on the ladder in the process.

"These shows would sell out without any of these bands except for Mumford," Dawes frontman Taylor Goldsmith lamented. "These bands are bands that nobody has really heard of, or only heard of remotely. It's not like they need Dawes to sell tickets, that's for sure. It just goes to show this is really Mumfords' way of saying, 'This is what we like and this is what we want to share with people.'"

In fiercely individualistic American culture, with its unspoken code of "every man for himself" – a country where raw ambition ruled and at times justified all kinds of disloyalty – the Mumfords' attitude towards their fellow groups might have seemed surprising. However this was at the heart of what they stood for – community spirit derived from a shared love of music.

The nights were also a chance for the group to get off the radar a little. The residents of the small towns they played in were not celebrity conscious and had barely heard of many British bands. After playing to a 15,000 strong audience, they could retreat to an inconspicuous bar and reminisce over the days before they were famous. "There was this one night where they just rammed as many people as possible into a small bar," one friend chuckled to the author. "It was just like the old plays playing Bosun's Locker, going to places that could only fit 30 or 40 people. They still have a soft spot for that type of thing and no matter how famous they get, I think they always will."

The Portland stopover – held at an outdoor park overlooking the sea – earned the town $54,000. What was more, the concert promoters reimbursed all expenses and even footed the bill for a clean-up team to remove the rubbish left behind afterwards. Ben did a spot of incognito DJing at local venue the Space Gallery, while the concert itself was brought to a climax by another rendition of the Band's 'The Weight'.

Other dates on the tour included a stopover in Bristol, Virginia/Tennessee. Unbelievably, the event would be held on State Street, the intersection that divided two different states from one another. For Winston, the location also held special significance as "the birthplace of country music". "Does it get any better?" he demanded on the Gentlemen of the Road website. "I think not."

To show their appreciation of the genre, $1 from each ticket sale was donated to the Birthplace of Country Music Cultural Heritage Center, which proudly tells the story of the town's musical past.

On August 25, the group moved on to Monterey, chosen by Marcus to honour the birthplace of his literary idol, John Steinbeck. Prior to the concert, the group took over a local theatre to passionately lead their own event – "Mumford & Sons In Monterey: A Salute To John Steinbeck". The multimedia tribute included live drama, music and a discussion led by the boys – together with a local literary scholar – on how the author had influenced and inspired their work.

Then it was off to the town's local fairgrounds, a location where Jimi Hendrix had famously first set his guitar on fire for the pleasure of a screaming crowd.

Yet it was the group's August 18 show in diminutive Dixon, Illinois, that meant most of all. Separated from Chicago by endless rows of cornfields – not to mention mile upon mile of relentless concrete motorways – Dixon finally emerges at the end of a blink-and-you'll-miss-it exit on the long Interstate 88. Outsiders might have been forgiven for believing its only claim to fame was its status as birthplace of the 40th American President, Ronald Reagan. Yet the Mumfords wanted to prove otherwise.

Their love affair with the tiny town began when an announcement was placed inviting candidates to come forward and apply to be part of a "major band tour of historic towns". Just who that major band was, the advert neglected to mention. In spite of the secrecy, the town's Main Street executive director, Josh Albrecht, happened upon the advert while he was browsing the National Trust For Historical Preservation website.

He immediately jumped at the chance – albeit with some trepidation. "When he heard it was a British band, he feared the worst and thought it might be One Direction," revealed one anonymous insider. "Folk round here are very traditional – they tend to like music that means something – and if it had been them, I don't think we'd have got the approval we needed to host them."

Fortunately, Dixon was more receptive to what one local would term the "British invasion" when it was Mumford-led. This sleepy town wasn't accustomed to receiving high-profile visitors at all – let alone those from outside American – but this group was sympathetic to American culture.

The last time a band all the way from Britain had caught Dixon's attention in any major way, it had been the Beatles – hence why the locals hailed the Mumfords "the Fab Four". For the boys' part, they seemed to take that message to heart when they performed the Beatles' track 'A Little Help From My Friends' for the encore.

Yet it was no accident that they chose that number for a joint sing-along with the other performers present that night. Once again they were emphasising the importance of community spirit and, to them, it was what the entire project had been about.

That night, the population of Dixon had swollen to 30,000, almost doubling it, and revellers had come from as far afield as the West

Coast and Canada – but it was a feat that the Mumfords and their tourmates had achieved together.

The end result was excitement that really had been akin to Beatlemania, with even the town's local Walmart putting a sign in store to honour them. What was more, during the set of the Very Best – a group the Mumfords had met on the Laura Marling tour of Australia four years previously – Winston lapped up the hysteria, throwing himself into the audience to crowd-surf. He'd later appear on the band's bonus track 'Tisamale' from their unusually named album *MTMTMK*.

Yet the group didn't just remember Dixon for the electric live show – it had also been the location for Marcus to secretly record a mini covers album. Together with Dawes frontman Taylor Goldsmith, Marcus recorded Bruce Springsteen's 'Atlantic City', Bob Dylan's 'I Was Young When I Left Home' and alternative rock band Toad & the Wet Sprockets' 'Reincarnation'. The two then collaborated on Texas-born folk-country singer Guy Clark's 'Partner Nobody Chose'.

Mirroring Marcus' passion for Robin Hood, the track 'Not In Nottingham' was also recorded – the same song that the cartoon rooster had sung in the Disney film version of Robin Hood. Another track was 'Angel Band' by American bluegrass duo the Stanley Brothers.

Marcus had first been introduced to the track when he'd watched the 2000 film *O Brother Where Art Thou?*, a comedy set in America's Deep South in the era of the Great Depression and simultaneously inspired by *The Odyssey*. It had inspired him in many ways since.

Also recorded was the traditional bluegrass classic 'Little Birdy' – and sandwiched in between the covers collection was a jam of 'Not With Haste', performed at the Dixon High School Auditorium. All of the other songs had been secretly created while squirrelled away on the tour bus in between their appearances in Dixon.

"Marcus was playing 24/7," a friend told the author. "Most people have work time and then leisure time, but for him there was no distinction between the two. He'd constantly be singing and writing and when he wasn't, he was reading books or watching films specifically chosen to inspire him for the next song he'd write, I would describe him as creatively restless, as his creative mind never really went to sleep. Oh, and the minute his hand healed – as soon as he could safely get back on the guitar – he was back on it."

It was no surprise then, that the band had already finished their second album by this stage. They'd wasted no time in showcasing as many songs as possible in a live setting and the next single they were planning, 'I Will Wait', was one of them.

The promotional video for the song was filmed on August 29 at the open air Red Rocks Amphitheatre in Morrison, Colorado. As its name suggests, the venue was backed by red rock structures, and this unusually scenic concert location also served as a lookout post, with abundant views of the Denver skyline clearly visible on the horizon. It was a legendary venue and commonly described as "the most beautiful in America". Given the success of past artists who'd performed there, it was an auspicious place to launch the next single too. The Beatles had been the first group to perform there, in 1964, followed by Jimi Hendrix in 1968.

Disaster struck in 1971 when 11,000 extra people had turned up to an already packed venue without a ticket and, in their desperation to see headliner Jethro Tull, had staged a mass charge at the line of police officers guarding the entrance. The stampede hurled rocks at their heads, momentarily disabling the entire police force and forcing them to respond by spraying tear gas. The carnage provoked a five year ban on rock concerts. However, when the venue's owners took legal action, it was eventually ruled that the state had acted "arbitrarily and capriciously" and the ban was finally lifted. Other high profile acts that subsequently graced the stage at Red Rocks included U2.

Now it was the turn of Mumford & Sons – and as the constant refrain of 'I Will Wait's chorus rang out, it echoed many listeners' thoughts. It was the next album they were waiting for and, as far as fans were concerned, it was now long overdue.

Chapter 8

The Trials And Tribulations Of Hopeless Wanderers

The day they'd all been anticipating so eagerly came on September 24, when follow-up album *Babel* hit the shops. The truth be told, recording it had been a challenge for the Mumfords, as they'd barely taken a break since the band had begun.

In true Communion spirit, the group members had spent much of their limited spare time over 2011 helping out some old friends. For example, Ted had played the double bass as a guest on the *Eye To Eye* EP by Emily & the Woods. A close friend of both the Mumfords and Laura Marling, the 23-year-old Emily Wood, whose band included her father and brother, could be described as a mixture of acoustic folk and British blues – it suited Ted's interests perfectly.

Then there was his guest appearance in the Moulettes, performing on their studio album, *The Bear's Revenge*. Even the album's title was a cheeky reference honouring their famous friend – back in the early days, Ted had been affectionately christened T-Bear.

Concurrently Ben had been expanding the reach of Communion club nights, adding artists to the record label – which by now could count more than 30 releases – and networking with promoters and venues. In some ways, he performed the roles of booker, performer, tour manager, business owner and A&R scout all in one.

The reality was that all four band members had been busy – albeit happily so – and then there was another overriding priority, the small matter of touring in Mumford & Sons. To create time where there was none, they'd resorted to snatching moments in the early hours of the morning after coming offstage to collaborate on new ideas. Consequently most of the songs had taken shape on the road.

The relentless cycle of making music at every opportunity – including offstage – had been inspired by tourmates Old Crow Medicine Show, for whom the process was as natural as eating, sleeping and breathing. "They're truly inspirational in the way they conduct themselves and the way they see music," Marcus had marvelled to CMT. "For them, it's not a job. It's not a career… they never put their instruments down. They were always playing [on tour]. We would be eating dinner and taking a rest and they'd have these guitars that were always around and they were just picking away in the corner and playing the whole time. That's the kind of attitude we aspire to maintain throughout our life as a band."

Due to this ethos, many of the songs the band had been working on had been added to the set list in the infant stages of their conception, without so much as a title, and had grown organically after several live outings.

However others, such as 'Hopeless Wanderer', had never been playing live at all. That track, which represented the start of their recording sessions, had been developed during Christmas 2011 at a tiny, rustic farmhouse in Nashville, Tennessee.

Nashville was a special place for the group. Not only was it inspiring due to its much-lauded status as the birthplace of country music – not to mention the acres of scenic farmland, the like of which had featured in many a Mumford & Sons song – but it was also the location where Marcus had reunited with the childhood sweetheart who would become his wife. Just as love had blossomed in Nashville, so would music. Yet that Christmas would be the first break the band had enjoyed since 2007 – and the long tour had produced some dark emotions.

The fact that they'd been living in each other's pockets in a cramped tour bus for so long was the least of their worries – after all, in Ben's words, they loved and knew each other "infinitely better than anyone else on the planet". What proved to be much more of a bitter pill to swallow was the crippling sense of loss and loneliness they felt so far away from home.

'Hopeless Wanderer' captured the ambivalence the group shared about touring – the contrast between the passion they had for following their calling and the price that they paid for doing so. The Mumfords loved life on the road – in fact, after one particularly memorable tour, an inebriated Ben had refused to leave the bus, clinging to the wheel and clutching his passport stubbornly in his hand at 4.30a.m., reluctant to go home.

Travelling had become such a large part of his life that it was often hard to adjust to normality again "We call it post-tour blues," Ben would recall. "We spend six weeks sleeping two feet from each other on the tour bus with the adrenalin of the gigs and meeting people. Then we come home and there is no itinerary. There isn't a shape to the day. I make a cup of tea in the kitchen and think, 'What am I doing today?' It's like the carpet has been pulled from under you."

Four friends travelling the world together, pouring out their souls on stage every night and getting paid for it might have seemed an enviable lifestyle on the surface – and even the band themselves admitted they loved it. Yet in spite of the elation of performing and the inevitable comedown on returning home afterwards, being on the road also had its downside. It was a struggle to maintain meaningful relationships – and even adopting an open door policy on the tour bus, allowing siblings, friends and partners to come and go at will, couldn't always shake off the emptiness.

"It really has been tough," Ben would admit. "We're all in relationships. And it's hard to be away from our families. It's hard when you don't get to see people you love as often as you would like, or as often as they would like [but] it's just the way it is – in this job, you can't expect to play gigs from your home."

In 'Hopeless Wanderer', the lyrics confess a yearning to grow old and live a simple lifestyle. They describe someone wrestling with the nomadic tendencies the youthful side of him desires and then remembering the problem they got him into in the first place, and the equally forceful need to stay by the side of someone he loves.

These conflicting emotions are also addressed in 'Reminder', a track which, according to Ben, "is very much about being away and trying to keep sight of the one you've left behind".

A shade slightly darker than its predecessor, the track also expresses someone's guilt at not knowing how much their prolonged absence is hurting a loved one, confessing that they have shut their eyes and ears to her suffering as they cannot bear to acknowledge it.

'Where Are You Now?', one of the album's bonus tracks, tackles another downside to being on the road alone – the temptation to cheat. The song details the ending of a relationship, speaking of a lover's pain when his girlfriend is cold and emotionless about the prospect of them parting. He questions, after the split, whether she still allows thoughts of him to occupy her mind, or whether he is now just a distant, fragmented memory, blurred and clouded by the passage of time.

Marcus' relationship with Laura Marling disintegrated – allegedly due to unfaithfulness on his part – and in the song, Marcus does seem to take on the role of a betrayer begging forgiveness and claiming to be "desperate" and "weak". Yet there is another hidden clue that the track is about Laura – the lyrics suggest that darkness can descend, a probable reference to the track 'Darkness Descends' from her 2010 album *I Speak Because I Can*.

Another dark song concerning the perils of temptation, on which Marcus' frustration is clearly audible, is 'Broken Crown'. He laments that he'll never be someone's chosen one and, parallel to that, admits that the pull on his flesh is overwhelmingly strong – a possible double entendre. It could refer to losing the love of a woman and the chance to be her "chosen one" because his sexual urges drove him to cheat and destroyed their relationship or, on the other hand, it could refer to earthly desires pulling him away from a relationship with God and making it impossible to keep to a righteous path.

The song features Biblical themes of temptation throughout. In the book of Matthew, Jesus fasts in the desert for 40 days and nights in the spirit of self-sacrifice, but each night the Devil tries to sabotage his plans. Firstly he encourages him to break the fast by making bread from stones and then, when that fails, he promises him all of the world's kingdoms if he submits to him instead of God.

Marcus takes up the theme of martyrdom when he talks of crawling on his belly, and he rejects the kingdoms spoken of by Satan when he sings that he'll never wear a broken crown. In this context, "broken" refers to something impure which has been tainted by evil.

The term "broken crown" is also mentioned in Jeremiah 2, which alludes to being invited into God's land, but then defiling it and making his heritage "an abomination". The lyrics also talk of taking a rope, perhaps a reference to Judas hanging himself out of guilt for betraying Jesus. Matthew 20 and 27 describe the moment when Judas accepts a bribe of 30 silver pieces in return for delivering Jesus to a group of priests to be executed. He later returns the money, claiming his guilt prevents him from accepting it. He then commits suicide.

In 'Broken Crown', the lyrics suggest that the conflicted character can take the rope, but that he has a choice – and that the choices he make will seal his fate. Whether the character's wrongs involve cheating on a partner or something more serious, he seems to have made a decision to change his ways. The guilt-ridden lyrics appeal for forgiveness, accept weakness and flaws and ask not to be condemned to "darkness" for the wrongs he has previously committed. By rejecting the broken crown, he is doing the best he can to rid his life of temptation, dishonesty and betrayal.

However, it seems that life is still a constant battle between the conflicting forces of good and evil, as 'Whispers In The Dark' implies. The lyrics claim that a lie is dead and that while something might taste holy, a brush with the Devil could clear someone's mind – a possible indication of someone turning away from religion and dismissing its scriptures as an elaborate lie.

Marcus ended the ambiguity when he declared to *The Big Issue*, "The lyric 'I set out to serve the Lord', no-one realises it's pluperfect tense. The lyric is, 'I HAD set out to serve the Lord'. It's looking back at a time when that happened."

While he seemed keen to disassociate himself from religion, adding, "I don't even call myself a Christian," the lyrics had an extraordinary amount of references to the Bible for a song written by a non-believer.

One lyric, which appeals for someone's sins to be spared for the ark, is a reference to Genesis 9, where God instructs Noah – a righteous man but one who is not without fault, whose sins are an inherent part of being human – to build an ark to protect himself and his family from flood. He had seen the extent of wickedness among His people and had decided to wipe it out with a flood that killed every human being on earth.

He asked Noah to bring two of every species of animal into the ark along with a generous supply of food and then the floods began – only those in the ark were saved. A year later, God invited him out of the ark and it was revealed that he had been chosen to be saved due to having a righteous heart.

The reference to the ark in the song lyrics seem to be a plea – even if a retrospective one – to be saved. The theme of guilt and forgiveness continues when Marcus sings that he's worried he's blown his only chance.

The title 'Whispers In The Dark' was inspired by a song of the same name released in 2006 by the devoted Christian group Skillet. The Mumfords had considered themselves big fans of their music and spiritual messages, even covering another song of theirs at their album launch party for *Sigh No More*. Additionally, the lyric about picking up clothes and curling one's toes seems to have been influenced by a similar lyric by Laura Marling on her album *I Speak Because I Can*.

However the song's most conspicuous theme is ambivalence towards religion, which repeats itself in 'Below My Feet'. The lyrics appear to use a metaphor for death to describe Marcus' rejection of God and of his former belief system. He talks of blood running cold and of being led by light – and traditional Christian symbolism depicts following a light through a tunnel as part of the transition into the afterlife. He talks of sleeping – another metaphor for death – and makes reference to "blackened holes", perhaps a euphemism for graves. Meanwhile the plea to keep the earth beneath his feet could be a confession that he is fearful of going to Hell.

For the first time, Marcus seems to be directly attacking religion when he claims that he was under a spell when he was told by Jesus that all was well. Those questioning the logic of belief in God often accuse preachers of brainwashing or hypnotising converts with their stories, and indeed Marcus' pastor parents had faced similar accusations themselves.

Marcus' sarcastic reaction to the comfort offered by Jesus suggests that it was not a human being that has died, but rather his faith. Elaborating to *The Big Issue*, he insisted that the album was "not a statement of faith", before adding, "We don't feel evangelical about anything really, other than music... spirituality is the word we engage with more."

However, almost all Mumford songs had contained a degree of Bible references, suggesting an unusual preoccupation with God for someone who didn't consider himself a follower of any faith. Was this repetitive Biblical imagery merely a side effect of growing up in a deeply religious home, an experience which he subsequently rejected for being too claustrophobic? Or was it that he DID retain his beliefs in God, but preferred to silence them as a strategic way of appealing to a wider, more secular audience?

Perhaps the group felt that fans might be alienated if they came across as prophets of God in their music and wanted to tone down their association with religion when it came to the public eye. Maybe they didn't want to see Mumford & Sons stereotyped as just another Christian band.

Or perhaps Marcus was reacting against the responsibility heaped upon him by Christian leaders who targeted him as the group leader to blog their concerns that he was leading a heathen lifestyle while claiming religious beliefs and publicly chastised him for not using his music to spread a more explicit message of faith.

Marcus would see his lyrics and character dissected and analysed by pastors of churches from as far afield as the USA – something he was probably not expecting when the band began – and instead of laying himself bare to insults about the way he followed his faith, he might prefer to publicly renounce it and avoid bearing the responsibility of his actions for the rest of the world. Put simply, he might have been tired of living his life under continual religious scrutiny, and distancing himself from the debate about whether or not he was a good enough Christian by opting out altogether might finally put a stop to it once and for all.

Whatever the reasons for Marcus distancing himself from God, towards the end of 'Below My Feet', he demonstrates defiance and general contempt towards those who seek to control him. He talks of his flesh being wrapped in twine, probably a metaphor for the Christian religion's perceived desire to restrain and suppress urges of the flesh and to keep people under control, obeying a strict code of conduct instead of giving in to their desires.

Perhaps his admission of faithlessness wasn't a surprise – especially after the revelations from one of Marcus' friends earlier in the book about his ongoing crisis of faith. Nonetheless, with both parents and a brother working as pastors and remaining dedicated to the ministry, becoming the black sheep of the family couldn't have been easy.

While his parents remained supportive of him and his career, was he fighting back feelings that he would always be a disappointment to them? Either way, it seemed he'd found something to believe in that transcended all boundaries – the music. To all four Mumfords, music was a universal language that required no prior understanding to appreciate and that brought everyone together regardless of their mother tongue or indeed their beliefs.

This notion of music becoming a universal language is made all the more intriguing in the context of songs such as the album's title track, 'Babel'. The word 'babel' comes from the Hebrew word 'balal' meaning 'to confuse' or 'to jumble'. One of the central stories in the Bible is that of the Tower of Babel, featured in Genesis 11. Until that part of the Bible, all of the world had used one language. However the people of the earth joined together to create a city with a tower so tall that it would lead them to Heaven. They wanted to use this "stairway to Heaven" to become closer to God and prevent their city from being scattered.

However, the Bible continues, "God came down to look at the city and tower and remarked that as people with one language, nothing that they sought would be out of their reach [so] God went down and confounded their speech, so that they could not understand each other, and scattered them over the face of the earth."

Some Biblical scholars have insisted that this was the moment when God divided the world into five continents. According to Genesis, the people had spent 43 years working in the tower before God intervened. This story might make for uncomfortable reading for those questioning their beliefs.

Firstly, it brings into question the universally held belief among Christians that God is all-powerful. God's words in the Bible on learning of the tower were, "If as one people speaking the same language, they have begun to do this, then nothing they plan to do will be impossible for them."

This statement alone implies that the power of God is not necessarily greater than the power of ordinary people, making his status as a figure of worship somewhat debatable. It also introduces an element of competition between God and humankind – did God feel threatened by His followers trying to reach Heaven on their own, fearing he would no longer have power over them? And if not, why was he seeking to disperse the people and destroy their work?

The Bible continually features a theme of unity, which appears to contradict the actions of God when he scattered the people and diversified their language so that they could no longer understand each other. This imagery seems unsettling due to its incongruence with most Christians' perception of a loving God.

Some theories suggest that God felt the need to limit people's powers to prevent them from using them in the future for the purpose of evil. However traditionally, people being divided has been the cause of war. Additionally, two chapters earlier in Genesis God had wiped out evil by destroying every living creature on the earth apart from those sheltered in the ark. If evil no longer existed, what was the purpose of scattering and confounding those making a tower merely to become closer to Him and be united in one spiritual purpose? The questions are endless, while the answers can never be definitive.

The reference to the Genesis story in the song 'Babel' is unmistakable, with lyrics about the walls of a town coming crumbling down. However the band's stance is more ambiguous. Parts of the song, such as the lyric that urges someone to come down from their mountain or the one that acknowledges being the weaker party from the start, seem to suggest deference to God. Likewise, the lyrics speak of a city that had nurtured someone's pride and greed, indicating disapproval of Babel.

The song ends with a promise that while someone builds their walls, the character will do his best to tear them down. This implies that he feels he has been unified in the words of Christ and that this is more important than building a tower to Heaven and existing independently of his faith. In Peter 123, the Bible claims, "The grass withereth and the flower thereof falleth away, but the word of the Lord endureth forever and this is the word by which the gospel is preached unto you."

Perhaps echoing this sentiment, the song is indicating that being scattered doesn't matter because the only language that is important is that of faith.

However, other lyrics could contradict this theory. Marcus sings that he believes in choice – perhaps as an alternative to accepting preordained destiny – and insists that he will be born without a mask, a possible symbol that he will no longer follow blind faith.

The lyrics also depict him laughing in spite of the walls of the city crumbling down. Could this be a signature of defiance, a feeling of victory and triumph that music had become a universal language, flying in the face of God's attempts to prevent a single language from existing? Perhaps the band saw music as something that could provoke an emotional response in those moved by certain sounds or chord sequences regardless of whether they knew what the lyrics meant. Could the song be a carefully shrouded middle finger to the regime of control that some felt living a God-fearing life represented?

That wasn't a question the Mumfords were likely to answer any time soon. "Honestly, we'd like not to be too prescriptive with the songs and their meanings," Ted had told *Rolling Stone* with skilful diplomacy. "It just feels a little bit like that was the song that was gonna say, 'This is like chapter two. It'll be like our best foot forwards.'"

Perhaps the group's reluctance to divulge exactly what the song meant to them reflected a desire for fans to interpret it according to their own individual understandings. Ironically, *The Library Of Babel*, a short story by author Jorge Luis Borges, is a tease imagining a library that contains every single possible book and so much information that those reading it can find no definitive meaning at all.

Meanwhile Ted claimed that all four Mumfords had related to the story of Babel, insisting, "It's such a human thing. As humans, we're such a discontented species. We're always trying to further ourselves, and you get all the way to the moon and then it's just discontent. You want to go to Mars. You know, there's so many stories in that story. There's definitely, like, analogies for our strange behaviour as a species that I consider interesting."

Perhaps even within the band, with its multiple differing faiths and personalities, there wasn't a single universal meaning for the song. Regardless, the track's ambiguous nature was a fitting accompaniment to the metaphor of people being confounded and scattered.

Another intense song on the album is 'Lover's Eyes', which depicts an all-consuming passion for someone, maintained by the casualty of a tragic love affair. While the Mumfords had been invited to contribute songs to the 2011 film version of *Wuthering Heights* – and had produced 'Home' and 'The Enemy' as a consequence – the film had ended with the death of the female lead, Catherine, omitting the second half of the book.

'Lover's Eyes' acts as a follow-on story, depicting scenarios that the film didn't portray. It echoes, for example, the moment when Heathcliff felt haunted by the ghost of his dead ex-lover. Referring to how he stubbornly ran away on hearing Catherine reveal that she could never marry him, leading both to ultimately wed others, the lyrics talk of a young headstrong couple that couldn't last the distance.

The words, written from Heathcliff's perspective, also confess that he sees ghosts that he believes wish him dead and, in a reference to how he finally died in Catherine's former bed, there is a plea to God to let him die beneath the curse of his lover's eyes. By the end of the song, he is begging to be helped on his way.

Overall, the track is every bit as dark and intense as the novel that inspired it – although, due to the nature of some of the other Mumfords lyrics, it might almost have seemed light-hearted in comparison.

'Not With Haste' was another song influenced by a movie, in its status as a version of 'Learn Me Right' from the Disney film *Brave*.

'Ghosts That We Knew' may also have been inspired by *Wuthering Heights*. Yet here the Mumfords rewrite the ending, averting tragedy and claiming that the ghosts of the past would flicker from view, leaving him and his lover free to pursue a long life. Meanwhile the talk of broken glass and blood running from a victim's veins could be a sinister allusion to self-harm, or simply a recollection of how Heathcliff was beaten and abused as he grew up.

Then there was 'Holland Road', a location that also cropped up in 'Home'. The title might refer to a road in West London which connects Kensington High Street to the Holland Park roundabout, but while these desirable postcodes were areas in which the Mumfords had spent plenty of time as they grew up, the road's significance in the song remains unclear.

According to the lyrics, however, it was a place where great hardship was experienced. Using the metaphor of a heart of stone, Marcus seems to express his guilt about a decision to turn away from

God. The Bible is replete with references to hardened hearts. Jeremiah 17 claims, "The heart is deceitful above all things and desperately wicked," adding that it is the fickle nature of the human heart that persuades people to break their faith. Additionally, Hebrews 3 warns against "unbelief", urging, "Do not harden your hearts... see to it, brothers, that none of you has a sinful, unbelieving heart that turns away from the living God... encourage one another... so that none of you may be hardened by sin's deceitfulness."

Yet it was this requirement to abandon both head and heart and surrender instead to blind faith that had forced Marcus to question his religious beliefs in the first place. To him, the rules were too rigid. For example, in the Christian faith, a person is said to have broken the second commandment if he "trusts in his own or another's reasoning and lives that way rather than the way God ordained or commanded".

What was more, modern living could see this type of commitment tested to the extreme. According to one sermon at Marcus' church, the burden on believers was to "make whatever sacrifice is necessary, even to giving up our lives, to submit in obedience to anyone, even the least of God's commands".

This wasn't merely an extreme interpretation of a Christian's obligations either. In Luke 14, Jesus states, "If anyone comes to me and does not hate his father and mother and wife and children, brothers and sisters and yes, his own life also, he cannot be my disciple."

To Marcus, this was a step too far: a life of unquestioning obedience – one that discouraged him from thinking for himself – bordered on unbearable. Clinging to independence, he'd rejected these responsibilities.

"He felt that giving himself fully to God and following the rules to that extent was the equivalent of having a lobotomy," a former friend from Marcus' church group told the author. "He thought it would make him impotent as a human being and that he'd be like a child without his own free will to make his own decisions. But when he chose autonomy, he gave up God's protection. A few people called him the lost sheep – they weren't sure of whether he was still living right and prayed for him to return to the flock. Looking back though, I don't think they really needed to worry!"

Yet did 'Holland Road' signify a change of heart? In the lyrics, after Marcus claims his heart of stone had put up no fight against a calloused mind, he then insists that it's not the end and that, in spite of the cracks in his soul, he's still a believer. Could this be the call of a born-again Christian to salvation? After all, Ezekiel 36 deals with someone returning to the faith, stating, "I will give you a new heart and put a new spirit in you; I will remove from you your heart of stone and give you a heart of flesh."

Could this be the passage to which Marcus refers when he sings of being cut down, only to rise again? He claims to have had a heart of stone – the Biblical symbol of "unbelief" – before ending the song with the reassurance that he *does* still have faith.

The sentence about delivering a new heart of flesh is relevant in relation to the teaching, "Too often the heart is easily led to satisfy its own desires rather than follow revealed knowledge, but God faithfully soothes and tests our hearts to rid us of all idolatries, so we will follow His way as clearly as possible."

Yet in subsequent interviews, Marcus was adamant that the album was a statement of spirituality, not of faith, suggesting that if he had returned to God, he had done so not within the tenets of organised religion, but rather on his own terms.

Marcus seems to continue his cautious flirtation with themes of born-again Christianity in 'Lover Of The Light', where he asks for his eyes and ears to be closed – the clearest indication on the album yet that he is deliberating on whether or not to submit again to blind faith. Meanwhile, his reference to being flawed by pride but also being a lover of the light runs parallel to Biblical phrases suggesting that, when exposed to the unforgiving glare of God's light, pride "melts like wax".

Someone who has "done wrong", as Marcus suggests he has in the song, might seek to run and hide from the light, fearful that it will illuminate all of their weaknesses and flaws. Yet he seems to feel that building up a defence against acknowledging his dark side is fruitless when he claims that there is no strength in the walls that he has grown.

Traditionally, Christians have believed that evil thrives in darkness because the absence of light enables misdeeds to be disguised and hidden – and that, without darkness, sins could not survive. Jesus warned in the Bible, "Walk while you have the light, before darkness overtakes you," and – indicating that a man is at his most vulnerable in the dark – he also stated, "If he walks at night, he stumbles, because there is no light to guide him."

Regardless of the level of Marcus' commitment to his faith, this song seems to be a promise to himself that he will live in the safety and sanctity of the light, rather than take the risk of being corrupted or abused by sin.

In addition to 'Where Are You Now?', Marcus' thinly disguised lament in memory of Laura Marling, the album contained two other bonus tracks – 'The Boxer' and 'For Those Below'. The former, originally a 1968 track released by American duo Simon & Garfunkel, was at that time notorious for allegations that it was a "sustained attack" on Bob Dylan. Intriguingly, in spite of the uproar in the press, Dylan responded by covering the song himself for his *Self Portrait* album. Songwriter Paul Simon later insisted the song was autobiographical. "I think I was reading the Bible around that time," he would say of the lyrics. "That's where I think phrases such as 'workman's wages' come from and 'seeking out the poorer quarters'. That was biblical. I think the song was about me: everyone's beating me up and I'm telling you now, I'm going to go away if you don't stop." Perhaps this explained the metaphor about a boxer, while the references to lies could have been a sardonic look at how Paul felt the public perceived him.

Like Bob Dylan before them, it was now the Mumfords' turn to cover the track – and, while Jerry Douglas would play the dobro, Paul Simon himself would take to guitar and backing vocals. It would mark the first time the Mumfords had ever included a special guest collaboration on one of their own CDs.

The other bonus track, 'For Those Below', could be yet another insight into how the Mumfords interpreted the *Wuthering Heights* tragedy. The lyrics speak of a man mourning a death who has since found himself "on top" as the leader of a flock. This could be a reference to Heathcliff's unexpected rise to wealth and fortune after fleeing Catherine's home, heartbroken, in his youth. The song talks of the burden bestowed upon a man who has built his life on love and, when it states that he is called to be wrong for those below, it implies that he bears not just his own guilt for Catherine's passing, but the weight of public disapproval too. The track concludes with an admission that his mind is just as broken, crippled and burned as the lover he has lost – a fitting description of Heathcliff's state of mind in his final hours.

Finally, there was the triumphant anthem 'I Will Wait' that would become the album's first single. Those familiar with the Mumfords' live shows might have witnessed the song's transformation from 'Untitled' to 'Nothing Is Writtten' and then to its final incarnation of 'I Will Wait'.

There are strong similarities between the Mumfords' track and '40 (How Long)' from U2's 1983 album *War*, which specifically mentions "waiting patiently for the Lord". The track came to fruition during a race against the clock after the band missed their deadline for completing the album. Their studio sessions had already overrun by a week and the clock was ticking, so lead singer Bono opened a Bible at random and found Psalm 40 and set about making an impromptu song version of the chapter. Despite coming to life accidentally, the track ended up becoming one of the most successful on the album. It was lyrically used as an encore for live shows and fans would often sing along up to 10 minutes after the lights had come back on and the band had left the stage. Psalm 40 includes the words, "I waited patiently for the Lord, he turned to me and heard my cry. He lifted me out of the slimy pit, out of the mud and mire; he set my feet on a rock and gave me a firm place to stand."

The Mumfords also seemed to be waiting for God – Marcus sings of kneeling down, as if in prayer, before appealing for someone to break his step and relent. Sometimes shepherds break a runaway sheep's leg before mending it again, to encourage it to trust and be dependent on its owner and not to wander away again. With the sheep by his side, the shepherd can nurture and care for it and, hopefully, will not abuse the bond between himself and his animals – whereas a runaway could face untold danger. This is where the phrase "being cruel to be kind" originates. Likewise, the Bible states that God is a shepherd to His people, with a verse that reads, "The Lord is my shepherd, I shall not want."

Isaiah 19 continues, "The Lord will strike Egypt with a plague; he will strike them and heal them. The reason? They will turn to the Lord." By punishing followers and then healing them again, the theory is that God is engendering their confidence in Him and using that confidence to guide them in the right direction. When Marcus asks for someone to break his step and forgive him, he seems to be appealing to be shown the way.

Subsequently he asks for his eyes to be fixed, a phrase which seems to correspond to a verse in Corinthians 4 – "So we fix our eyes not on what is seen, but on what is unseen, since what is seen is temporary but what is unseen is eternal."

Previously Marcus had reacted angrily against the idea of surrendering his heart and head to obey God unconditionally, yet in 'I Will Wait', he speaks of blind faith in positive terms. He then follows on by asking for his spirit to be painted gold, which relates to a line in Job 23 – "When He is at work in the north, I do not see Him; when He comes to the south, I catch no glimpse of Him. But He knows the way that I take; when He has tested me, I will come forth as gold."

Marcus seems to be giving in to faith in something unseen, something his logical mind cannot probe. He speaks of finding strength and courage anew and asks for his flesh to be tamed, but – as if answering to some of the complex emotions aired in 'Holland Road', he says that he will use his head *alongside* his heart. He seems to have found a resolution between not wanting to give up his head and heart and not wanting to follow purely his heart either, due to the temptations it brings up to follow "unworthy" urges. While the Bible indicates that the heart and its desires are at the root of all sin, that can be mitigated by finding a balance between the heart and the head – which Marcus seems to have achieved here – while integrating faith as well. While his complex relationship with faith was ongoing and ever-changing, the conclusion of 'I Will Wait' suggested that, at least for now, he'd found a way to embrace religion on his own terms.

Despite Marcus' religious proclivities being the dominant theme on some songs, in stark contrast, for example, to Winston's interests ("I don't really feel this stuff") – the writing process had nonetheless been much more collaborative the second time around, with the group working on many ideas together.

Plus what Winston, a self-confessed bookworm, and the others certainly could relate to was the literary inspirations that ran throughout the album. These included a line that Marcus mischievously admitted in the media was stolen from Hilary Mantel's *Wolf Hall,* a lengthy tome that had kept him occupied during the band's last Australian tour. The Booker Prize-winning book is a fictional account of the life of Thomas Cromwell, a trusted minister to Henry VIII and his attempts to arrange the king's marriage to second wife Anne Boleyn. Yet while one of Cromwell's lines had buried itself in a Mumford song – a form of plagiarism which Marcus had blushed "might be illegal" – it was just one of the literary references hidden on the album.

"You just have to listen to Bob Dylan to realise that's what people do when they write songs," he'd reasoned during an interview with the BBC. "Or even the old spirituals and the old blues guys. A lot of the time, writers are just sponges for what's around them, so books are helpful for focusing your mind and literally putting it into words."

Now the big day had arrived and their second studio album was out for the world to see. It was a nerve-racking moment – after all, they'd sold over 2.5 million copies of *Sigh No More* in the USA alone, so the pressure was on to deliver the same result with *Babel*. However, they needn't have worried – the formula that one journalist coined "banjo-plucking austerity indie" would this time bring them more success than ever.

Barely daring to hope for a number one album, Ted had told the *NME*, "Obviously no-one's going to work against a number one record, but I know Green Day and Muse also have albums out and they're pretty big hitters. If you'd told me in the nineties that I'd be in a chart battle with Green Day, I probably would just have laughed at you."

Yet it wasn't just these groups that Mumford & Sons would be successfully competing with. In the UK, *Babel* sold 159,000 copies in the first week of its release, a feat which not only led to a number one debut in the album chart but also made it the fastest-selling album of 2012.

Simultaneously, it was flying off the shelves in the USA, selling 600,000 copies in the first week. It dwarfed Justin Bieber's *Believe*, which had previously held the record for highest-selling album of the year on a debut week, with 374,000 copies.

The album also saw the Mumfords nearly double the result of Madonna's hugely popular album *MDNA*, which had sold just 359,000 copies in its first week. It also set a new record stateside on download website Spotfiy for the highest number of streams ever of an album in a one-week period. In that first week of release, the group's songs had been streamed over eight million times, with 10% of all visitors to the website downloading at least one Mumford song.

Perhaps the residents of Dixon, Illinois, had been prophesising accurately when they spoke of a British invasion. To top off their success in America, the Mumfords scored more download purchases than almost any other artist since the digital era of music had begun, coming second only to Lady Gaga's 'Born This Way'.

Yet the biggest victory of all would come in early October, when the Mumfords would make history by achieving six songs on the US *Billboard* chart simultaneously – a feat unmatched by any UK act for nearly 50 years. The tracks were 'I Will Wait', 'Babel', 'Lover's Eyes', 'Whispers In The Dark', 'Holland Road' and 'Ghosts That We Knew'.

Originally the group had conservatively hoped simply to match the success of *Sigh No More*, yet not only had their surpassed it, beating their previous records, but they'd set new ones USA-wide in the process. Contact Music responded to the furore by publishing a headline that teased, "Are Mumford & Sons the new One Direction?", a title which in itself might have been enough to induce horror for "real music" puritans. Yet what the website had intended to highlight was the fact that the Mumfords were now vying for pop giants in the mass market – and in doing so, seemed to have brought acoustic music back into fashion.

Recording an entire album without so much as a traditional drum beat on some songs came in stark contrast to the electronically produced, drum machine-dominated hits that filled the modern music charts. It was a veritable victory for those who sought to see a resurgence of more organic-sounding songs – those that could be performed without endless Auto-Tune or overdubbing. This moment was a celebration, led by the fans, of raw folk 'n' roll. It captured the contentment of the days before electronic music existed, the days when the Beatles could fill a stadium armed with nothing more sophisticated than simple instruments and the voices with which they were born.

This winning combination attracted thousands of hysterical teenage fans – although that wasn't a notion with which the shy and modest Mumford quartet were necessarily comfortable. In fact, to them, it still came as a surprise that they had found fame at all. "We don't want to be as big as Oasis," Ted told the *NME*, although it might have been a little late for that. "I think we're bigger than we ever wanted to be. I don't think we want to get any bigger now."

As their popularity continued to explode, he added that the group's ultimate destiny was a life of solitude in the country – perhaps one similar to the snapshots of farm life delivered in some of the songs.

"Pretty much all of our dreams sit around the countryside," he explained, "and having a little bit of land to do something with. I think when that desire takes over our desire to travel and play gigs, that's probably where we'll end up. Celebrity holds no interest for us."

There were clues leading to that state of mind in 'Hopeless Wanderer', when the band reveal that, in spite of their cravings to travel the world and be musical prophets, they long for the day when they can simply grow old contentedly with their loved ones.

As for Winston, Marcus predicted that he'd end up "about 58 miles away from Nashville on a pig farm, playing banjo to the pigs and chewing tobacco".

That said, their ambitions were far too voluptuous to suggest retirement any time soon. In fact, according to Marcus, the third album would be coming sooner than fans might think.

"We want to make one quicker than we did with this one," he revealed. "We want to get in the studio quicker and get another album out a bit sooner. The wait [for *Babel*] was just because we didn't have time," he added, referring to the group's relentless touring schedule. "It wasn't like we were sunning ourselves. We've been playing music the whole time."

And long may that continue.